D1084809

PLACE IN RETURN BOX to remove this checkout from your record.
TO AVOID FINES return on or before date due.

DATE DUE	DATE DUE	DATE DUE

TRADE, DEVOTION AND GOVERNANCE

TRADE, DEVOTION AND GOVERNANCE

Papers in Later Medieval History

Edited by
DOROTHY J. CLAYTON, RICHARD G. DAVIES AND
PETER MCNIVEN

ALAN SUTTON

First published in the United Kingdom in 1994 by
Alan Sutton Publishing Ltd · Phoenix Mill · Far Thrupp · Stroud · Glos

First published in the United States of America in 1994 by
Alan Sutton Publishing Inc · 83 Washington Street · Dover · NH 03820

Copyright © D.J. Clayton, R.G. Davies, P. McNiven, E. Powell,
S. O'Connor, P.H. Cullum, H. Bradley, J.D. Milner, N. Jamieson,
J.L. Watts, T.R. Adams, M.-R. McLaren, J. Carnwath

British Library Cataloguing in Publication Data
A catalogue record for this book is available from the British Library

Library of Congress Cataloging in Publication Data applied for

ISBN 0 7509 0594 8

Typesetting and origination by
Alan Sutton Publishing Ltd.
Printed in Great Britain.

Contents

Acknowledgement

The publication of this book has been assisted by a grant from the Scouloudi Foundation in association with the Institute of Historical Research.

Editors' Introduction

The 1989 Conference on Recent Research in Fifteenth-Century History, one of the biennial series of gatherings primarily geared towards hearing and discussing the work of newer recruits to the study of fifteenth-century British history, was hosted by the University of Manchester from 7 to 9 July. Based at Needham Hall of Residence in West Didsbury, the conference was marked by a number of distinctive features. Most important, in its conception and organisation it represented a particularly fruitful cooperative effort between the Department of History and the John Rylands University Library of Manchester. The second of these elements came to the fore in the Saturday afternoon session held in the Library's special collection repository, the original John Rylands Library on Deansgate in the city centre. A major exhibition on the theme of 'England in the Fifteenth Century' was mounted to coincide with the conference. Participants were able to view a selection of printed books, manuscripts and archives illustrating aspects of that period. Subjects included the dominant rôle of the Church in society and the growing desire for greater freedom in worship; the late medieval chronicle and the transition from manuscript to printed book, with examples from the Library's magnificent collection of incunabula; and illustrations of the life and culture of members of fifteenth-century English society ranging from kings and queens through the landed gentry to the humble citizens of the then insignificant town of Manchester. A visit to the nearby Chetham's Library, a seventeenth-century foundation in a fifteenth-century building, provided additional authentic medieval flavour to three days of wide-ranging and enthusiastic discussion of topics which found echoes in the books and manuscripts on display.

After the participants had been welcomed on behalf of the History Department by Professor Jeffrey Denton, Edward Powell delivered the conference's keynote lecture. A stimulating and sometimes provocative contribution to the debate on contemporary developments in the interpretation of English fifteenth-century political history, and the significance for past, present and future historians of the work of K.B. McFarlane, appropriately produced the most vigorous debate of the weekend. Subsequent conferences have continued to carry forward this seemingly inexhaustible theme, and it is thus a particular source of satisfaction to the editors that this long-awaited contribution to the study of the broader issues of fifteenth-century studies is at last in print.

Dr Powell takes as his starting-point the pervasive emphasis, in contemporary studies of the period, on the importance of patronage, noting by way of illustration that the word appears in the titles of three previous volumes of fifteenth-century conference proceedings. He then invites his audience to reconsider what the term actually means, and to note the difference between 'personal' and 'institutionalised' patronage. His survey of the pitfalls of concentration on collective biography and detailed study of local history as tools to interpret both patronage and political society in general leads him to warn of the tendency towards reductionism in this approach, and ultimately of the 'poverty' of excessive reliance on this form of historical analysis. In proposing a re-examination of the constitutional and political framework within which patronage operated, he challenges the thesis that 'government' and 'patronage' were mutually exclusive systems and recommends the study of the interaction between them, a process which he characterises as 'reconstructing the political culture'.

While all the conference papers were submitted as completely independent contributions, and while the title somewhat arbitrarily attached to this volume does not claim to be all-embracing, themes emerge which link certain of the papers both to each other and to Dr Powell's introductory address. Of the thirteen papers originally presented, it would not be expected that every one would be offered for subsequent publication, and it is a source of some satisfaction that ten of them are reproduced here. In these pages, it is hoped, may be seen something of the balance between great matters of state and the minutiae of local studies which Dr Powell so cogently advocated. The order of the papers in the volume is, in so far as this is possible, approximately chronological; a format which perhaps highlights the diversity of the themes covered.

Coincidentally pursuing Dr Powell's advice to continue the exploration of the conceptual basis of kingship, John Watts finds in the minority of Henry VI the ideal opportunity to pursue such a study. In a meticulous step-by-step overview of successive expedients employed to deal with a constantly evolving situation where the one constant element was the gulf between the theoretical rôle of the Crown and the all too human occupant of the throne, he examines the dilemmas faced by those who sought or were obliged to exercise royal power on Henry's behalf. Seeking insight into the political traumas which beset the whole reign, he charts the transition from the necessary creation of an artificial royal *persona* while the king was indisputably a minor, to the premature claims of the emergence of a true royal will, which were initially to founder on factional dispute and ultimately on the inadequacies of an adult monarch who may have been scarcely more competent than a child to assess the merits of the counsel offered to him.

The issue of the public perception of the discrepancy between Henry's royal status and private personality is also touched upon by Mary-Rose

McLaren in her study of the fifteenth-century chronicles of London. Re-appraising the pioneering work carried out by C.L. Kingsford in this field in the early twentieth century, she assesses the way in which the chroniclers employed selectivity, manipulation of material and conventional literary and symbolic devices to convey what they regarded as an essentially accurate 'message'. Their presentation of details of three politically-crucial processions serves to illustrate the contrast between the triumphantly assertive Richard, duke of York, in 1460 and the passive Henry VI during the Readeption in 1470–1, and the central theme that a successful ruler needed to project a positive self-image and to be seen by his subjects to be doing so. As a more general survey of the sources and preoccupations of this first generation of English laymen to record the events of their times on a systematic basis, Dr McLaren's paper provides insights into the chroniclers' perceptions of themselves and their society as well as their attitudes to those who sought to wield authority over them.

The history of the English Crown's military campaigns may be regarded by some contemporary students of the period as somewhat unfashionable, but the critical significance of the French wars for the Lancastrian kings cannot be denied, and two papers present research in this field which spans virtually the whole era of conflict in the fifteenth century. John Milner's study of the English expedition to France in 1412 looks at a neglected precursor of Henry V's successful campaigns, while drawing attention to one of the least studied members of the House of Lancaster. Henry IV's second son, Thomas, spent the whole of his relatively short life in the shadow of the elder brother whom McFarlane acclaimed as the greatest of English kings, and his career serves to illustrate the reverse side of the glory sought and temporarily attained by Henry V. While Thomas's campaign may, by a number of criteria, be regarded as a success or a failure, Mr Milner identifies factors, such as the exposure both of the weakness of the French and the hazards of English dependence on alliances with French noble factions, and the revival of an interest in campaigning abroad for material gain, which laid military and diplomatic foundations for the Agincourt campaign. He also draws attention to the hard practicalities of mounting a major assault on foreign territory, and this theme is at the heart of Neil Jamieson's study of the involvement of northern manpower in the Lancastrian efforts to conquer and occupy France. His examination of the various methods of recruitment demonstrates the different requirements of the years 1415–22, when identifiable northern troops on militia service formed a high proportion of Henry V's conquering armies, and the long struggle to maintain the occupation, when long-serving contract troops gradually lost their regional, or even English, identities. Both papers offer correctives to the air of glamour which still tends to surround Henry V's military achievements.

While ecclesiastical history as conventionally understood is not represented in these papers, two contributions help to counter Dr Powell's charge that 'secular' historians tend to take too little account of the rôle of the Church in shaping the events of which they write. Patricia Cullum considers the ways in which Christian teachings on society's duty towards its poorer members led to the foundation and endowment of the Yorkshire almshouses known as maisonsdieu. She considers the changes in the perception of poverty from the fourteenth century and demonstrates the various ways in which men and women from a wide spectrum of social class organised their acts of charity in accordance with local needs and their own often modest means. Julia Carnwath's study of churchwardens and other, lesser officials in an Oxfordshire town, a century or more later, looks at the contribution of the laity to the administration of the parish in the years immediately preceding the Reformation. Her research provides evidence of the types of person who acted as wardens, their status and their secular involvements in their community, the functions of minor office-holders, the ever-topical issue of Church funding and the possible motives of those who served.

The continuing need, acknowledged in Dr Powell's critique, to seek insights into the dynamics of society at the local level, and to link this study to higher politics, is met effectively in Stephen O'Connor's paper on the rise to 'gentry' status of the London merchants John Pyel and Adam Fraunceys. Noting the importance of such factors as birth, income, local standing, aristocratic patronage and above all the ownership of landed estate as prerequisites for social advancement, Dr O'Connor charts the successful careers of two men whose quests for self-improvement took rather different forms. Trade is the more explicit theme of the contributions of Helen Bradley and Terence Adams, and both offer new perspectives on an essential element in late medieval society. While the close trading links between England and the merchants of the Italian city-states are well documented, Dr Bradley's extensive examination of Italian archives has enabled her to offer a Florentine perspective on fifteenth-century commerce. She thus provides fresh insights into such issues as the English wool and cloth trades, the fluctuations in the English markets, the hazards of the sea passages, and anti-alien activity. Further understanding of the international trade of the period is provided by Mr Adams's analysis of the accounts of the water-bailiffs of Great Yarmouth. These reveal not only a flourishing trade with the Low Countries, which in turn linked Yarmouth with the Baltic and southern Europe, but the sophisticated network of trade along the rivers of the Norfolk hinterland. He discovers clear evidence of an agricultural society geared to the production of a regular surplus for the export market, and to the organised distribution and sale of imported Continental supplies within the county.

The conference organisers and volume editors would like to take this opportunity to acknowledge the assistance and encouragement of all those who were in any way involved in the gathering in Manchester in 1989 and in the present publication. Particular thanks are due to the Department of History and the John Rylands University Library for practical and moral support; to the staff of Needham Hall for providing what was generally agreed to have been a particularly congenial venue; and to Dr Michael Powell, Librarian of Chetham's Library, for giving conference participants a privileged viewing of that institution. We are very grateful to the Scouloudi Foundation (formerly the Twenty-Seven Foundation) for a generous grant towards the costs of publication; to the staff of Alan Sutton Publishing for their helpful and sympathetic approach to the production of the volume; and to Dr Barry White of the John Rylands University Library for the index. In conclusion, we would like to offer our thanks to the contributors in the hope that they will feel that their patience has been rewarded.

Dorothy J. Clayton
Richard G. Davies
Peter McNiven

January 1994

Contributors

EDWARD POWELL was Fellow and Director of Studies in History, Downing College, Cambridge, 1982–9. He is now practising as a solicitor.

STEPHEN O'CONNOR is Assistant Editor of the Medieval Latin Dictionary.

PATRICIA CULLUM is a Lecturer in History at the University of Huddersfield.

HELEN BRADLEY is Research Assistant to the Saddlers' Company, London.

JOHN MILNER is a Senior Officer at the Northern Examinations and Assessment Board, Manchester, and a part-time research student of the University of Liverpool.

NEIL JAMIESON is a Visiting Lecturer in History at Chester College.

JOHN WATTS is a Lecturer in Medieval History at University College of Wales, Aberystwyth.

TERENCE ADAMS is a former research student of the University of Birmingham. He is now a management consultant.

MARY-ROSE MCLAREN is a former research student of the University of Melbourne.

JULIA CARNWATH is a full-time research student of the University of Manchester.

Abbreviations

Add.	Additional [MS]
AN	Archives Nationales
BIHR	*Bulletin of the Institute of Historical Research*
BL	British Library
BN	Bibliothèque Nationale
CCR	*Calendar of the Close Rolls*
CFR	*Calendar of the Fine Rolls*
Ch.	Charter
ch.	chapter
CPR	*Calendar of the Patent Rolls*
CRO	County Record Office
CSP	*Calendar of State Papers*
DKR	*Annual Report of the Deputy Keeper of the Public Records*
EcHR	*Economic History Review*
EETS	Early English Text Society
EHR	*English Historical Review*
HMC	Historical Manuscripts Commission
POPC	*Proceedings and Ordinances of the Privy Council of England*, ed. N.H. Nicolas, 7 vols (London, 1834–7)
PRO	Public Record Office
RC	Record Commission
RP	*Rotuli Parliamentorum*, ed. J. Strachey and others, 6 vols (London, 1767–77)
RS	Rolls Series
TRHS	*Transactions of the Royal Historical Society*
VCH	*Victoria County History*

Other abbreviations are defined in the notes for the particular papers to which they relate.

1

After 'After McFarlane': The Poverty of Patronage and the Case for Constitutional History

Edward Powell

'It is the duty of every generation of historians', wrote K.B. McFarlane in 1938, 'to rewrite the broad outlines of our subject in the light of those specialised studies which are our prime concern'.[1] In that paper McFarlane identified what he called 'the collapse of the Stubbsian framework' of the constitutional history of late medieval England, and suggested ways forward to the construction of a new framework, namely local surveys to investigate the power of the great noble families, and collective biographies of the gentlemen who sat in parliament.[2]

McFarlane may not have rewritten the history of late medieval England in his own hand, but he certainly exercised a direct and very considerable influence over the generation of historians who did.[3] It was their work, much of which was published in the late seventies and early eighties, which consolidated the revival of fifteenth-century studies in this country. Professor Colin Richmond eloquently captured the spirit of the revival in his 1983 review article 'After McFarlane', upon which the title of the present paper is a rather ponderous play.[4] 'The fifteenth century', Richmond rightly asserted, 'is McFarlane's century',[5] and it was the implementation of the McFarlane agenda which gave the work of his successors an overall cohesion and unity. There remain, as Richmond's review demonstrated, areas of disagreement and differences of emphasis, but far more significant is the general consensus on fundamentals.

The fundamentals of the McFarlane agenda were as follows: a rejection of traditional constitutional history focused narrowly on the institutions of government and their apparent progress towards parliamentary democracy; instead, detailed study of English society in the age of bastard feudalism through the careers, estates and finances of the nobility; complemented by careful reconstruction of the workings of patronage – the ties of lordship and clientage which bound political society together and enabled it to function.

Patronage has of course been the catchword of the 'After McFarlane' generation. The term appears in no less than three of the published proceedings of previous Fifteenth-Century History conferences;[6] and if

1

essays at Cambridge are anything to go by, the term has acquired an almost mystical significance for students as a key to unlocking the mysteries of late medieval politics. This view may be, as Dr Christine Carpenter has put it to me, nothing better than 'Bastard McFarlanism', but on the other hand it may plausibly claim the authority of the Master. 'Patronage and service', McFarlane wrote in the paper of 1938 cited above, 'were the essence of contemporary society', and this was a maxim he repeated in almost identical terms thirty years later in the conclusion to his final lecture in Oxford in 1966.[7]

Until recently I should have said that McFarlane's victory was complete, and that the spectre of Stubbsian constitutional history had finally been laid to rest. This can no longer be said with confidence, however, since the publication of A.L. Brown's book, *The Governance of Late Medieval England, 1272–1461*.[8] Here is a work with which Stubbs and Tout would have felt thoroughly at home, and it provides admirable corrective reading for any student who interprets the problems of medieval government purely in terms of patronage. There is a striking resemblance, in structure if not in form, between Professor Brown's book and Lodge and Thornton's *English Constitutional Documents, 1307–1485*, published in 1935 to plug the gap between Stubbs's *Charters* and Prothero's *Tudor Constitutional Documents*.[9]

Such rugged individualists apart, few historians would now discount the importance of patronage in the governance of medieval England. Indeed, in recent years it has come to be seen as a significant factor in British history in every age from the twelfth to the nineteenth century. Without wishing to diminish McFarlane's contribution, we must acknowledge that it was not so much his influence as that of Sir Lewis Namier which was instrumental in bringing about this far-reaching change of historical perspective. Namier's most influential work, *The Structure of Politics at the Accession of George III*, examined the workings of eighteenth-century politics through detailed investigation of the composition of the House of Commons.[10] By means of such rigorous structural analysis he demolished the traditional Whig interpretation of the period, in the process setting off a revolution in British historiography.[11] In his study of the exercise of royal patronage in the twelfth century, Sir Richard Southern described Henry I as a 'devoted Namierite', and observed, 'it was Namier's greatest service to English history that he described with sympathy and vast knowledge the system of patronage and its place in the work of government at the moment of its fullest articulation before the rise of parties and principles forever destroyed it'.[12] Professor J.C. Holt for the twelfth and thirteenth centuries, McFarlane for the fifteenth century, Sir John Neale for the sixteenth century, and most recently J.M. Bourne for the nineteenth century, have all followed Namier's example.[13] McFarlane explicitly acknowledged Namier's influence, comparing the late medieval magnate affinity with the eighteenth-century 'connection' anatomised by Namier. 'There was', he wrote 'the same element of voluntary interdependence, the same competition for "place" and the same absence of any separate fund of political principle'.[14]

What is the relevance of this potted history of historiography to a conference on Recent Research in Fifteenth-Century History? I return to the quotation of McFarlane's with which I opened, that every generation of historians has the duty to rewrite the broad outlines of our subject. It is a valuable, indeed indispensable exercise for us, particularly at such a gathering as this, to reflect from time to time upon the general direction that our researches are taking. How will the research students and successors of the 'After McFarlane' generation rewrite the history of England in the late middle ages?

There is no shortage of advice as to how we should proceed. Professor Richmond, in the review already cited, and Dr Gerald Harriss, in his introduction to McFarlane's collected essays, are in no doubt; we must pursue the McFarlane agenda a stage further, and examine gentry society in close detail, particularly through the systematic compilation of gentry biographies. 'It is at this level of society that we should be looking', argues Richmond, 'in town and country where the active gentry were most active. It is there that McFarlane directed us, and it is there, if we want a deeper understanding of fifteenth-century England, that we should be'.[15]

Up to a point Richmond and Harriss are obviously correct in their advice: gentry studies are a logical development of the historiographical trends over the last thirty years, and work already done in the area reveals how fruitful they can be.[16] Yet such an approach carries with it certain risks. As we plunge ever deeper into the thickets of late medieval political society, we must take care not to lose sight of the wood for our concentration on the leaves on the trees.[17] Our assumptions about the centrality of patronage, and our pursuit of detailed structural analysis of gentry society, raise important conceptual and methodological problems which have so far received little discussion. Nevertheless we all wrestle with them, as we compile our card indexes and pound our word processors, and they deserve our considered attention. It is these problems which I want to address in this paper.

The pitfalls of such an exercise are only too obvious. The last thing I want is to be seen as castigating the reader for shortcomings of which he or she is not guilty. On the contrary, I must emphasise that this paper grew out of a sense of dissatisfaction at the limitations of my own research and teaching, and a desire to clarify the reasons for that dissatisfaction. This will inevitably involve a certain amount of theoretical discussion, which I hope will not occasion too much impatience. British historians, and medievalists in particular, instinctively recoil from theory, preferring a healthily pragmatic and empiricist approach. Professor Richard Cobb, I suspect, spoke for many of us when he wrote:

> I do not know what history is about, nor what social function it serves. I have never given the matter a second thought. There is nothing more boring than books and articles on such themes as 'What is History?', 'The Use of History', 'History and Something Else'.[18]

I must confess a certain regard for Cobb's cheerful nihilism, but ultimately such unreflectiveness creates more problems than it solves. I do not intend to ask, 'What is history?', but I do suggest that we should give careful thought to the question: 'What is patronage?'

That question is far from being a simple one. I propose to explore it in three different ways: to consider how the term patronage may be defined; the methods of historical research particularly associated with it, namely prosopography and the local study of shire or affinity; and finally the problems of its use as a tool of historical analysis.

Definitions of Patronage

In my attempts to find satisfactory answers to these questions, I have encountered a remarkably large canon of literature on patronage. This covers practically every historical period from the ancient world to the present day, and embraces several academic disciplines apart from history, notably anthropology, political science and sociology.[19] Predictably the approach to the analysis of patronage differs according to discipline. Anthropologists tend to investigate patronage in rural, pre-industrial societies, examining patron-client relations in a localised context and assessing their impact on village life. As a rule such studies pay little attention to the place of patronage within any formal structure of government which may exist. Political scientists, by contrast, concentrate on the existence of patronage within a political system, especially the workings of political parties in the distribution of offices and favours. For sociologists patronage provides the opportunity to construct a model of the exchange theory of interpersonal relationships.[20] The work that I have found most helpful, however, is that of historians of the ancient Greek and Roman world, which has the advantage of being written in terms that a medievalist can readily comprehend. The alertness of ancient historians to the concept of patronage is probably attributable to two factors: the fact that the very terminology of patron and client originated in Rome;[21] and the influence of Sir Ronald Syme's seminal study *The Roman Revolution*, published in 1939, which changed the direction of Roman history in the same way that Namier's work changed that of British history, and for the same reasons: Syme reinterpreted the collapse of the Roman republic and the establishment of the Empire under Augustus in terms of factional struggle and patronage.[22]

The term 'patronage' has several shades of meaning. Its original use, and the only one current in the late middle ages, was ecclesiastical – the right of presentment to a benefice. By the eighteenth century at the latest this usage was extended to the right of appointment to offices and honours in the royal gift. Beyond this limited sense, historians and social scientists conventionally use the term to denote a particular kind of relationship between two parties. Professor Richard Saller provides a tripartite definition of this relationship which has found general support among ancient historians:

> First it involves the reciprocal exchange of goods and services. Secondly, to distinguish it from a commercial transaction in the marketplace, the relationship must be a personal one of some duration. Thirdly it must be asymmetrical, in the sense that the two parties are of unequal status and offer different kinds of goods and services in the exchange – a quality which sets patronage off from friendship between equals.[23]

To summarise, Saller's definition sees patronage as a personal relationship involving reciprocity, intimacy and inequality.[24] It is perhaps necessary to add a fourth point, namely that patronage is a transaction entered into voluntarily and not through coercion or legal constraint, by contrast with slavery or serfdom.[25] This provides us with a tolerable working definition of patronage, and one indeed implicit in Dr Horrox's valuable analysis of service in her important new study of Richard III.[26]

There remains a third, still broader definition of the term, where patronage describes the nature of a political system. Patronage may not merely be a relationship between consenting adults in public, therefore, but may characterise the workings of the social, political, and governmental institutions of an entire society. Historians have not always been careful to distinguish between these two definitions;[27] as medievalists we have been inclined to subsume the latter within the former, and to suppose that the existence of patronage relations automatically implies the existence of patronage as a political system. A wider perspective suggests, however, that patronage relations represent an almost universal element in human society, to be found even in modern industrial democracies. It is not sufficient, therefore, for historians merely to document the existence of patronage relations within a society; it is necessary also to examine how they function as part of the wider social and political system. Failure to do so may result in excessive concentration on patronage at the expense of alternative forms of social organisation, such as kinship, neighbourhood or bureaucracy, and this is a point to which I shall return.

It might be argued that an unbridgeable gap exists between patronage as an intimate personal relationship on one hand, and patronage as a political system on the other. This is particularly true of highly centralised systems of power, where the ruler or his ministers are constantly inundated with requests for office or favour, often from petitioners of whom they have little or no knowledge. For Lord Burghley, Elizabeth I's chief minister, 'it was his disease . . . to have too many servants'; while on becoming Prime Minister in 1841, Sir Robert Peel spent six hours a day for his first few weeks in office writing letters in reply to applicants for civil service posts.[28] Those in power devised various strategies for dealing with the deluge of petitions: Colbert, the servant of Louis XIV, was notorious for his extreme rudeness and the duke of Wellington, lacking Peel's conscientiousness, simply had a printed slip made up, brusquely refusing assistance.[29] One wonders what strategy the duke of Suffolk adopted.

In order to bridge the gap between personal and systemic patronage, some historians have introduced the concept of the broker, that is, a middleman, who is both patron and client, based in the locality but with personal ties to those in power at the centre.[30] The concept has obvious applicability to late medieval England: here one thinks not so much of the higher nobility as of figures like the Stanley family in the North-West in the early fifteenth century, and Sir John Conyers, the steward of Middleham, whom Professor Pollard suspects was choosing retainers for Richard, duke of Gloucester in the early 1470s.[31]

Before leaving the subject of definitions, it is worth noting that, on the whole, ancient and early-modern historians have explored the terminology of patron-client relations within their period of study far more systematically than medievalists.[32] This provides a rich body of comparative material for us to consult: for example, Saller suggests how the terminology of friendship could be used in early imperial Rome as an oblique means of expressing patronage relations where the use of 'patron' and 'client' might have been dishonourable to the latter; while for seventeenth-century France Professor Sharon Kettering's analysis of the term '*crédit*' calls to mind the fifteenth-century concept of 'worship'.[33] More than that, however, it suggests that we might subject to closer scrutiny the use of patronage terminology in our own sources. The concept of 'good lordship' has become familiar to the point of cliché, but as Dr Horrox has recently shown it continues to repay sympathetic inspection.[34] Other terms like 'worship', 'friendship', 'mastership' and 'lover' deserve fuller analysis.[35]

Patronage and Prosopography

Let us now move on to a consideration of the methodologies used to investigate patronage as an historical phenomenon. If, as McFarlane claimed, patronage and service were the essence of late medieval society, then the obvious method for studying such a society is prosopography, or collective biography. This method was pioneered by Namier for the eighteenth century and Syme for the Roman world, and must now be one of the most widely used forms of historical research.[36] Precisely because of its popularity we must be all the more aware of its pitfalls and limitations. It is a peculiarly demanding methodology, because in order to claim validity it aims at comprehensiveness – the reconstruction as far as the sources will allow of the profile of an entire social group, individual by individual. Of course the difficulties of the source materials – their sheer volume, their incompleteness, or both – frustrate the aim of comprehensiveness, and turn it into a constantly receding mirage. The toll of collective biography on its original devotees was heavy: we may suspect that it was the demands of their method, as much as their perfectionism, which prevented McFarlane and Namier from producing the authoritative treatment of the subject to which their lives were devoted.[37]

One of the chief problems of collective biography, then, is that it is easy to lose control of one's material and to allow it to fragment into a thousand little histories, and at worst into antiquarianism. This is particularly the case when dealing with a large group like the late medieval gentry. A second is knowing where to stop. We are advised to study the lives and careers of the English gentry, but why should we confine ourselves to this class? Is it not arbitrary and elitist so to do, especially in view of the fact that as our knowledge of the gentry grows, so the line between the minor gentleman and the substantial yeoman becomes increasingly indistinct? Surely if the key to an understanding of the nobility lies in the relationship with their retainers and dependants, the same must apply *mutatis mutandis* to the gentry? And if we attempt a collective biography of the yeomanry, why not the entire population? That of course is a *reductio ad absurdum*: the sources would not allow it. But the logic of the prosopographical method implies that conclusion.

The final problem of collective biography is that its subject matter is dependent on the types of sources which survive. For the late medieval gentry, needless to say, they relate overwhelmingly to matters of family and business – the ownership, management and transmission of landed estates, and the workings of government – and this inevitably focuses our attention on dynastic and material concerns. As Professor Richmond suggested, we can remedy the deficiency to an extent by looking beyond the archives to other sources such as books, tombs, wills and churches;[38] but even here we remain largely in the world of externals, of acquisition, consumption and display, touching only indirectly upon the internal world of reflection and motivation. This problem has no solution, barring the discovery of a vast new cache of fifteenth-century letters, but we must constantly bear it in mind because it sets limits on the usefulness of the methodology for an understanding of fifteenth-century history. Prosopography, like patronage, is not enough.

Closely related to prosopography is the county or provincial study. Here we are following in the footsteps of seventeenth-century historiography, where a series of local studies revolutionised understanding of the civil-war period, focusing particularly on the importance of the county community.[39] The same is now happening for the fifteenth century. One hazard to note here is what one might call the 'Morrill effect', after the civil-war historian Dr John Morrill. After the publication of his book *The Revolt of the Provinces*, which deals with the phenonemon of 'neutralism' in the localities at the beginning of the Civil War, Morrill was accused, half seriously, of explaining why the war did not break out in 1642.[40] This illustrates neatly the centrifugal force that local studies can exercise. Furthermore the county boundaries may set artificial limits to such studies, and the administrative machinery of the shire may impose an artificial sense of cohesion on gentry society.[41] But these are well recognised problems, and do not need labouring.

The Poverty of Patronage and the Case for Constitutional History

Finally I want to consider patronage as a tool of historical analysis. As we have seen, in the hands of Namier, Syme and McFarlane, it has been an immensely powerful one, transforming the historical landscape. Its great disadvantage as an analytical device is that it has been accompanied by a marked tendency towards reductionism: the reduction of constitutional history to politics, of politics to patronage, and of personal motivation to material self-interest. That, in essence, is the poverty of patronage.

Since my theme is the case for constitutional history, I propose to discuss the use of patronage in the light of the constitutional interpretations of history which it has largely superseded. For there is nothing inherently reductionist about patronage; it is merely one type of social and political relationship among several which command our attention. The fact that it has become so has been due largely to the distinctive development of historical writing over the past century. The preoccupation with patronage was born out of disillusionment with traditional constitutional history, 'that far from helpful abstraction', as McFarlane called it,[42] the central concerns of which were the institutions and workings of government and the development of the principles and conventions regulating their use. The whiggish tone of much constitutional history, its emphasis on the age-long struggle between tyranny and liberty, culminating in the triumph of British parliamentary democracy, was particularly unconvincing for historians writing after the First World War under the shadow of fascism. For young Turks like Syme the concept of patronage provided a razor-sharp weapon, cutting through the cant of constitutional verbiage to the underlying historical reality:

> The Roman constitution was a screen and a sham. Of the forces that lay behind or beyond it, next to the noble families the knights were the most important . . . [T]hrough patronage exercised in the law courts and ties of personal allegiance contracted in every walk of life, the political dynast might win influence not merely in Rome but in the country-towns of Italy . . . Whether he held authority from the State or not, he could thus raise an army on his own initiative and resources.[43]

How familiar it all sounds! The attraction of the concept of patronage, which struck this generation of historians with all the force of a revelation, was that it appeared to lay bare the naked realities of political power. Politics was not about the workings of institutions but about relationships between men; what mattered was not men's words but their deeds; the principles they espoused were a meaningless façade adopted to conceal their calculating self-interest and lust for power.[44]

Because of the circumstances in which it was adopted, therefore, patronage as an analytical tool entailed not so much the modification as the root-and-branch rejection of constitutional history. The consequences of this rejection for the historiography of late medieval England have been profound. Not only has there been a wholesale diversion of research away from constitutional theory and the institutions of central government (is there an historian under sixty who has written a book on the late medieval parliament?); the assumption has also taken root – bastard McFarlanism though it may be – that constitutional issues are peripheral to our understanding of the period. To take an example at random, here is Dr Horrox on the usurpation of Richard III:

> The constitutional issues thus become not much more than flourishes to a *fait accompli*. Gloucester's justification is presented as the armed force at his disposal, and it is against this background that he was petitioned to take the throne by the three estates.[45]

Might, in effect, was right and rested, not on constitutional propriety but on military support. This depended on the extent and effectiveness of a ruler's 'good lordship', which in turn relied upon satisfying the self-interested demands of retainers whom McFarlane, in a famous passage, portrayed as fickle and footloose:

> In this loose-knit and shamelessly competitive society it was the ambition of every thrusting gentleman . . . to attach himself for as long as it suited him to such as were in a position to further his interests . . . Lordship lasted only so long as it was found to be good lordship, or until it was ousted by a better.[46]

I now intend to attempt a refutation of those assumptions, and argue the case for constitutional history. I must emphasise at once that I am not advocating a reconstruction of the Stubbsian framework, nor a return to institutional history for its own sake. Neither am I proposing that we reject the concept of patronage as an analytical tool. What I suggest is that we need to set patronage in its proper perspective; and that in order to do so we must pay closer attention first to the values, ideals and conventions governing political life and the exercise of authority in late medieval England, and secondly to the machinery of law and government through which that authority was exercised.

The first essential is to re-establish the importance of political and constitutional principles as a subject for study in relation to political action. The case has been most powerfully argued by the historian of political thought Professor Quentin Skinner.[47] Skinner's argument took the form of a refutation of Namier's assertions that the profession of political principles formed no guide to the underlying realities of politics, and that political behaviour was governed solely by the desire to acquire and exercise power.[48] Skinner pointed out that Namier's reasoning was flawed in that it ignored the content of such principles. Why should a political figure adopt one set of principles in preference to another? Skinner's answer is that he does so to legitimise his actions and to gain acceptance and support for them among the political community. The politician's freedom of manoeuvre is therefore constrained by the limited range of recognised principles he can employ to justify his actions and provide favourable interpretations of them.

The relevance of this analysis for fifteenth-century history is self-evident, particularly for our assessment of the cases put forward by royal usurpers, and the positions adopted by 'opposition' figures like Richard, duke of York. One great advantage of Skinner's argument is that the vexed question of a political figure's sincerity in espousing certain principles becomes irrelevant. Thus it does not really matter whether or not York was a passionate believer in his manifestos for governmental reform, or Richard III had as profound a commitment to justice as he claimed. What is important is that they operated within a specific political culture and had to reconcile their actions to its values. Their success or failure therefore turned not just on the might at their disposal but on their ability to convince political society of the righteousness of their cause. To put it another way: their might could in part depend upon their being seen as right.

In exploring the values and principles of the political culture of late medieval England, we should not define our terms too narrowly. Thus in my view constitutional ideas should be taken to include not merely such matters as the inalienability of the royal prerogative or the necessity of parliamentary consent to taxation, but also the advice given to rulers in 'mirrors of princes' literature – for example the exhortation that the prince should cultivate the virtues of justice, piety, mercy, patience and so on.[49] Perhaps even the horoscopes of kings are appropriate subjects for treatment: there is a particularly interesting one cast for Henry VI in 1441 during the proceedings against Eleanor Cobham for necromancy.[50] Equally relevant is the chivalric ethos which governed the behaviour of the nobility. This point was borne in upon me by a reading of Dr Jones's important article on the feud between the dukes of York and Somerset, in which he argues that York's hostility to Somerset, and his attempts to bring him to trial for the mismanagement of the defence of Normandy in 1449, stemmed from his anger at Somerset's dishonourable conduct of the campaign and his desire to vindicate his own reputation.[51] The aristocratic code of honour clearly influenced the manner in which the public affairs of the realm were conducted, and its effect on late medieval politics merits further study.[52] The Church also formed an integral part of late medieval political culture, as the career of Wyclif and the response to Lollardy makes only too clear;[53] but this is a point which it is easy for 'secular' political historians to overlook.[54]

Much of the argument outlined above can be adduced to support a revival of research into the workings of the machinery of law and government.[55] Thus the development of legal institutions and due process of law inevitably regulated and constrained the exercise of royal power. An equally powerful case can be constructed on different grounds, however, by challenging one of the basic assumptions deriving from the use of patronage as a tool of historical analysis. This is the belief that the formal machinery of government and the informal machinery of patronage formed two distinct and exclusive systems: on one hand an official bureaucracy and judicial structure theoretically dedicated to the enforcement of royal power and the maintenance of the public interest in justice and defence; on the other hand a web of personal relationships devoted to private gain and self-advancement.[56] The effectiveness and probity of governmental institutions were fatally undermined by the patronage networks which infiltrated them. As Dr Carpenter put it:

> the outward forms of a highly developed bureaucratic system concealed a riot of mutual back-scratching.[57]

Such a view is closely allied to Syme's view of the constitution as a 'screen and a sham',[58] implying that the machinery of government was a mere façade, and that what matters is not how it worked but who worked it.[59]

Once again, it is not my intention to discount the rôle of patronage in the workings of government, least of all in the administration of justice. On the contrary, my argument is exactly the opposite. Without patronage, and the corruption that went with it, royal government could not have functioned. Far from undermining bureaucracy, patronage complemented and reinforced it. The Crown used royal officials such as sheriffs and J.P.s to administer the localities, but institutional procedures alone were insufficient to ensure effective government. In consequence the Crown supplemented its authority by cultivating patron-broker-client ties, which functioned both inside and outside the institutional framework.[60] A key to the understanding of the exercise of royal authority therefore lies in the *interaction* between bureaucracy and patronage.

If we cease to regard patronage and bureaucracy as mutually exclusive systems of power, the balance between them may be restored. Traditional constitutional history emphasised institutions at the expense of the men who worked them, prosopographers the men at the expense of the institutions. Perhaps we can agree at last that both are equally worthy of study, and that most fruitful of all is the relationship between the two. No doubt I am guilty of special pleading in this matter, speaking as a legal historian concerned to set the workings of the law in their social context; but one needs only to be briefly acquainted with medieval law to realise how difficult it is to reduce its operation merely to the play of patronage. It was too open, too complex a system, expectations of it were too high, and its rules and procedures had a logic and momentum of their own which restricted, though it did not exclude, manipulation. Perhaps we have been misled by the innumerable petitions alleging the power and undue maintenance of an opponent: the fact that the petitioner's voice is heard at all should make us sceptical, and in any case the allegation was a standard ploy – one of the moves of the game. Similarly the chorus of complaint in contemporary poems and songs against maintenance and corruption is a healthy sign that the system was open to popular pressure. The fate of those, like Despenser and Suffolk, who attempted to subordinate law to patronage, is another reminder of that fact. *Pace* the chronicler John Hardyng, the law was not really:

. . . lyke vnto a Walshmannes hose,
To eche mannes legge that shapen is and mete . . .[61]

It was more like a suit of armour: it provided sterling defensive facilities, and gave certain room for manoeuvre, but there were some points at which it would not bend.

The argument in favour of the history of institutions is in fact very similar to that in favour of the study of patronage systems. They represent alternative structures of organisation regulating the distribution of power and authority. Where they interact, bureaucratic forms and procedures may determine the character of patronage as much as patronage influences institutional decision-making. We may expect them, as alternative systems generating different loyalties and values, to compete and conflict with one another on occasion. It does not follow, however, that one will predominate so completely over the other as to nullify it and render negligible its historical significance.

The case for constitutional history, then, is essentially the case for reintegrating the history of late medieval England. Of course we need a better understanding of local gentry society, but it is not an end in itself. There is an urgent need to create a more complete and rounded historiography, in which analysis of the economic position of the landowning classes and the workings of patronage can be related to institutional and administrative changes, and to those developments in political theory which influenced relations between the king and his subjects. This is the most pressing task which awaits the successors of McFarlane's successors. It is perhaps best described as reconstructing the political culture of late medieval England. Some of the materials already lie to hand: there is a growing interest in the conceptual basis of kingship, in the chivalric ethos of the nobility and gentry, and in popular attitudes to law and government displayed in poems and ballads and in protest movements. An appreciation of patronage and an understanding of the dynamics of local society are of course indispensable. Much remains to be done, however. In the field of legal history the more technical aspects of law remain astonishingly neglected, and a great mass of legal literature goes unexamined. Familiar problems of the late medieval period, such as violence and corruption, require more rigorous and penetrating analysis than they have so far received. We should also be more receptive to the ideas of historians of other periods and scholars of other disciplines: the urban historians have given us a lead here in their discovery of ritual in the late medieval town.[62] Finally (heretical thought!) is it not time that we climbed down from the giant's shoulders, dwarves though we may be, and stepped forward by ourselves to see what lies beyond the horizons of McFarlane's work?

Notes

1   K.B. McFarlane, *The Nobility of Later Medieval England* (Oxford, 1973), p. 279.
2   Ibid., pp. 296–7.
3   C.D. Ross, ed., *Patronage, Pedigree and Power in Later Medieval England* (Gloucester, 1979), p. 8.
4   C.F. Richmond, 'After McFarlane', *History*, 68 (1983), pp. 46–60.
5   Ibid., p. 46.
6   Ross, ed., *Patronage, Pedigree and Power*; R.A. Griffiths, ed., *Patronage, the Crown and the Provinces in Later Medieval England* (Gloucester, 1981); R.B. Dobson, ed., *The Church, Politics and Patronage in the Fifteenth Century* (Gloucester, 1984).
7   McFarlane, *Nobility*, p. 290; idem, *Lancastrian Kings and Lollard Knights* (Oxford, 1972), p. 226.
8   A.L. Brown, *The Governance of Late Medieval England, 1272–1461* (London, 1989).
9   *English Constitutional Documents, 1307–1485*, ed. E.C. Lodge and G.A. Thornton (Cambridge, 1935); *Select Charters*, ed. W. Stubbs, 9th edn (Oxford, 1913); *Tudor Constitutional Documents*, ed. J.R. Tanner, 2nd edn (Cambridge, 1930).
10 L.B. Namier, *The Structure of Politics at the Accession of George III* (London, 1929).
11 J. Cannon, 'Lewis Bernstein Namier', in J. Cannon, ed., *The Historian at Work* (London, 1980), pp. 136–40.
12 R.W. Southern, *Medieval Humanism and Other Studies* (Oxford, 1970), p. 209.
13 J.C. Holt, *The Northerners* (Oxford, 1961); idem, 'Feudal Society and the Family in Early Medieval England III: Patronage and Politics', *TRHS*, 5th series, 34 (1984), pp. 1–25; J.E. Neale, 'The Elizabethan Political Scene', *Proceedings of the British Academy*, 34 (1948), pp. 97–117; J.M. Bourne, *Patronage and Society in Nineteenth-Century England* (London, 1986).
14 K.B. McFarlane, 'Parliament and Bastard Feudalism', *TRHS*, 4th series, 26 (1944), p. 71.
15 Richmond, 'After McFarlane', pp. 59–60; G.L. Harriss, 'Introduction', in K.B. McFarlane, *England in the Fifteenth Century* (London, 1981), pp. xxvi–vii.
16 E.g. M.J. Bennett, *Community, Class and Careerism: Cheshire and Lancashire Society in the Age of Sir Gawain and the Green Knight* (Cambridge, 1983); M.C. Carpenter, 'The Beauchamp Affinity: a Study of Bastard Feudalism at Work', *EHR*, 95 (1980), pp. 515–32; S.M. Wright, *The Derbyshire Gentry in the Fifteenth Century* (Chesterfield, 1983).
17 See the quotation from Namier cited in Cannon, 'Namier', p. 148.
18 R. Cobb, *Second Identity* (London, 1969), p. 47; cited in J. Cannon, 'The Historian at Work', in J. Cannon, ed., *The Historian at Work*, pp. 5–6.
19 See A. Wallace-Hadrill, ed., *Patronage in Ancient Society* (London, 1989), pp. 1–13; S. Kettering, *Patrons, Brokers, and Clients in Seventeenth-Century France* (Oxford, 1986), pp. 3–11; Bourne, *Patronage and Society*, pp. 1–8.
20 S.N. Eisenstadt and L. Roniger, 'Patron-Client Relations as a Model of Structuring Social Exchange', *Comparative Studies in Society and History*, 22 (1980), pp. 42–77.
21 R.P. Saller, *Personal Patronage under the Early Empire* (Cambridge, 1982), pp. 7–15; idem, 'Patronage and Friendship in Early Imperial Rome: Drawing the Distinction', in A. Wallace-Hadrill, ed., *Patronage in Ancient Society*, pp. 49–61. I am most grateful to Dr P.C. Millett of Downing College, Cambridge for several very helpful discussions on patronage in the ancient world, and for guidance on reading.
22 R. Syme, *The Roman Revolution* (Oxford, 1939).
23 Saller, *Personal Patronage*, p. 1; Wallace-Hadrill, *Patronage in Ancient Society*, pp. 3–4.
24 See also Kettering, *Patrons, Brokers, and Clients*, p. 13; Bourne, *Patronage and Society*, pp. 5–8.
25 P. Garnsey and G. Woolf, 'Patronage of the Rural Poor in the Roman World', in A. Wallace-Hadrill, ed., *Patronage in Ancient Society*, pp. 158–9.

26 R. Horrox, *Richard III: A Study of Service* (Cambridge, 1989), pp. 1–26.
27 T. Johnson and C. Dandeker, 'Patronage: Relation and System', in A. Wallace-Hadrill, ed., *Patronage in Ancient Society*, pp. 219–42.
28 Neale, 'Elizabethan Political Scene', p. 104; Bourne, *Patronage and Society*, p. 58.
29 Kettering, *Patrons, Brokers, and Clients*, pp. 42–3; Bourne, *Patronage and Society*, p. 66.
30 Kettering, *Patrons, Brokers, and Clients*, pp. 40–67.
31 Bennett, *Community, Class and Careerism*, pp. 215–23; A.J. Pollard, 'The Richmondshire Community of Gentry During the Wars of the Roses', in C.D. Ross, ed., *Patronage, Pedigree and Power in Later Medieval England* (Gloucester, 1979), pp. 53–4; Horrox, *Richard III*, p. 49.
32 Saller, *Personal Patronage*, pp. 7–39; Kettering, *Patrons, Brokers, and Clients*, pp. 13–22.
33 Saller, 'Patronage and Friendship', pp. 49–62; Kettering, *Patrons, Brokers, and Clients*, pp. 43–4.
34 Horrox, *Richard III*, pp. 1–12.
35 For a discussion of the distinction between 'lordship' and 'mastership', see K.B. McFarlane, 'The Wars of the Roses', *Proceedings of the British Academy*, 50 (1964), p. 114, n. 2.
36 L. Stone, 'Prosopography', in L. Stone, *The Past and the Present* (London, 1981), pp. 45–73.
37 K. Leyser, 'Kenneth Bruce McFarlane, 1903–66', *Proceedings of the British Academy*, (1976), pp. 485–6; Cannon, 'Namier', pp. 148–50.
38 Richmond, 'After McFarlane', p. 60.
39 E.g. A. Everitt, *The Community of Kent and the Great Rebellion* (London, 1966); A. Fletcher, *A County Community at Peace and War: Sussex, 1600–1660* (London, 1975).
40 J.S. Morrill, *The Revolt of the Provinces*, 2nd edn (London, 1980), p. x; C. Holmes, 'The Concept of the "County Community" in Stuart Historiography', *Journal of British Studies*, 19 no. 2 (1980), pp. 54–73.
41 Ibid., pp. 56–61.
42 McFarlane, *Nobility*, p. 1.
43 Syme, *Roman Revolution*, p. 15; compare Neale, 'Elizabethan Political Scene', p. 97.
44 Syme, *Roman Revolution*, p. viii. See also L.B. Namier, *Personalities and Powers* (London, 1962), pp. 4–5; Stone, 'Prosopography', p. 54.
45 Horrox, *Richard III*, p. 120.
46 McFarlane, 'Parliament and Bastard Feudalism', p. 70.
47 Q.R.D. Skinner, 'The Principles and Practice of Opposition: the Case of Bolingbroke against Walpole', in N. McKendrick, ed., *Historical Perspectives: Studies in English Thought and Society in Honour of J.H. Plumb* (London, 1974), pp. 93–128. I am grateful to John Watts of the University of Wales at Aberystwyth for drawing my attention to this article.
48 Namier, *Structure of Politics*, p. vii; idem, *Personalities and Powers*, pp. 4–5.
49 E. Powell, *Kingship, Law, and Society: Criminal Justice in the Reign of Henry V* (Oxford, 1989), pp. 126–34; see, for example, T. Hoccleve, *The Regement of Princes*, ed. F.J. Furnivall, EETS, extra series, 72 (1897), pp. 89–196; B. Guenée, *States and Rulers in Later Medieval Europe* (Oxford, 1985), pp. 69–74.
50 Cambridge University Library MS Ee. III. 61, fos 159–75; see H.M. Carey, 'Astrology at the English Court in the Later Middle Ages', in P. Curry, ed., *Astrology, Science and Society* (Woodbridge, 1987), pp. 52–3.
51 M.K. Jones, 'Somerset, York and the Wars of the Roses', *EHR*, 104 (1989), pp. 285–307.
52 But see A.J. Pollard, *John Talbot and the War in France, 1427–53* (London, 1983), pp. 122–30.
53 See, for example, M. Aston, 'Lollardy and Sedition, 1381–1431', *Past and Present*, 17 (1960), pp. 1–44; repr. in eadem, *Lollards and Reformers* (London, 1984), pp. 1–44;

P. McNiven, *Heresy and Politics in the Reign of Henry IV: the Burning of John Badby* (Woodbridge, 1987).

54 A point made forcefully with regard to the present paper by Dr B. Thompson of Sidney Sussex College, Cambridge, in discussion at the Manchester conference.

55 See Powell, *Kingship, Law and Society*, pp. 1–9.

56 Johnson and Dandeker, 'Patronage: Relation and System', pp. 219–42.

57 Carpenter, 'The Beauchamp Affinity', p. 525.

58 See above, p. 9.

59 Cf. the comments of Professor Hilton on the late-medieval legal system: 'what was important in an inevitably decentralized state was not so much what the law was as who administered it and in whose interests' (R.H. Hilton, *A Medieval Society: the West Midlands at the End of the Thirteenth Century* (Cambridge, 1967), p. 219).

60 Kettering, *Patrons, Brokers, and Clients*, p. 5.

61 Quoted in V.J. Scattergood, *Politics and Poetry in the Fifteenth Century* (London, 1971), p. 321.

62 C. Phythian-Adams, 'Ceremony and the Citizen: the Communal Year at Coventry, 1450–1550', in P. Clark and P. Slack, eds, *Crisis and Order in English Towns, 1500–1700* (London, 1972), pp. 57–85; E. James, 'Ritual, Drama and Social Body in the Late Medieval English Town', *Past and Present*, 98 (1983), pp. 3–29.

2
Adam Fraunceys and John Pyel: Perceptions of Status Among Merchants in Fourteenth-Century London

Stephen O'Connor

'It is one of the commonplaces of English social history to remark upon the successful merchant's traditional ambition to become a gentleman.' So wrote Sylvia Thrupp in a book which celebrated the fortieth anniversary of its publication in 1988, and which remains the most comprehensive and detailed work yet produced on London mercantile society in the middle ages.[1] If such a remark was commonplace in 1948, it can hardly be less so today. We are all familiar with the theme of the humble provincial who set out for London to seek his fortune, went on to amass great wealth, and purchased in the process a large country estate where he eventually retired to enjoy the fruits of his enterprise. Indeed the seemingly eternal mirage of London as a city of gold, where large sums can be made by anyone with ability and energy, has done nothing to dispel this compelling vision of 'rags-to-riches' opportunity. But making money and becoming a gentleman are not necessarily synonymous in any age. Nor is it self-evident that gentry status was the ultimate goal to which all who embarked on a mercantile career in the fourteenth century aspired. It is the intention of this paper, therefore, to look again at the question of social mobility among London merchants in the later middle ages from the perspective of two case studies, namely two London mercers, John Pyel and Adam Fraunceys, and in so doing I should like to consider three questions. First, what factors defined a person's social status in the fourteenth century? Secondly, how and to what extent was a mercantile career instrumental in enabling men to transcend their social origins? And lastly, what can we tell of Fraunceys' and Pyel's aspirations and self-image, and how far did these accord with the reality of their status in English society?

The fourteenth century has been identified as a period of great social mobility. Several factors are held to account for this; falling population, particularly after the Black Death; growth in the land market, which resulted partly from dynastic failure among landowners, but also from the pressure to sell or lease estates as landed families faced economic decline and debt; and the rise in the numbers of men able to profit from the newly available land, including some lesser landowners, to be sure, but also upwardly-mobile careerists, lawyers, administrators, retainers of the rich and powerful, and merchant traders. There was the impact of the Hundred Years War, which probably acted rather as a catalyst to changes that were already afoot, contributing further to the impoverishment of landholders whose resources were already overstretched, boosting the fortunes of retainers by means of military service, and providing opportunities of pure gold to merchant financiers like William de la Pole. Whatever the causes, the effects were keenly felt.

In 1363 sumptuary laws were introduced to regulate expenditure on clothing and food.[2] Too many people of lesser estate, it seems, were aping their betters in what they wore and, presumably, in the delicacies with which they graced their tables. All this was forcing up prices 'to the great damage of the lords and commons', but, more especially, it threatened to erode the social barriers that separated the established hierarchy, the knights and above, from what might be called the 'other ranks'. Nigel Saul, in his book on the Gloucestershire gentry, refers to the gradual differentiation which was taking place among that hotch-potch of ill-defined groups that were, as it were, bubbling under the rank of knight. These were identified by the Latin nouns *armiger, valettus, serviens ad arma,* and *scutifer.* At the end of the thirteenth century there was seemingly little to choose between them in order of precedence. During the fourteenth century, however, these distinctions became less fluid, as the *armiger,* or esquire, approached the knight in local status, and the *valettus* drifted down towards the stolid smallholder who came to be represented by the English word yeoman.[3] But these more discrete classes do not make the picture any less complicated. Dr Saul has noted, for example, that the Gloucestershire poll tax returns identify four *armigeri* who were assessed at quite different rates of tax. Two of them were lords of manors, while the others were broadly equivalent to those middle-ranking freeholders known as franklins.[4] The sumptuary laws of 1363 subdivided both esquires and knights by income, but even more significant for our purposes is the way in which the same legislation was forced to take into account wealthy townsmen who possessed no land.[5] Clearly men of such substance could not be ignored, but to compensate for their lack of land, income requirements were raised considerably. So merchants, citizens, burgesses and the like, in London and elsewhere, with goods and chattels worth £500, could wear clothes permitted to esquires and gentlemen worth £100 a year. To qualify for parity with the upper division of esquire and gentleman, worth £200 a year, goods to the value of £1,000 were stipulated.[6] In social terms, unearned income from land, 'livelihood', was still at a premium.

Income and land were therefore crucial in determining personal status, but in view of the considerable overlap that continued to exist between classes, other factors were evidently in force. A third criterion must have been the function a man fulfilled in his region: lordship of a manor, holding local office as sheriff, for example, or serving on commissions of the peace or on the grand jury. Active participation in local government would have made an important contribution to an individual's reputation in his locality.[7] A fourth element was birth. The extent to which birth mattered is less easy to define than levels of income, but there were numbers of families who were considered knightly, whether or not knighthood was taken up in every generation, and Sylvia Thrupp has pondered the status of the man of gentle birth fallen on hard times, compared with the *nouveau riche* on his newly acquired estate.[8] Chris Given-Wilson provides a partial answer by saying that many in the fifteenth century who described themselves as 'gentlemen' were not themselves possessed of land, but were either in service or in trade, yet he does not believe that contemporaries regarded them as socially inferior, say, to a merchant who had acquired land to the value of £10–£15 *per annum*. Gentle birth, he concludes, was every bit as important as landed income.[9] This point may be illustrated in reverse by a quotation from Froissart. Froissart has a reputation as a narrator of colourful and dramatic stories which occasionally coincide with historical fact. On a point of social standing, however, we might expect that Jean, who was, after all, something of a snob, knew what he was talking about. In a famous episode, the Norfolk insurgents at the time of the Peasants' Revolt press Sir Robert Salle to lead them with these words:

> 'Robert, you are a knight and a man of great weight in this country . . . but notwithstanding this, we know who you are. You are not a gentleman, but the son of a poor mason, just such as ourselves. Do you come with us and be our commander.'[10]

This story illustrates two important points; first that native origins were significant in determining a man's place in society, and secondly that social status was as much conferred by the acknowledgement of others as assumed by the individual himself, or, for that matter, granted by the king.

Social status in late medieval England depended upon a combination of factors, including landed wealth, function in the locality, good birth and acceptance by one's peers,[11] which gave to the upper ranks of society a measure of flexibility and openness that allowed those at the lower end to ascend, those from outside to enter, and inevitably, those at the top to subside.

Perhaps one further general comment should be made before turning to Adam Frraunceys and John Pyel. When social mobility among merchants is discussed, it is generally assumed that this implies movement from the town to the countryside, from merchandise to land. This was undoubtedly the route that most social climbers took. As Michael Bennett has remarked, the only way of registering social advancement in medieval England was through the acquisition of the landed estate, and by attempting to rejoin the tenurial hierarchy at a higher level.[12] Perhaps the best-known example of mercantile mobility, William de la Pole, though he eventually fell foul of the king, died possessed of a mosaic of properties in Yorkshire, Lincolnshire and Durham, and he bequeathed to his son a legacy rich enough to sustain the dignity of an earldom, and to make him one of the most powerful men at court.[13] Yet not all successful merchants were so anxious to follow the yellow-brick-road to gentility. Richard Whittington was the younger son of a gentry family in Gloucestershire who became, as we all know, one of the wealthiest and most influential London citizens of his day, yet he neither invested in a large estate nor retired to a country seat, though he lived into his sixties at least. His bequests were directed towards London. He endowed almshouses there and a college of priests, and made provision for the rebuilding of Newgate gaol and work to be carried out on Guildhall library.[14]

Whittington is obviously exceptional; he had no children to provide for, and few seem to have followed his example. What his career illustrates, however, is partly that wealth might be considered its own reward, but, more cogently, that civic interest, culture and vision could so colour an individual's world picture that he could resist the lure of a place in the landed social hierarchy. The influence of city life on these great merchants was doubtless deeper than the often over-simplified accounts of gentrification might lead us to suspect.

Adam Fraunceys and John Pyel were, as far as I can tell, newcomers to London. The evidence for Fraunceys is admittedly negative, but in the absence of any reference to his parentage, and given the high incidence of immigration into London, it is likely that he was new to the city or at most a first generation Londoner. With Pyel we are on firmer ground. He came from Irthlingborough, on the banks of the River Nene in Northamptonshire, where his family had originally been bondmen of Peterborough abbey, but had perhaps become well-to-do peasants by the time John left for London.[15] Fraunceys and Pyel emerge in the records, the one in 1339, the other in 1346, as well-established and already moderately wealthy merchants.[16] They were mercers, business partners and personal friends, often acting together in the purchase of land. They were presumably apprenticed at some time in the 1320s, and would have received at least a rudimentary education. Pyel may have been educated in Northamptonshire with his younger brother, Henry, who went on to study at Oxford, and eventually became archdeacon of Northampton.[17]

The most important asset these merchants possessed for advancement was their conspicuous wealth, which was created first by their trade as mercers, and secondly through their rôle as financiers. They were able to invest heavily in real property, both within the city, where they acted largely as rentiers, and outside. Large sums were spent in acts of piety during their lifetime, and more was provided for the same purpose in their wills. But the quantities of money each was able to advance in loans is ample testimony of the resources that they had at their disposal. In the course of his career, Adam Fraunceys, either on his own or with others, lent in excess of £11,000 to the king alone, and Pyel in the region of £22,000, excluding contributions to corporate loans or gifts made by the city. Many of these loans, it is true, were advanced through a consortium, or raised as a form of brokerage, but even to contemplate offering a sum as large as 10,000 marks, as Pyel did in 1372, suggests he had sufficient reserves to cover it.[18] Along with the other merchant capitalists, they made themselves virtually indispensable to the king, and part of the reward for their reliability was the award of office under the Crown. Pyel served in the royal exchanges in the early 1350s, a common post for royal financiers, and throughout his career he was involved in diplomatic service. In 1364 he was appointed, with Adam Fraunceys, to a commission of enquiry into the administration of Calais, where he evidently spent some time, as he was granted a licence to ship foodstuffs there to support his household.[19] Pyel was less interested in London affairs. He represented the city twice in parliament, in 1361 and in 1376, but he did not become an alderman until 1369, and was sheriff in 1369 and mayor in 1372.[20] Fraunceys, by contrast, was catapulted into office in 1352, when he was elected alderman and mayor in the same year, and was thus burdened with civic responsibilities almost twenty years before his friend.[21] Fraunceys, too, was summoned to perform services for the Crown, where he was often called upon to give the benefit of his experience. Hence in 1369 he was asked to make recommendations to the council for the protection of merchant shipping against French attack.[22] He was also appointed to serve on several commissions and was on one occasion entrusted with a mission of some delicacy. In 1369, the king of Scotland, David II, summarily set aside his wife, Margaret Logie, in the expectation of marrying a younger and, it was hoped, more fruitful queen. His hopes were in vain, however, and he died in 1371 without heir.[23] The following year, Edward III, or his officials, in an effort to make matters even more uncomfortable for the new Scottish king, encouraged Margaret to travel to Avignon to appeal in the curia against her divorce.[24] Margaret had had a long-standing quarrel with the steward of Scotland, now Robert II, whom she blamed for her disgrace, and she possessed endless reserves of enmity, which could usefully be tapped by the English king. Unfortunately, she had only limited reserves of cash, since she had been left with a less than generous pension by King

David, and Edward was able to tempt her to Avignon by paying her 500 marks, over three times her annual pension, which was delivered in the guise of a loan from three London merchants, Adam Fraunceys, his son-in-law, John Aubrey, and William Walworth, and paid through the agency of two Italian bankers. The merchants were repaid in cash directly from the exchequer.[25] A further 1,000 marks was made over in 1374, and payment was executed by the same device.[26] This rather long-winded, not to say costly, attempt at political sabotage was very nearly successful. Margaret was on the point of winning her appeal, and there was talk of placing Scotland under an interdict, when she died suddenly in 1375, and the case was allowed to drop.[27]

Despite his engagement by the king on a matter of such sensitivity, Fraunceys' activities seem less weighted towards the court than Pyel's, who used the services he had rendered to the Crown to avoid shouldering other responsibilities. In 1360 he received a letter patent from the king granting him exemption from all form of judicial or civic office against his will, a concession of which he made full use.[28]

Office-holding under the king reflected status as much as conferred it. The same could be said of the patronage extended to merchants by members of the gentry and aristocracy. Such links are well-known; for example, those of the Celys with Sir John Weston, prior of the order of St John of Jerusalem in England, in the fifteenth century, and John Philpot with the earl of Arundel in the fourteenth.[29] Often the service required was financial, as in the case of currency exchanges provided by Philpot and Nicholas Brembre for John of Gaunt.[30] There was no question of social equality being assumed by these associations, but powerful and prestigious patrons conferred a dignity and honour upon their clients, which may have been, as Thrupp says, incalculable, but cannot have been negligible. Adam Fraunceys is known to have had links with several aristocratic families, including the Montagu earls of Salisbury, and the Bohun earls of Hereford, Essex and Northampton. Fraunceys' connections with the Montagus are to be inferred mainly through the marriage of his daughter, Maud, to John Montagu between November 1381 and May 1383, possibly after his father had become heir to the Salisbury title.[31] Montagu succeeded to the earldom in 1397, and suffered the double misfortune of losing Richard II's Welsh troops in 1399, and his own head after the ill-conceived rebellion of 1400. There is no evidence of a close association between the families before the marriage.

Fraunceys' closest ties with the aristocracy were with Humphrey de Bohun, earl of Hereford. It is not known when and how the connection was made, but it is interesting to note that Adam became friendly with Peter Favelor, a trusted retainer of Humphrey's father, William de Bohun, earl of Northampton. George Holmes describes Favelor as one of the most

active of Bohun's servants, and he was attorney, and later executor, for the
earl. He was certainly highly favoured by his lord and received from him a
number of manors in Dorset, Oxfordshire, Essex and Kent.[32] Favelor also
owned property in London and was co-founder of a chantry at Guildhall
with Fraunceys and Henry Frowyk.[33] More significantly, in the 1350s he
purchased, jointly with Adam Fraunceys, land in Edmonton which was
later to form the core of the Fraunceys estate in Middlesex, part of which
bordered Humphrey de Bohun's own manor of Enfield. In return, Adam
completed and endowed a chantry chapel which Peter had founded for
himself in the parish church at Edmonton.[34] In 1366 Earl Humphrey
nominated Adam Fraunceys to be one of his attorneys during his absence
overseas, and in 1371 Bohun made over a number of manors and
reversions to a group of feoffees, one of whom was Adam, his neighbour
and by this time his friend.[35] Some of the feoffees, including Simon
Sudbury, bishop of London, Sir Guy de Bryan and Sir Philip de Meldreth,
were appointed Hereford's executors in December 1372, but to Adam was
accorded the especial honour of supervising his will, in company with
Bohun's widow, Joan, and her father Richard Fitzalan, earl of Arundel.[36]
Whatever the degree of intimacy which existed between them, Fraunceys'
relationship with Hereford was founded at the very least on deep trust and
mutual respect. There can be little doubt that Adam was able to exploit
this connection to gain social credibility as a newly-arrived tenant-in-chief
of the king.

John Pyel did not cultivate links with aristocratic families in quite the
same way, though as we shall see, he was closely associated with John of
Gaunt, which may partly account for his more particular interests at court,
especially in the 1370s.

Marriage does not seem to have played much part in the advance of
either man's career. Both married capable and resourceful women of whose
background we know nothing. After Adam's death, Agnes Fraunceys
continued to act as a property trustee in concert with friends and associates
of her husband, such as William Walworth, Nicholas Brembre and John
Philpot, and presumably helped to look after the family interests. She took
over the guardianship of Paul, son of Sir Thomas Salesbury, a near
neighbour of the Fraunceys at Walthamstow,[37] and in 1388 lent £700 to
the king in her own right.[38] Joan Pyel, as a widow, resumed her husband's
attempt to found a college of secular priests at Irthlingborough, despite stiff
opposition from the bishop of Lincoln, and six years after her husband's
death successfully completed the foundation which he had begun.[39] Pyel's
son, Nicholas, married into an apparently solid but undistinguished
family,[40] while the Fraunceys' heirs aimed somewhat higher. Adam
Fraunceys junior married Margaret, the widow of Thomas Tudenham,
London citizen, and later Margaret, sister of Sir John Holland.[41] Young

Adam's sister, Maud, married three times, each husband representing in cameo a step up the social ladder; first a prominent London citizen, John Aubrey, grocer, second, a courtier and chamberlain of the royal household, Sir Alan Buxhill, and third, John Montagu, the future earl of Salisbury.

The biographical details outlined so far have described little more than career development and associations with men of high degree. The evidence does not demonstrate enhanced status conclusively, although the implications are clear. Nevertheless, it is perhaps possible to move closer to the social aspirations and achievements of these men, by looking at aspects of their lives which are more suggestive of their social awareness, such as their adoption of armorial bearings, their attitudes to religious piety, but most especially their acquisition of land.

Settlement on estates outside London does not prove that a merchant desired to become a gentleman. Admission into a network of traditional social and political affiliations cannot have been an easy or inevitable consequence of land purchase. It is necessary, therefore, to try to determine at what level merchants entered society in the counties, and what influence they brought to bear in their new *loci operandi*. As so often in medieval history, the question is infinitely easier to ask than to answer. We need to know how merchants operated in the countryside, what responsibilities they undertook, and with whom they consorted. In the case of Adam Fraunceys and John Pyel there is virtually nothing to show how they spent their time on their manors, nor, indeed, how much time they spent there at all. However, we do have two cartularies, books of charters drawn up some time after both had begun to acquire land, which indicate a rationale behind each merchant's purchases, and provide, in the case of Pyel at least, a more complete corpus of witnesses than we would otherwise have. They also, by their very existence, give some clue to the Londoners' personal response to their move to the countryside.

Adam Fraunceys bought or received land in a number of counties, but for his principal holdings he tended not to stray too far from London. His earliest foray into the land market outside the city was the manor of Wyke, including tenements in Hackney and Stepney, which he bought from his fellow mercer John Causton in February 1349. Causton had inherited these lands from Simon de Abyndon, yet another Londoner, by marrying his widow, Eve. It was in fact Abyndon who had built up the manor, which consisted of at least two messuages and some 150 acres of land by the time it came into Fraunceys' hands.[42] Fraunceys continued to expand his holding by buying up small parcels through clerical agents or by purchasing directly himself. Those who held the land previously often turn out to have been London citizens. Richer de Refham, a mercer and former mayor, had sold land to Simon de Abyndon, and Fraunceys himself bought land from Walter Turk, who had been mayor in 1349–50.[43] Not surprisingly, Hackney Wick was a desirable prospect for Londoners, given its proximity to the city, and it had no doubt been colonised by citizens from an early date.

Ruckholts and Chobhams were manors in Essex, within a few miles of each other and of Wyke. Ruckholts was a small manor in the parish of Leyton, which two agents of Adam Fraunceys obtained in 1350 and passed on to Adam nine years later.[44] The Chobhams estate comprised lands in West Ham, East Ham and Barking, and a small amount of pasture and meadow in Stratford. It had been purchased and consolidated in the early 1330s by John Preston, corder, a man of considerable wealth, whose granddaughter married John of Northampton, one of the principal protagonists of London politics in the 1380s.[45]

The centrepiece of Adam's estate was at Edmonton in north Middlesex. Initially he bought lands there piecemeal. Between 1351 and 1360, he and Peter Favelor acquired two manors, which had been held by the Londoners William Causton and Roger Depham, both mercers, and a further 550 acres of land in smaller parcels.[46] In 1361, William de Say, lord of the manor of Edmonton itself, came of age and took possession of his lands. Finding himself in severe financial straits, he first leased, then mortgaged the manor to Adam Fraunceys in March 1362 for £1,000, before granting it to him in perpetuity.[47]

The pattern of Fraunceys' land purchases, therefore, shows quite clearly their London orientation. Starting close to the city, his acquisitions gradually fanned out, but remained within close contact of London. Those selling to him were frequently Londoners, and Fraunceys can hardly be said to have moved outside the sphere of city influence; the colonisation of Middlesex by Londoners is well documented, as is their use of the land for direct exploitation.[48] While I would not like to suggest that Fraunceys was using his estate merely as an adjunct to his commercial activities, neither can the motives which lay behind his appropriations be explained simply in terms of gentrification. They reveal complex cultural, social and economic influences, which were closely intertwined, and the common thread which bound them was London.

The creation of John Pyel's estates, on the other hand, betrays different forces at work. Pyel began to make his purchases at roughly the same time as Fraunceys. In 1348 he inherited land from his father in Irthlingborough and in the same year received the manor of Cransley, also in Northamptonshire, from Lady Elizabeth Wake, probably as a result of debt.[49] His lands were situated in the east of the county and consisted mostly of a group of manors clustered within a five- to six-mile radius of Irthlingborough. Smaller parcels of land were added to consolidate the holdings, and Pyel was evidently aiming for a moderately-sized but compact estate. The reasons for Pyel's estate building had little to do with

London. It cannot be certain how much time he spent at Irthlingborough before his eventual retirement from the city around 1378–9, yet he does seem to have maintained an interest in the region, which no doubt had something to do with his trading activities, but also reveals where his loyalties ultimately lay. Apart from buying up quantities of cereals in the east midlands and Yorkshire to ship to London, Pyel was appointed in 1370 to a commission to investigate obstructions of the River Ouse in Huntingdonshire, which were seriously hampering the passage of goods from neighbouring counties.[50] In the early 1350s he and Fraunceys had a contract to buy wool from the abbey of Sulby in the county, and he also had a receiver in Northampton to look after his interests there.[51] In 1347 Pyel and a neighbour, John Curteys of Higham Ferrers, had been appointed collectors of wool for the customs farmers in the counties of Huntingdon and Northampton.[52] Given the general paucity of evidence concerning Pyel's trading activities, the east midlands would seem to feature quite prominently, suggesting a distinct bias towards that region, and the possibility that Pyel spent a sizeable proportion of his time there.

What sort of a figure did Pyel cut in his county? Middlesex we noted as being very much London-dominated in the fourteenth century, but Northamptonshire was different. Sylvia Thrupp has observed that a number of Londoners had bought lands in the county, and in the east midlands and East Anglia in general, but the turnover in land was likely to have been smaller than in the home counties, and newcomers probably made a greater impact.[53] There are no extant court rolls relating to the manors which Pyel held at the time, nor do we know of any local office that he held. The men with whom he associated are known almost entirely from the witness lists on his charters, apart from a few who appear in his will. Those who appear most frequently are all described as 'of Irthlingborough', and none is of any great standing. The names of the leading families of the locality, the Draytons, for example, or the Zouches of Harringworth, seldom appear, and then only when transacting business with Pyel, or supporting each other in the process. Politically, however, Pyel's place in the county was determined by the proximity of his lands to the Northamptonshire estate of John of Gaunt. Gaunt held the neighbouring manors of Higham Ferrers, Raunds, Rushden and Irchester, ranged on the opposite bank of the River Nene from Irthlingborough.[54] Others have drawn attention to Pyel's connection with Gaunt. Ruth Bird and Chris Given-Wilson both note a letter in Gaunt's register written in April 1375 and addressed to the duke's officials in Northamptonshire, ordering them not to make purveyance of Pyel's goods or those of his tenants, and to extend to him 'all ease and comfort'.[55] Miss Bird deduces from this that Pyel held a seigniory of Gaunt, and Given-Wilson describes Pyel as 'a friend of Gaunt, with whom he went to Bruges for the peace negotiations of 1374', and cites him as an example of those London merchants who were in close contact with the court clique.[56] On this last point Given-Wilson is undoubtedly correct. Pyel was heavily involved with men like William Latimer and Richard Lyons who were impeached in the Good Parliament of 1376, and was himself interrogated in the same parliament, though he escaped on a technicality.[57] Whether Pyel could be described as a friend of Gaunt is less certain. Gaunt's letter refers to him as '*nostre tres cher et bien ame Johan Pyel*', though that could be construed as conventional phrasing. And while it is true that Pyel was in Bruges at the same time as Gaunt's delegation, he was in fact taking part in talks with Flemish merchants as he had done earlier in the decade, and there is no evidence that he was directly involved in the peace negotiations with France.[58] Yet he was very friendly with the lawyer, John Holt, who was Gaunt's steward at Higham Ferrers from 1377 until at least October 1382, and one of the men whom Pyel made supervisors of his will.[59] And in July 1364, a commission of oyer and terminer was appointed to inquire into 'trespasses, extortions, damages and grievances' perpetrated in Northamptonshire against the king, Gaunt, Pyel and three other Irthlingborough men, as well as Lancaster's retainers and servants.[60] The inference is that the main target of these attacks had been the duke and that the inclusion of Pyel and those in his circle probably implies close political links with Gaunt.

The patterns of land purchase therefore suggest that while Fraunceys was keen to remain in contact with London, Pyel ultimately intended to cut all ties with the city. Fraunceys bought land in areas where Londoners had previously settled in large numbers. There was no desire to go back to the land of his forebears, whereas Pyel returned not only to his native county, but to his ancestral village. Fraunceys' friendship with his neighbour, Humphrey de Bohun, is mirrored by John of Gaunt's patronage of Pyel. For Pyel, London was a means to an end; it was the trading, financial and political centre of England. When he felt that he had finally outstayed his welcome after 1376, he retired to the estate that he had created for himself, well away from the city.

Rank, of course, brings with it responsibility, and the status of both men is reflected in the obligations which they recognised towards God and to those of His creatures who were beholden to them. In several places in his will, Pyel referred to those '*a queux je sui tenuz*'. He and Fraunceys evinced a strong commitment to their religious lives. What the spiritual content of that commitment was is an open question. The endowment of a church or the foundation of a chantry presupposes a level of Christian faith, but equally it demonstrates a response to prevailing social conventions. So, both men signalled their intention to go on pilgrimage to Rome in the jubilee year of 1350, but whether in response to a genuine religious fervour, or, to borrow the words of Jacques de Vitry, 'out of mere curiosity and novelty', who can tell?[61] Indeed, it is equally possible that they commuted their visit, while retaining the indulgence, by payment of a sum of money.[62] Jonathan Sumption, however, identifies the late fourteenth century as the beginning of a second phase of the 'noble pilgrimage', and it is possible that, even by the middle of the century, travel to exotic parts was regarded as an activity in which an aspiring individual might wish to engage, especially if it was undertaken with a degree of ostentation.[63] In 1363 John Pyel made elaborate preparations for a second pilgrimage, this time to Galicia.[64] Santiago had become a thriving commercial centre, and Pyel may have been intending to combine business with penitence. In terms of religious or social kudos, however, it apparently did not rank among the shrines most popular with noble pilgrims, who favoured the Holy Land, as well as Mont St Michel and Le Puy.[65]

It was not uncommon for those who had the resources to found chantries, where one or more priests would be employed to say daily masses and to recite prayers and psalms for the repose of the soul of the founder and his family. Men of substance tended to provide for these endowments in their wills, but occasionally chantries were set up for charitable purposes during their founders' lifetimes. Shortly before November 1356, Adam Fraunceys, Peter Favelor and Henry Frowyk founded a chantry in the chapel of St Mary, Guildhall, which was to be maintained by a college of five priests and endowed by lands and rents in a number of city parishes.[66] Some years later, in 1363, Fraunceys built a chapel to the Holy Ghost adjoining the church of the convent of St Helen's, Bishopsgate, where he had his London residence, and in November 1364 he successfully petitioned for an indulgence on behalf of those who made visits there on the principal feast days.[67] In his will, Fraunceys instructed his executors to instal two further chantries at St Helen's, where he was to be buried, and to enlarge the chantry in the parish church at Edmonton, which Peter Favelor had founded.[68] Although Fraunceys had established his estate at Edmonton long before his will was drawn up, he provided no chantry there for himself or his family, but chose, rather, to be buried and prayed for where he had lived, within the precincts of a London nunnery.

Pyel's acts of piety reveal a similar disposition, but in a different direction. He made no religious foundations in the city, although he did bequeath money to certain London ecclesiastical institutions in his will. In 1375 the abbey of Peterborough was granted, at Pyel's behest, a licence to erect the parish church of St Peter at Irthlingborough into a college of six secular canons, including a dean, and four clerks.[69] This is Pyel's greatest monument, and it was not achieved easily. Pyel himself did not live to see its completion, and it was left to his redoubtable widow to fulfil the wishes of her husband. As well as the physical expansion of St Peter's to accommodate the college chaplains, the church underwent a period of rebuilding in the mid- to late-fourteenth century, which included the addition of a tower at the west end, on which are displayed the Pyel arms, a bend separating two mullets.[70] These arms are also to be found prominently placed either side of the west door which give the church a distinctly proprietorial air. Pyel's reasons for founding the college included those intentions which lay behind the establishment of chantries. There was to be a continuous stream of liturgical prayer rising to heaven for the repose of his soul. But an important part of the college's function was to enhance the religious life of the parish. The college was to provide masses and canonical services at which parishioners could assist, and may have been intended to offer some elementary education for the young of Irthlingborough and the surrounding parishes.[71]

The founder evidently saw himself both in the mould of the great lay patrons of the past, and also as fulfilling the rôle of lord in his county. Historians have remarked on the tendency among the upper ranks of late medieval English society to transfer their patronage away from monasteries towards the parish church, a move which was often signalled by the appearance of heraldic decoration. Nigel Saul provides a good illustration of this in his account of the Etchingham family in Sussex.[72] In the 1360s William de Etchingham rebuilt his parish church, which he emblazoned with coats of arms representing men of every social rank, from the king and princes of the blood royal, down to members of the local gentry, allowing due prominence to the arms of his own family. There had been an earlier dispute between the Etchinghams and the monks of Robertsbridge abbey, who had been the principal religious beneficiaries of their patronage, but grants to the abbey had subsequently been resumed, and Dr Saul concludes that the decision to rebuild Etchingham church rested on the fact that 'after the fashion of the time, [William de Etchingham] chose to make the parish church . . . the focus of the religious and to some extent the social aspirations of his family'.[73]

Such parish consciousness was also reflected in Pyel's will. Both churches in Irthlingborough received vestments and liturgical books and vessels, and sums were provided for the maintenance of a further seventeen local churches and the charitable support of their parishioners. Two of these churches received slightly more than the rest, and in recognition of his munificence, St Mary's, Little Addington, carries the Pyel arms on its restored belfry.[74] At a more mundane level, Pyel set aside money for the repair of Irthlingborough bridge and the highway and the erection of thirteen stone crosses in and around the village, and among other charitable works, he left £25 to be distributed among his poor relatives in the county. Whatever his true place in Northamptonshire society, Pyel had sufficient resources to ensure a conspicuous contribution to his locality in death, and this shows more clearly than anything else his identification with his native region and his desire to be remembered there with honour and respect.

John Pyel, with his compact estate in the east midlands and his assumption of many of the facets of patronage, appears to have been more conscious of his gentry status than Adam Faunceys. But in a subject of such complexity, impressions can be misleading. As great burgesses, holding senior civic office in London, both men would have displayed the trappings of gentility which were accorded to their status within the city, and which in some cases corresponded to a similar rank outside. We have already noted the equation between merchants and esquires devised by the sumptuary laws of 1363.[75] Merchants could also bear arms, a concession which had been known and accepted in Europe by the thirteenth century, and the higher echelons of the merchant class in London enjoyed a quasi-military status equivalent at least to that of a knight. During the earlier part of the fourteenth century, aldermen were buried with full baronial honours, a rider appearing in the cortège mounted upon a richly caparisoned horse, displaying the armour of the deceased, his banner and his shield.[76] Arms were also adopted for use on seals, serving not only as status symbols, but also a necessary practical function, and while it was common in the fourteenth century, and almost universal in the fifteenth, for aldermen to bear arms, this did not preclude their adoption by merchants who had not attained that rank.[77] Faunceys and Pyel had armorial bearings of heraldic device, which both had adopted before they became aldermen, and which, as we have seen, Pyel chose to display in a very gentry-like fashion on the churches in his locality.[78] Adam Faunceys, too, would have thought of himself as equal to a knight of the shire at least, even though he neglected to take up knighthood itself. That his gaze was directed towards London did not reduce the consciousness of his own dignity or that of his family, and it is the family which provides the key to Faunceys' attitude to status.

What links Pyel and Faunceys, apart from their friendship and business association, is that both produced cartularies, that is, books of charters relating to their land-holdings. I have not time here to describe in detail these two interesting documents. Suffice to say that the survival of mercantile cartularies is exceedingly rare. Most cartularies were drawn up by monasteries and other ecclesiastical institutions with large estates.[79] Some lay cartularies survive, usually belonging to the greater landowning families. That these two merchants should have seen fit to produce them argues strongly that they were concerned to create a landed estate for future generations. This is more clearly visible in the case of the Faunceys cartulary. It was compiled in 1362, two years after Peter Favelor's share of the Edmonton properties reverted to Adam, and the very year in which William de Say alienated the manor of Edmonton itself. The muniment was systematically organised and professionally executed, and while doubtless useful as a work of reference, that was not its primary purpose. Once completed, no new charters were transcribed, although Adam continued to consolidate his holdings. Rather, the cartulary signalled Adam's intention to establish himself as a substantial landowner outside London, marking out Edmonton as the seat on which he was aiming to settle his dynasty. Although Adam senior spent little time in Edmonton himself, his son took up knighthood, unlike his father, and settled on the manor, serving as knight of the shire for Middlesex and sheriff of Hertfordshire and Essex.[80] Pyel's son, Nicholas, however, is a shadowy figure, and evidently failed to live up to the elevated model provided by his father. Neither family had male heirs surviving to the third generation, and their lands eventually passed to the gentry, or in the case of Maud Fraunceys, the aristocratic, families into which the daughters married.

The material I have considered in this paper as evidence of actual social mobility and perceived notions of status has necessarily been mostly indicative or suggestive, yet certain patterns of thought and behaviour have emerged. One can broadly distinguish between Adam Fraunceys, on the one hand, primarily a merchant and citizen of London, concerned with civic affairs, prepared to undertake civic office and to foster the development of his career through his commercial and city connections; and on the other, John Pyel, who never completely severed his Northamptonshire roots, eschewed civic office for as long as he decently could, became embroiled in court factional politics, and eventually left London, if not in disgrace, certainly under suspicion, to invest his heart, soul and money pouches in the soil of his native county. But Pyel could not entirely cut his ties with London. So in his will he entrusted his two sons' upbringing and education to Nicholas Brembre, grocer and mayor of London and John of Northampton's rival in the 1380s, he acknowledged his debt to John de Wesenham, Adam Fraunceys and William Halden, all of whom he had met and associated with in London, and he patronised St Helen's Bishopsgate, the Charterhouse and the friaries of London.[81] Pyel had spent the whole of his working life in the capital; friends, acquaintances, business interests, the city way of life, all would have had a profound influence upon him which could not simply be shaken off like dust from the feet. And for all his grand gestures in Irthlingborough, there is no evidence that Pyel had a major rôle to play in the life of his county. Moreover, the established families of his corner of Northamptonshire, who had controlled local office for generations, may have had to deal with Pyel on a business level, but showed little sign of welcoming him as a friend and equal.

Fraunceys, too, looked further than the confines of London. He fraternised with the nobility and undertook important missions for the Crown. He knew well senior figures at court, even if the focus of his attention did not lie there. And as I have intimated, his estate at Edmonton was not just a convenient country retreat to which he could retire when life in the city became impossible. We can detect in these men subtleties of emphasis, priority and loyalty which were fashioned by a variety of often conflicting cultural, social and political influences to which each was exposed during his career as a London merchant. The term 'merchant class' embraces such a wide group of disparate individuals, with their own perceptions and aspirations, that we need to take a longer look at the men who so often lie entombed within its anonymous corporate image. By putting some flesh on the statistical skeleton, we may hope to create a more three-dimensional picture of city life, and, more especially, of the men who dominated it.

Notes

1   S.L. Thrupp, *The Merchant Class of Medieval London 1300–1500* (Chicago, 1948), p. 234.
2   *RP*, II, p. 278.
3   N.E. Saul, *Knights and Esquires: the Gloucestershire Gentry in the Fourteenth Century* (Oxford, 1981), pp. 16–18.
4   Ibid., p. 19.
5   *RP*, II, pp. 278–9.
6   Ibid.
7   See Saul, *Knights and Esquires*, p. 20, and R.H. Hilton, *English Peasantry in the Later Middle Ages* (Oxford, 1975), pp. 26–7.
8   Thrupp, *Merchant Class*, p. 246.
9   C. Given-Wilson, *The Nobility of Later Medieval England: the Fourteenth-Century Political Community* (London, 1988), p. 72.
10 M.H. Keen, 'Robin Hood – Peasant or Gentleman?' in R.H. Hilton, ed., *Peasants, Knights and Heretics: Studies in Medieval English Social History* (Cambridge, 1976), p. 265.
11 Among others, service and association with men of high degree, for example.
12 M.J. Bennett, 'Sources and Problems in the Study of Social Mobility: Cheshire in the Later Middle Ages', *Trans of the Historic Soc. of Lancashire and Cheshire*, 128 (1979), p. 84.
13 For a recent biography of Pole, see E.B. Fryde, *William de la Pole, Merchant and King's Banker* (London, 1988).
14 C.M. Barron, 'Richard Whittington: The Man behind the Myth' in A.E. Hollander and W. Kellaway, eds, *Studies in London History Presented to P.E. Jones* (London, 1969), pp. 197–248.
15 *Carte Nativorum: a Peterborough Abbey Cartulary of the Fourteenth Century*, eds C.N.L. Brooke and M.M. Postan, Northants. Record Society, 20 (1960), nos 65–8, 389. John Pyel inherited land in Irthlingborough from his father in 1348 (Pyel cartulary, College of Arms (hereafter CA), Vincent 64, fo. 46r).
16 *Wardrobe Book of William de Norwell 1338–40*, eds M. Lyon, B. Lyon, H. Lucas (Brussels, 1983), p. 289; *CCR, 1338–40*, p. 405; *CCR, 1346–9*, p. 166.

17 J. Le Neve, ed., *Fasti Ecclesiae Anglicanae 1300–1541*, 1: *Lincoln Diocese*, rev. edn by H.P.F. King (London, 1962), p. 11.
18 *CCR, 1370–4*, pp. 196–7. Pyel made a second, even larger loan to the Crown in August 1374, jointly with the wealthy vintner, Richard Lyons, which was called into question during the Good Parliament of 1376 for the excessive rate of interest levied. For a general discussion of these loans, see G.A. Holmes, *The Good Parliament* (Oxford, 1975), pp. 69–79.
19 T. Rymer, *Foedera*, 4 vols in 7 (London, 1816–69), III part 2, pp. 722, 741.
20 *Return of Members of Parliament* (London, 1878, reprinted Munich, 1980), I, p. 167; R.R. Sharpe, ed., *Calendar of Letter Books of the City of London A–L* (London, 1899–1912) (hereafter *Letter Book*) H, p. 20. Adam Fraunceys served as an M.P. at least six, and probably seven, times between 1352 and 1366, as well as representing the city at the council of 1369.
21 A.B. Beaven, *The Aldermen of the City of London, temp. Henry III–1908* (London 1908), I, p. 189.
22 *Letter Book G*, p. 255.
23 R. Nicholson, *Scotland: the Later Middle Ages* (Edinburgh, 1974), pp. 182–3.
24 *Calendar of Documents relating to Scotland*, ed. G. Burnett (Edinburgh, 1878), IV, p. 401.
25 *Foedera*, III part 2, p. 938; PRO E403/444, 20 February 1372.
26 PRO E403/451, 25 March 1374.
27 Nicholson, *Scotland*, p. 183; *Calendar of the Exchequer Rolls of Scotland*, ed. J. Bain (Edinburgh 1888), II, p. lxv.
28 *CPR, 1358–61*, p. 433.
29 Thrupp, *Merchant Class*, pp. 183–4; K.B. McFarlane, *The English Nobility in the Later Middle Ages* (Oxford, 1973), pp. 90–1.
30 Thrupp, *Merchant Class*, p. 259.
31 G.E. Cokayne, *The Complete Peerage*, ed. V. Gibbs and others (London, 1910–59), XI, 391–2.
32 G.A. Holmes, *The Estates of the Higher Nobility in Fourteenth-Century England* (Cambridge, 1957), pp. 69–70.
33 *Letter Book G*, p. 67.
34 Will of Adam Fraunceys, enrolled in the Court of Husting, Corporation of London Record Office (hereafter CLRO), HR 103/79.
35 *CPR, 1364–7*, p. 303; Holmes, *Estates of the Higher Nobility*, p. 56.
36 J. Nichols, *Collection of Royal Wills* (London, 1780), p. 57.
37 *Letter Book H*, p. 170.
38 PRO E403/425, 20 January.
39 *CPR, 1385–9*, p. 428. See below, pp. 28–9.
40 He married Elizabeth, sister of Roger Lychefeld, possibly a London skinner, who for a while secured for himself an interest in the Pyel manors (BL Add. MS 25288 (the register of William Genge, abbot of Peterborough), fo. 44v; *CPR, 1405–8*, p. 121).
41 CLRO, HR 101/107. For the information on Fraunceys' second marriage I am indebted to Dr Carole Rawcliffe, who has kindly shown me a copy of the biography of Adam Fraunceys junior, now published in *The House of Commons 1386–1421*, eds J.S. Roskell, L. Clark and C. Rawcliffe (Stroud, 1992), III, pp. 118–20.
42 Hatfield House, CP 291.1 (Fraunceys cartulary), no. E9 (fo. 10v); ibid., fo. 9v.
43 Ibid., no. B4 (fo. 6v); BL Add. Ch. 40513.
44 Hatfield, nos 10, 15 (fo. 2v).
45 Ibid., fos 3r–4v; R. Bird, *The Turbulent London of Richard II* (London, 1949), p. 8.
46 Westminster Abbey, WAM 27, 40, 44, 52, 59, 65, 126, 132.
47 Hatfield, CP 291.1, nos 1101–1103 (fos 105v –106r).
48 See D. Bolton's discussion of this point in *The Victoria History of the Counties of England*

(hereafter *VCH*) *Middlesex*, V, ed. T.F.T. Baker (Oxford, 1976), p. 163. See also D. Moss, 'The Economic Development of a Middlesex Village', *Agricultural History Review*, 28 (1980), pp. 109, 111, on the grazing of cattle in Tottenham and the exaction of tolls from goods traffic between Edmonton and Shoreditch.

49 CA, Vincent 64, fo. 40r–v.
50 *CPR, 1350–4*, p. 253; *CPR, 1367–70*, p. 363; *CPR, 1370–4*, p. 35.
51 CA, Vincent 64, fos 14r–15r; *CPR, 1354–8*, p. 205.
52 *CFR, 1347–56*, p. 8.
53 Thrupp, *Merchant Class*, p. 118.
54 R. Somerville, *History of the Duchy of Lancaster*, I (London, 1953). p. 7.
55 *John of Gaunt's Register*, ed. S. Armitage-Smith, Camden Society, 3rd series, 20–1 (1911), I, no. 374.
56 Bird, *Turbulent London*, p. 28; C. Given-Wilson, *The Royal Household and the King's Affinity* (Yale, 1986), p. 153.
57 *Anonimalle Chronicle 1333–1381*, ed. V.H. Galbraith (Manchester, 1927), pp. 89–90.
58 For documents relating to these talks see *The Anglo-French Negotiations at Bruges 1374–77*, ed. E. Perroy, Camden Miscellany, 29 (1952). Particulars of the account for Pyel's journey in 1375 survive among the household records (PRO E101/317/2). He was 'to treat of certain articles pending between the king and the town of Bruges', a mission he had undertaken at least twice earlier in the decade (PRO E403/446, 19 July 1372).
59 Somerville, *Duchy of Lancaster*, I, p. 371; Pyel's will, enrolled in the Register of John Buckingham, bishop of Lincoln, Lincoln Archive Office (hereafter LAO), Episcopal Register XII, fo. 242.
60 *CPR, 1361–4*, p. 544.
61 *CPR, 1348–50*, p. 560; *CCR, 1349–54*, p. 267; J. Sumption, *Pilgrimage: an Image of Medieval Religion* (London, 1975), p. 257.
62 Ibid., p. 241.
63 Ibid., pp. 263–4.
64 *CPR, 1361–4*, p. 335; CA, Vincent 64, fo. 27r.
65 Sumption, *Pilgrimage*, pp. 166, 264.
66 *Letter Book G*, 67. The college was refounded in 1368, and the document for this later foundation survives (BL Harleian MS 79, G. 38).
67 *Calendar of Papal Petitions*, I, pp. 445, 505; *Calendar of Papal Letters*, IV, p. 49.
68 CLRO, HR 103/79.
69 *CPR, 1374–8*, p. 72. A detailed account of the foundation and early years of the college is to be found in A. Hamilton Thompson, 'The Early History of the College of Irthlingborough', *Reports and Papers of the Northampton and Oakham Architectural Society*, 35 (1920), pp. 267–85. I am most grateful to Mr N.A. Groome for drawing my attention to this article.
70 *VCH Northants.*, III, ed. W. Page (London, 1930), p. 210; N. Pevsner and B. Cherry, *The Buildings of England: Northamptonshire* (Harmondsworth, 1973), pp. 267–8.
71 Hamilton Thompson, 'College of Irthlingborough', pp. 281–4.
72 See the chapter on Etchingham Church in N.E. Saul, *Scenes from Provincial Life: Knightly Families in Sussex 1280–1400* (Oxford, 1986), pp. 140–60.
73 Ibid., p. 145.
74 *VCH Northants.*, III, p. 163.
75 Above, p. 18.
76 Thrupp, *Merchant Class*, pp. 249–50; G.A. Unwin, 'Social Evolution in Medieval London' in Unwin, ed., *Finance and Trade under Edward III* (Manchester, 1918), p. 7.
77 Thrupp, *Merchant Class*, p. 250.
78 The seventeenth-century compilations of aldermanic arms (BL Stowe MS 860, Harleian

MS 1464) portray Fraunceys' arms as a lion rampant. One of his seals depicts a shield bearing a bend with lion's face in sinister chief (BL Add. Ch. 50.D.52). A second (and seemingly later) seal device shows a bend with annulet in chief on a shield resting within a letter 'A' (WAM 11, 55; BL Harleian Ch. 79.G.38).

79 For the ratio of ecclesiastical to lay cartularies, see G.R.C. Davis, *Medieval Cartularies of Great Britain* (London, 1958).

80 *CCR, 1381–5*, p. 227; *CFR, 1391–9*, p. 56.

81 LAO Episcopal Register XII, fo. 242.

3
'For Pore People Harberles': What was the Function of the Maisonsdieu?

Patricia H. Cullum

After 1300, and especially after 1350, most new hospital foundations could be divided into three groups based on the type of founder. The first were aristocratic foundations. There were relatively few of these, and they were more often created by the nouveau-riche seeking to establish themselves than by older noble and gentry families. The second type were guild foundations, created by both religious and trade guilds (where these two functions did not overlap in one organisation). These became increasingly common with the wider extension of corporate status. They were more a feature of larger and wealthier towns, and catered primarily, though often not exclusively, for members of the guild. Thirdly there were the individual foundations of merchants, mercers and a few other wealthy tradesmen, their wives and widows, and occasionally clergy; these were probably the most common type of foundation in this period. Both of the first two types were usually endowed and both were still usually called hospitals, whereas the third group were usually, though not exclusively, known as maisonsdieu, or masendewes in Yorkshire, whereas elsewhere they might be called almshouses. As this paper is largely based upon Yorkshire evidence that terminology has been continued here. Maisonsdieu might or might not be endowed, depending on the wealth or intentions of the founder. Whereas aristocratic and guild founders could individually or corporately afford, and might think worthwhile, a licence in mortmain, this was rarely true of the founders of maisonsdieu. Despite the restrictions of the Statute of Mortmain, the first two types of foundations were often like the traditional type of hospital, albeit generally smaller, making comprehensive provision for their inmates. Maisonsdieu, with their limited or non-existent resources, could not do this.

It is proposed to deal here only with the maisonsdieu. Maisonsdieu are often obscure, undocumented except for chance references, lacking foundation documents, internal records, and, because they were secular institutions, any kind of episcopal supervision. At best they are referred to in some detail in the founder's will, provided that these arrangements had not been made in life, and in bequests in other wills. It is possible that such establishments might be found referred to in property deeds, and occasionally in the civic records, where the mayor and corporation had been made trustees of the maisondieu. The latter arrangement was more common in the case of endowed maisonsdieu, and seems to have been particularly popular in Hull, where a number of such foundations coincided with the incorporation of the civic government. As most references are in wills, there is a bias towards seeing them as primarily post-mortem foundations. However, this is no more true of maisonsdieu than it is of chantries, which were regularly established during the founder's lifetime.

Most maisonsdieu were shadowy because, often unendowed, they were poor and relatively short-lived. They provide little material for the historian to work on. As a result they have largely been ignored, or where considered usually dismissed as failures because of their lack of permanency. This attitude, which fails to do justice to the importance of these institutions, arises partly from the shortage of material, and partly from the fact that the model which has been used to look at them is inappropriate. Maisonsdieu have generally been considered as part of the hospital tradition, which had a monastic model and sought to provide totally for the inmate for the duration of his or her stay. While the maisonsdieu were undoubtedly a development of that tradition, they were also a step away from it. Only a few of the maisonsdieu made any attempt to make total provision for their inmates; for the majority a roof and possibly a regular dole were as much as could be provided. A parallel can probably be drawn here with the Florentine *spedaluzzi*, parish charities which consisted simply of a room and bedding, supported by the voluntary labour and alms of the parishioners.[1] However, the English maisonsdieu were almost invariably established by individuals or families rather than the parish. For many founders the concern was the fulfilling of one of the seven works of mercy: receiving the stranger. Although this might be a permanent and all-encompassing activity in the home, it was generally regarded as being only a temporary and partial one: after a few days the stranger moved on.

A better model for understanding maisonsdieu is the chantry. Chantry foundations were familiar to the people who established maisonsdieu. Many of them founded both, sometimes in conjunction. Chantries were established to pray for the living and for the souls of their dead; they might last for a year, or a few years or in perpetuity, if the founder had the resources for such a foundation. Perpetual chantries were only a small minority of all the chantries founded, though they are disproportionately well-recorded, because of the records generated by such foundations.[2] Perpetual chantries were only ever a minority of such foundations because only a very small number of people had the resources available for such an arrangement.[3] This is recognised, and nobody would consider a chantry which was established for a lesser period than eternity to be a failure.

People established chantries to the extent of their abilities and resources. The same is true of maisonsdieu. The wealthiest might establish a permanent and endowed house, but those less well-off could not afford that, however much they might wish it, and so they made a lesser provision, within their capacity: a room in their house to be reserved for the poor; the house itself to be inhabited by the poor, or the house to be left with an endowment for a certain number of years to house the poor. The part of the house, the unendowed house, and the limited period, did not indicate failure, but ingenious efforts to assist the poor with limited resources. Moreover, they existed in a context in which it was not expected that any one individual or group could make an adequate and comprehensive provision for the poor. Each individual made their contribution in the expectation that there would be others able and willing to take up the burden. Miri Rubin has suggested that 'few charitable foundations ever offered more than short-term alleviation of need'.[4] While this is in itself a debatable statement, it also misses the point that often provision was not expected to be long-term, either because the need was not such or because others would take up the burden. It has been suggested that the regular lack of provision for children and more distant relatives in chantry foundations indicated a lack of concern for these at the expense of spouses, parents and patrons, but the latter were less likely than the former to be in a position to make further provision for themselves through death, whereas younger relatives were in such a position. In the same way founders could expect others to follow in their footsteps.[5] Social values relating to charitable provision were well developed, as can be seen by the regular appearance of a range of charitable practice in wills and by the frequency with which dispositions were left to the discretion of executors. This provided reassurance in that area.[6] We should not expect to find very much evidence for this attitude in didactic works of the period which were concerned to emphasise individual responsibility, but this does not mean that it was not there.

Despite the paucity of information about individual maisonsdieu, and the difficulty of knowing how many there were, so many being known only from a single and sometimes ambiguous reference that it is difficult to know whether the same institution was being called by different names, it is clear that they were very common. In York there were at least a dozen, including a civic maisondieu, and almost certainly not less than eighteen, as well as five guild hospitals. In Hull there were fifteen maisonsdieu, perhaps more; Beverley, already well-provided with hospitals by 1300, had another half dozen or so; Scarborough had not less than four and probably more.[7] Nor was it only in Yorkshire that this phenomenon could be found: in Cambridge four almshouses and a leper-hospital were all established despite the relatively small size of the 'town' as opposed to 'gown' elements of the population.[8] In London Stow recorded at least twelve, not counting guild hospitals, and he was probably biased towards remembering the better-endowed and more permanent houses than the transitory ones.[9] If Norwich could only manage one almshouse after 1370, that was at least partly a result of its already very comprehensive provision.[10] Winchester produced none, but Winchester, like Norwich, had had a number of hospitals from an early date, and was throughout this period going through a steady and inexorable decline.[11] All these figures are minima. If the Yorkshire towns appear to have produced a greater number of maisonsdieu than towns elsewhere, that is less likely to be a reflection of what was actually happening than that writers on other towns either did not notice or failed to appreciate the significance of this kind of provision. Almshouses and maisonsdieu were established in many larger, and some smaller, towns. Although in themselves often not very substantial, as a 'movement', as an indication of the priority placed on care for the poor, they clearly show that the poor were considered important. Foundations of monasteries, and even friaries, were rare after 1350, but the establishment of almshouses was common. If the change was at least partly due to the saturation of the market for monasteries, and partly to the exigencies of the Statute of Mortmain, it was also partly the result of a growing importance placed on the care of the poor, an importance which had not seemed so great since the twelfth century.

At the most basic level, if one could not afford to found a maisondieu, it might be possible to support one or more through donations in life or, in one's will, after death. It is clear from a survey of wills that this was very popular. The most popular group of hospitals were the leper-houses of York: in Prob. Reg. 1 (1389–96) 34 of 125 wills with any kind of charitable content, or 27% of such wills, gave to this end; in Prob. Reg. 2 (1397–8, 1440–59), 91 of 414 charitable wills, or 22%, did so. These figures are from all wills within the sample, not just York wills; as a proportion of York wills it was much higher. The York leper-houses were clearly regarded as the paradigm of the hospital, receiving the stranger, the pauper and the sick, but the maisonsdieu were also frequent recipients of gifts. In Prob. Reg. 1 testators clearly preferred to name individually each maisondieu which they wished to receive a donation, but by the 1440s it had become usual to make a single bequest to 'all the maisonsdieu of York', although it was still not uncommon to pick out particular houses for special attention. In Prob. Reg. 2 14% of all bequests were of this comprehensive nature. This change was a local one, and suggests something of the relative sophistication of the system of probate administration in York, as this change did not occur in Beverley, Hull or Scarborough. This was fortunate, for the all-encompassing bequest, though easy to record, is less informative than the individualised one. Comparison

of the two Probate Registers shows that there was also something of a
chronological divide between York and the other towns. York had acquired
the majority of its maisonsdieu by 1400, and already had two by 1353,
whereas Hull had only three by 1410, and another dozen or so would be
founded in the succeeding 120 years. Clearly in the early 1390s the habit
of giving to maisonsdieu was not yet established in Hull, for in 1396 Peter
Steller gave a large endowment to the hospital of St James in
Whitefriargate but mentioned neither of the other maisonsdieu in the
town, and in the previous year Robert de Crosse of Hull gave bequests to
St Giles in Beverley, and two hospitals in Scarborough, but nothing in
Hull.[12] Beverley, and perhaps Scarborough, probably partook more of the
York than the Hull pattern.

Amounts varied tremendously and could be directed either to the
maisonsdieu separately or collectively, or to their individual inhabitants. In
York bequests varied from as much as two marks to each maisondieu to as
little as 4d.[13] Bequests to individuals within the maisonsdieu usually ranged
between one and four pennies. In Beverley it was usual to give to the
maisondieu rather than the individuals within it, and sums were generally
in the region of 3s. 4d. Much the same is true of Hull. While most gave
money some gave in kind: gifts of coal were common in Hull and
Beverley, particularly in the mid-fifteenth century, but rare in York.[14] In
York, however, it was more common to make gifts of food and drink.[15]

For those who could manage more than a bequest to an existing
maisondieu but were still of limited means there were various possibilities:
these ranged from supporting a particular individual within a maisondieu
to taking the poor into one's own house, or making part or all of that
house available for the use of the poor. Alice de Bridford of York, widow
(d. 1390), left a tunic to Magota de la maisondieu; Richard Ledys of York
(d. 1390) left a gown, hose and shoes to Grogson de masyndieu; and in
1459 Joan Cotyngham left to Joan Day, a poor little woman in a certain
maisondieu, a lined russet gown and a linen chemise.[16] The lack of
specificity about the location of these maisonsdieu suggests that the
individuals concerned were so well-known to testator and executors that
further identification was unnecessary. This in turn suggests that these
individuals had also been supported during the life-time of the testator.

A few were able to establish a bed within a maisondieu, to which the
testator's heirs might retain the right of presentation. Roger de Rilleston of
York (d. 1402) left his brother eight marks to establish a bed in a hospital.
As Rilleston's executors included William de Ottelay, master of Holy
Trinity Hospital in Fossgate, and Warmabald van Harlam, patron of the
maisondieu in St Peter Lane Little, it is likely that it was in one of these
that the bed was placed.[17] Richard Kirketon of York, chaplain (d. 1486),
left a garden in Blossomgate to sustain the poor in the maisondieu of John

Bedford, gentleman, in Little St Andrewgate on condition that his heirs should have the right to present a pauper chosen by them to a bed in the maisondieu.[18] More basically, John Garton of Hull (d. 1455) left 10*s.* and two beds with bed-linen to the Beverleygates maisondieu. In 1447 Margaret Hansforde of Hull, widow, had been able to give only 12*d.* and an ancient featherbed and two old covers. In 1524 Dame Joan Thurscrosse, vowess, similarly gave a bed and bedding to the same maisondieu.[19] John de Scheffeld of York, skinner (d. 1395), left a set of bedding to St Thomas's Hospital.[20]

Bequests towards receiving the poor and feeding them on certain days over a period of a year or more probably also reflected life-time practice and were part of this continuum of care for the poor.[21] Cecily Giry's request that three beds in her guestchamber be used for receiving the poor is another stage in this process.[22] Agnes Brome of Scarborough (d. 1400) had a little more space, but not a spare tenement, so she built a maisondieu at the bottom of her garden. She required her heir to endow it with six quarters of coal annually, but did not apparently require him to maintain or repair the building.[23] Unless her maisondieu can be identified with one of the otherwise unknown maisonsdieu in John Stokdale's will of 1468 it is unlikely that it could have survived longer than the building stayed up.[24] Agnes de Whitflete of Hedon in 1396 left a tenement to a couple for their lives which was afterwards to be demised to the poor.[25] In fact it seems to have been vested in the mayor and corporation, as so many Hull maisonsdieu later were, for the poor inhabiting the house were to return an annual rent of 15*d.* to them. This may indicate that Agnes was concerned less for the absolutely destitute than for those too poor to be able to afford any other housing. The rental may also have been used to maintain the tenement, which may mean that it was kept up for some time, but the dearth of wills from Hedon makes this impossible to check. A similar bequest may lie behind the gift of Thomas de Kent, mercer (d. 1397), to the poor women lying in the house of Cecily Plater in St Andrewgate in York.[26] Although anything up to three different maisonsdieu may have existed in St Andrewgate and Little St Andrewgate from the late fourteenth to early sixteenth centuries, it seems likely that this house survived throughout the period.[27] In 1428 John Spoo of Beverley, tanner, left to his wife two tenements in Fleminggate, to be inhabited free of charge by the poor, for the sake of charity.[28]

The prominence of female founders or donors of this type of provision for the poor was no accident. Women were apparently more likely to be charitable than men, even with the generally more limited means at their disposal. Also, these more basic forms of housing for the poor were provided by women who did not have the same resources as the wealthier men like the merchant brothers, the Holmes. This is not to say that women did not provide more substantial housing for the poor when they could. Both Ysolda de Acaster in York and Joan Gregg in Hull were clearly the founders of the maisonsdieu which at the time generally bore their names, though later generations have sometimes credited their husbands with these foundations.[29] Where women were widows or single their part in founding such houses is not too ambiguous, but in the case of married women no such certainty is possible. Nevertheless it seems unlikely that women would only develop this interest in widowhood, and it is probable that at least some of the maisonsdieu regarded as founded by men were at least as much the interests of their wives. An example of this may be found in the higher social circle inhabited by Robert and Constance Knollys, who founded Knollys Almshouse in Pontefract. Both are named in all the documents relating to the house, but the location of the almshouse in Pontefract suggests that it may have been more Constance's concern than her husband's. Robert's home was in Cheshire, and he had acquired property in London, but he had no obvious connections with Pontefract, while there was a tradition that it was Constance's home.[30] As Constance predeceased her husband there is no evidence of her independent interest in the hospital, but the choice of location is probably significant. Other, more tangential evidence, may be the records of wives being left the supervision of hospitals, as in the case of John Armstrong of Beverley, who left the supervision of his maisondieu to his wife Juliana and others, or Katherine de Holme of York, who was left the supervision of the Castlehill maisondieu by her husband Thomas.[31] Richard Bedford of Hull (d. 1451) left the almshouse next to Holy Trinity chapel to his wife Agnes, and only after her death to their son, Richard.[32]

Some maisonsdieu appear to have been established in particularly poor areas of a town, and would thus have benefited the most needy. The concentration of maisonsdieu in and around St Andrewgate in York has already been noted. This was a poor part of the city not far from the 'red-light' district, and seems to have had a relatively high proportion of female inhabitants.[33] It is noteworthy that the only maisondieu dedicated throughout its life to the housing of women was here. At least one testator seems to have made no distinction between the inhabitants of the maisondieu and other poor people in the street: Lady Joan Spenser, widow (d. 1407), left to 'the poor widows and my tenants in St Andrewgate, 13s. 4d. divided among them'.[34] In Scarborough in 1468 John Stokdale left 3s. 4d. to the poor living around the castle ditch and the poor living in the hospice of St Mary Magdalene.[35] Wodlane may have been a similar area in Beverley.[36] It is unclear if there was such a place in Hull, though the apparent concentration of maisonsdieu in Whitefriargate may be significant. In Bristol the Chestres left doles to prisoners, lepers, almspeople and the poor in 'Long Rewe'.[37] While Winchester had no maisonsdieu, it is fairly clear that the hospital of St John the Baptist did provide cheap rented accommodation both on its own site and in some of its property in poorer areas of the town.[38] In London the almshouses provided for the sick poor in Houndsditch drew charitably-minded visitors to the area, and a similar effect may have been experienced in St Andrewgate and the poor parts of other towns.[39]

The more substantial citizen could afford to set up a maisondieu in a separate building during his lifetime. Although the greater part of information about a particular maisondieu may come in the will of the founder, it is clear that the majority of these foundations, like chantries, were established during life. The most extreme example of this is the hospital founded by Robert de Holme, merchant of York, in Monkgate, just outside the city. Robert made quite detailed provision for his maisondieu in his will of 1396, but it is clear from the will of Adam de Hibernia that it was under construction in 1353.[40] Similarly, John de Craven, also of York, died in 1416, but his maisondieu near Layerthorpe bridge had received a bequest in 1407.[41] Thomas de Holme, brother of Robert, had also established a maisondieu, in Castlehill, also known as Hertergate, by 1389, but did not die until 1406.[42] Likewise, John de Darthyngton made arrangements for his maisondieu in St Peter Lane Little in his will of 1402, but it had been receiving bequests since at least 1390.[43]

The apparent sudden appearance of a large number of maisonsdieu in York in the 1390s is probably more to do with the survival of the Probate Registers of the Exchequer court from 1389 than with the actual distribution of foundations. It is only the chance recording of Adam de Hibernia's will in an act book of the Dean and Chapter that indicates the surprisingly early foundation of Robert de Holme's maisondieu in Monkgate, and the possibly even older maisondieu of Thomas Duffield (unlike Holme's it was already built) which may be identified with the maisondieu of Richard Duffield in Little St Andrewgate, existing in 1398.[44] Nevertheless a brief survey of the Dean and Chapter Probate Register which covers this period and extends backwards to the earlier fourteenth century does not disturb this picture. It is possible that a more detailed study might serve to fix more precisely the foundations of some of these maisonsdieu, but it seems likely that the majority of York's almshouses were founded in the two decades before, and one after, 1400. This would fit the period of York's economic boom after the Black Death. Ironically, most provision was made at a time when there was relatively little need for it, though most of these would survive into more needy times.

This pattern serves to refute Miri Rubin's suggestion that there was a falling away in charitable giving and hospital foundations after the Black Death. It was precisely in the sixty years or so after the Black Death that a great wave of foundations of small almshouses and maisonsdieu took place.

Indeed Dr Rubin's own book provides evidence that Cambridge itself saw an expansion of hospital provision in the post-Black Death period. From a pre-Black Death situation of one hospital supporting between three and twelve poor, and a leper-house, there was an expansion to a post-Black Death position of an additional leper-house (replacing the earlier one) and at least four almshouses (one of which was a refoundation) supporting at least fourteen almsfolk. This alone must cast some doubt on the Rubin thesis.[45]

While there is no denying that some literary and legislative sources indicate a hostility towards the rural and urban wage-labourer who was seeking to improve his or her lot in a period of increasing labour scarcity during the thirty-odd years after the Black Death, that is a quite separate matter from attitudes towards the poor. The poor were understood to be those who through sickness, accident, infirmity or age were not in a position to support themselves by their own labour. In these circumstances the improving status of the peasant or wage-labourer was irrelevant, and understood to be irrelevant, to the situation of the poor, because they were by their nature debarred from participating in it. The only way in which it was relevant was that it threw into even starker relief the plight of those who were not in a position to benefit from the opportunities around them. Here Paul Slack's observation, derived from de Tocqueville, on the early nineteenth century, is a more useful interpretation of the picture than that provided by Rubin:

> As material circumstances improved, changing definitions of what was a minimum acceptable standard of living led to an expansion in the number of people classed as 'poor' . . . the comfortably off now recognised new needs among the lower orders and had the wealth and moral inclination to try to meet them.[46]

Another reason for the high proportion of foundations in this period, particularly before about 1390, may lie in concern about St Leonard's Hospital. This was an old-established hospital in York, probably the largest outside London, providing around 200 places. Visitations in 1364 and 1377 had revealed that the hospital's finances were not holding up in the face of the economic changes of the times. These problems were exacerbated by the appointment of a series of unsuitable masters who wasted the substance of the hospital and caused dissension within the community, by blocking the attempts of the more responsible of its members to attack practices which were leading the hospital to the verge of bankruptcy. Knowledge that St Leonard's was suffering financial problems, and that it was increasingly selling rather than giving freely places within the infirmary, may well have prompted the wealthier citizens and their wives to found maisonsdieu which would continue or replace in some measure the care which St Leonard's had formerly given.[47]

There seems to have been another small 'boom' in York foundations in the late 1430s and 1440s, with the establishment of St Christopher's maisondieu in Fishergate, later moved to the Guildhall; of the Tanners' maisondieu; St Anthony's, Peaseholme Green; John Marton's maisondieu, later supported by the Cordwainers' guild of which he was a member; and the Whitefriars or Stonebow maisondieu.[48] It is perhaps significant that these later maisonsdieu were mostly founded by guilds, perhaps anxious to protect their more vulnerable members from the effects of developing recession. However, a similar pattern of a high number of foundations in the 1430s and especially 1440s can be found in Hull, where it may have had something to do with the incorporation of the city in 1440 and subsequent decisions by founders to vest their institutions in the mayor and corporation.

Those who founded the more substantial maisonsdieu did sometimes endow them with property, but even when they did they rarely managed to make the income extend to paying any kind of pension to the poor inhabitants. As these almshouses were usually set up during the lifetime of the founder it is perhaps possible that arrangements for endowments went unmentioned because they had already been made. It is not clear whether either of the maisonsdieu in North Street in York were endowed. Certainly such endowments were rarely discussed in much detail. The will of John Armstrong of Beverley, tailor (d. 1502), was unusually precise in describing the five cottages in Awmond Lane, two tenements in Eastgate, the horsemill and five other tenements which were the endowment of his maisondieu dedicated to St John the Baptist.[49]

John de Darthyngton apparently did not endow his maisondieu in St Peter Lane Little, though he left a tenement in the same street to be sold to provide masses and other works of charity.[50] The two Holme brothers and John de Craven, however, all specifically mentioned endowments for their hospitals, but were unspecific about their nature or extent. Robert de Holme directed that his son, also called Robert, should have all his tenements and buildings which belonged to the hospital to repair and conserve it. These included his capital messuage in Goodramgate, a rent of 3s. 4d. from a tenement or messuage in Goodramgate which he held of St Leonard's hospital, and all his other lands and tenements in York. It is unclear whether the property of the hospital was clearly differentiated from that descending to the family. As the maisondieu was to revert to the family after 100 years, and the family was in the meantime responsible for its upkeep, such a differentiation may not have been considered necessary.[51] His brother Thomas had already enfeoffed property to the trustees of the hospital, which apparently consisted in part at least of rental income, for the chantry chaplain had a responsibility to collect the farm.[52] John de Craven bequeathed all his lands and tenements to his son William, from which he was to pay an annual rent to support the poor in the maisondieu. If he failed to do so for forty days the mayor and corporation were empowered to take all the lands and tenements and to pay the poor in perpetuity.[53] Thomas de Holme, like Darthyngton, does not appear to have paid a pension to the poor in the hospital, but both Craven and Robert de Holme did. Robert paid at the rate of 1*d*. per day, which would probably have been just enough to support a pauper entirely, whereas Craven paid 3*d*. a week to twelve of the poor, and 4*d*. to another in return for morning and evening prayers. In Hull, in the hospital founded by Robert de Selby, his wife, Emma, and Richard de Ravenser in 1375, each of the twelve poor men was to receive ½*d*. per day.[54]

Craven was unusual in expecting that his maisondieu should exist in perpetuity; most founders made no stipulations, but both Robert de Holme, founder of the Monkgate maisondieu, and Thomas Preston of Hull, merchant (d. 1451), set limits to their foundations. Holme directed that his should last for 100 years after his death. The maisondieu was still receiving bequests in the 1440s, and presumably continued to function as such for its full term, and then reverted to the family. In 1562, a descendant, Thomas Holme of Elvington, gentleman, sold some land in Monkgate which included 'one cottage called le Meason Dieu'.[55] Raine suggests that Duffield's maisondieu in Little St Andrewgate may have had a similar limit and that this would explain why it bore the name of a different founder from about 1485. While this is possible, it is not certain that Duffield's and Bedford's maisonsdieu were the same building.[56] Thomas Preston of Hull had established a tenement in St Nicholas Street in Hedon for three poor people, who were to remain there for ten years after his decease, receiving 1*d*. each per week.[57] It is not clear what was to happen after that period, but presumably Preston's executors, who were to supervise the maisondieu, would receive it back for the estate. These examples, and the unendowed maisonsdieu mentioned above, all point towards the conclusion that most of the maisonsdieu were not permanent institutions because they were never intended to be.

Except in the case of Robert de Holme, even in the rare cases where some kind of dole or pension was provided to the inhabitants it was never enough to be the whole support of the poor recipient. How then did the paupers within the maisonsdieu support themselves? While they received some donations in money and food from bequests, and more from those who gave during their lifetimes, it is likely that their main source of income was begging from door to door. Alice de Bridford of York, widow (d. 1390), left 1*d*. to each infirm pauper in each maisondieu who was not able to beg. Bernard de Everton of York, chaplain (d. 1407), left 6*s*. 8*d*. to the poor in the *domus dei* of Thomas Howme, 4*d.* to each bedridden pauper unable to go out and beg within the parish of St Mary (within which Howme's maisondieu lay), and 2*d.* to each pauper who was able to go out and beg daily from door to door within the parish.[58] While Everton appears to have drawn a distinction between the poor within the maisondieu and those without it, it is clear from Bridford's will that she envisaged begging as the usual form of maintenance of the inhabitants of the maisonsdieu if they were able to perform it. Both wills give preferential treatment to the bedridden poor, who are not only precluded from working but even from begging because of the state of their health. Thus even where some dole was attached to a place within a maisondieu, it was usually intended to supplement an income from begging, rather than to replace it. It was never intended to provide total support for the recipient.

There is some evidence to suggest that testators may have discriminated between maisonsdieu where the inhabitants received a dole and those where they did not. Neither Craven's nor Robert de Holme's maisonsdieu received much in the way of bequests: Holme's received four in Prob. Reg. 1 (one of those being from the founder), and one in Prob. Reg. 2 dated 1398; Craven's (not in existence in the 1390s) received two in Prob. Reg. 2. By contrast Thomas de Holme's maisondieu received nine bequests in Prob. Reg. 1 and seven in Prob. Reg. 2; while Acaster's maisondieu received seven in each of these Probate Registers. Part of the reason may lie in the location of Robert de Holme's and Craven's maisonsdieu; the one outside the city at the far end of Monkgate, the other in a relatively poor and underpopulated area in Layerthorpe. However, it seems unlikely that this is the sole reason for the difference. It may also be significant that of donations to the maisonsdieu in the two St Andrewgates 60% in Prob. Reg. 1 and 50% in Prob. Reg. 2 were from women, suggesting that, as women were never more than 25% of the total number of testators, they were disproportionately interested in giving to houses which had wholly or principally female inhabitants.[59]

A few maisonsdieu may have had gardens or small plots of land upon which the inhabitants could grow vegetables for food. Tickell quotes from what he alleges to be the founders' rules of Gregg's maisondieu in Hull, which included the provision of a garden 'common to alle the brothyrs and systers . . . in herbs . . . and in dewe tyme þay to manour and garto set and sow the same garden by þair best avyle for þe welefare of þem alle'.[60] And in 1486 Richard Kirketon of York, chaplain, left a garden in Whitefriarlane to the use of the poor in the maisondieu of John Holme, gentleman. While Kirketon had erected latrines in this garden, perhaps for the use of the poor, during his lifetime, it is unlikely that the land was entirely taken up by this purpose.[61]

Who were the people who were being supported in the maisonsdieu? Mostly they were described as 'the poor' – *pauperes*, as in John Craven's description of the *personia pauperibus* who were to be received into his maisondieu, but the majority were poor because they were unable to work.[62] They were those who, for reasons of health or age, were unable to support themselves. Robert de Holme's maisondieu was *hospitandum pauperes impotentes*, to support the impotent poor.[63] In Hull James de Kyngeston, king's clerk, received a licence in mortmain in 1344 to establish a habitation for thirteen poor men and women, broken by age, misfortune or labour, who could not gain their own livelihood.[64] As Alice de Bridford's bequest indicates, a significant proportion were bedridden and unable even to beg. John Close of York, goldsmith (d. 1442), left 12*d.* to the poor men and women lying and existing in the maisondieu in North Street. Thomas de Rigton of York (d. 1394) left money to the poor and languid in the hospitals and elsewhere. John Lamley of York, butcher (d. 1442), left 2*d.* to each man and woman in the maisonsdieu of York, and 4*d.* to each blind man and woman in the city except those in the maisonsdieu and 2*d.* to each bedridden man and woman in the city except those in the maisonsdieu.[65] Clearly Lamley was trying to ensure that the blind and bedridden within the maisonsdieu did not get two handouts, but he also clearly thought that these two groups comprised at least a part, perhaps a large part, of the population of the maisonsdieu.

That population comprised both men and women, and although a few maisonsdieu, such as that in St Andrewgate, were specifically for women, it is less clear how many were limited to men. Even when a maisondieu was described as for *homines* this did not necessarily mean that its inmates were exclusively male. It is probable that the number of women in the maisonsdieu was increasing from the mid-fifteenth century, as a result of economic depression reducing the number of jobs for women.[66] Somewhere between 1433 and 1445, the dates of the two nearest surviving Chamberlains' Accounts, the Ousebridge maisondieu ceased to take both sexes and thereafter the records refer only to the *pauperes mulieres* for which it provided.[67] Sometime before the 1380s, St Nicholas's, which had formerly been a leper hospital, ceased to have male brothers and held only sisters thereafter. By 1545 the maisondieu of Northallerton was housing thirteen widows, although when it was founded some time in the mid-fifteenth century there is no evidence that it was intended to be specifically for women.[68] And in 1506 Alice Neville of Leeds reminded her son that he had sworn that he would 'trewly whilst he lives gyff those ij howses in Holbek that I bygged to ij pore women in his primary gyfft to charge thame that they pray duly for me and all my good doars and when on Woman dyes to put in an othr Woman *but put in no man*.' (My italics). Each woman was to receive 13*s.* 4*d.* annually; like most such doles, it would not have been enough to support the recipient entirely. Alice clearly believed that there was a specific need for housing for women.[69]

Some were elderly relatives or servants of those who provided them with a place. Isabella Burgh (d. 1451) left a russet gown to Katherine Burgh living in the maisondieu in Little St Andrewgate. William Melburn of Beverley, merchant (d. 1411), left 3*s*. 4*d*. to Agnes, formerly the servant of William Fulthorp, now a sister in St Giles.[70] Some maisonsdieu were founded specifically for the elderly: Adryanson's hospital in Hull was established about 1485 for four honest elderly men.[71]

In some cases the inmates were travellers or immigrants to York. In 1392 Richard Bridesall of York left 6*s*. 8*d*. to William Candeler and his son, of Doncaster, staying in Ousebridge maisondieu.[72] Both St Anne's maisondieu, Ripon, and St Thomas's, York, specifically reserved some beds for pilgrims. Richard Kirketon of York, chaplain (d. 1486), had established a bed in the Whitefriar Lane maisondieu, which was for poor people coming to the city from outside.[73] John Carre, a former mayor of York (d. 1487), bequeathed fifty beds to poor men and women of the city, one of which 'I bewitte . . . to pore people harberles to be harberd in the maisondewe at the White Freers Lane'.[74]

In 1455, when it was described as being newly-built, a married couple were placed in the hospital established by the will of John Aldwick of Hull (d. 1444) for two people.[75] It is also likely that two married couples were the four poor inhabitants of the two little almshouses next to the Friars Preachers in Scarborough established by John Storior, to whom Robert Wardale bequeathed 16*d*. in 1457 in perpetuity, to be paid from rents by his heirs.[76]

While most maisonsdieu were not as small as Aldwick's or Alice Neville's, which each supported only two people, few were very large. In most cases numbers were not specified, but where they were, twenty-four seems to have been the largest. Craven's maisondieu provided for twenty, Robert de Holme's for thirteen; and in Hull Gregg's housed thirteen and Selby's and Ravenser's twelve. John de Ake, merchant of Beverley (d. 1398), founded a maisondieu known as Holy Trinity on Crossbridge for twenty-four.[77] Thomas de Holme of York wanted thirteen men from his maisondieu to carry torches at his funeral, but as the house clearly had female inmates as well, it may have held as many as twenty-six. In 1443 Richard Usflete of York, alderman, left 12*d*. to each maisondieu which had more than twelve inhabitants and 6*d*. to each maisondieu which had less than twelve.[78] For most maisonsdieu, however, the lower rather than the upper figures were probably more likely.

While most founders left their maisondieu in the hands of wives or sons, this was not always possible. Many, indeed most, of the founders came from the aldermanic circle of their respective towns, or its equivalent, and looked to these, either formally or informally, to supervise their creations. In Hull Aldwick's, Bedforth's, Gregg's and Holy Trinity maisonsdieu were all supervised after 1444 by the corporation, which appointed the poor to vacancies as they arose.[79] In Hedon Agnes de Whitflete seems to have vested her house for the poor in the mayor and council.[80] In York Craven directed that the mayor and corporation should take over his maisondieu if his son failed to pay the poor their due.[81] John de Darthyngton made no formal assignment of his maisondieu to the corporation, but one of the witnesses to his will was William de Selby, a former mayor, and another Henry de Preston, a future mayor.[82] Selby may have taken more than a passing interest in the maisondieu, for his daughter Laurentia van Harlam left 4*d*. to each bed within it, and described it as belonging to her husband Warmabald, who had presumably taken over the patronage at some time after Darthyngton's death.[83] In 1495 the maisondieu of Ysolda de Acaster, widow of a mayor of York and M.P., was recorded as being farmed to the Weavers' guild by the city.[84]

In a number of cases, however, although the city had ultimate responsibility for the maisondieu, its day-to-day running lay in the hands of someone else − a chantry chaplain. Here the analogy of the maisondieu with the chantry reappears only to turn into something more like a fusion. In several cases founders made a close association between their chantry and their maisondieu. This was in some ways not surprising: a chantry chaplain was frequently the same person as the family chaplain, particularly where, as so often, the chantry was established during the lifetime of the benefactor. As such the chaplain might well be involved in administering his employer's estates, and helping to run his business. He might write, or at least witness, his will, and could act as an executor, or assist the executors. He might be expected to take a wider responsibility for his employer's soul than simply saying his daily mass, and direct other work for his spiritual benefit. He might indeed have had a hand in suggesting the most suitable forms of spiritual and charitable activity which his patron could perform. And once his only responsibility was to his chantry he would have time on his hands. Who more suitable to supervise a maisondieu?

Robert de Holme, while not giving his chaplain such a job explicitly, did make him an executor; John de Darthyngton made John Hertford, chaplain, the first of his two executors.[85] Thomas de Holme had enfeoffed property to his executors Robert Yneflete, chaplain, Robert Gamell, chaplain, and Peter de Appilton, clerk, part of which was to be sold for ministering to the poor. His chantry priest, probably one of these, was to have his ease in his chantry in hall, chamber and garden and 100*s*. p.a.[86] As the last building which had been mentioned was the maisondieu it is likely that it was located there. This assumption is strengthened by the fact that he was also to be responsible for collecting the rents and for repairs to the house. John Craven, too, seems to have housed his chantry in his oratory in his tenement by Layerthorpe Bridge, which was the location of his maisondieu.[87] In Beverley John de Ake housed his chantry and his maisondieu in the same house on Crossbridge.[88] Aldwick's hospital in Hull consisted of a house in which the chaplain had the room on the first floor and the poor people had the ground floor.[89]

In some cases it may even have been that the chantry chaplain had been left the sole charge of a maisondieu, to dispose of as he saw fit. Richard Kirketon of York, chaplain (d. 1486), was closely associated with two maisonsdieu: John Bedford's in Little St Andrewgate and John Holme's in Whitefriar Lane. To both he left plots of land on condition that his executors should have supervision of the maisondieu and the poor, and he explicitly stated that this was at the mandate of Bedford. In both cases on the death of his executors the governance was to go to one of the chaplains (apparently two different ones) of the nearby parish church of St Saviour.[90] In 1481 John York, canon of North Ferriby, was appointed to a chantry in St Mary, Castlegate, York by the death of Henry Medunsell, last incumbent and custodian of the hospital in the same street. The hospital can only have been that of Thomas de Holme, which lay on the corner of Hertergate and Castlegate. Seventy-five years after Holme's death the custody of the hospital and service of his chantry were still being associated, and it was not because the family were still appointing to both, as the patron of both was now the earl of Northumberland.[91]

The reason for this association of chantry and maisondieu was not simply one of administrative convenience. Both establishments benefited the soul of the founder: the chantry through the efficacy of the mass; the maisondieu because its charitable work was inherently beneficial, but also because the prayers of the grateful poor were particularly pleasing to God. It was not usually made explicit that the poor inhabitants should pray for their benefactor, at least not in the form of the lengthy daily prayers sometimes required by aristocratic founders, but the expectation of spiritual thanks was implicit. Craven made a distinction between the majority of the inmates of his maisondieu who received 3*d.* per week and the thirteenth who received an extra penny for saying prayers daily, morning and evening. Thomas de Holme asked that the poor in his maisondieu should pray specially for the souls of William Johnson and John Dedrikson. Presumably he assumed that they would in any case pray for himself.[92] Chantry and maisondieu made a coherent spiritual unit.

Notes

1   B. Pullan, 'Support and Redeem: Charity and Poor Relief in Italian Cities from the Fourteenth to the Seventeenth Centuries', *Continuity and Change*, 3 (1988), p. 188.

2   C. Burgess, '"By Quick and By Dead": Wills and Pious Provision in Late Medieval Bristol', *EHR*, 102 (1987), p. 846 points out that William Canynge's almshouses are far less well documented than his chantries – despite the fact that the latter were far cheaper to establish.

3   R.B. Dobson, 'The Foundation of Perpetual Chantries by the Citizens of Medieval York', *Studies in Church History*, 4 (1967), pp. 35–6.

4   M. Rubin, *Charity and Community in Medieval Cambridge* (Cambridge, 1987), p. 293.

5   J.T. Rosenthal, *The Purchase of Paradise* (London, 1972), p. 18.

6   For further material on this point see chap. 6 of P.H. Cullum, 'Hospitals and Charitable Provision in Medieval Yorkshire, 936–1547', York D.Phil. thesis, 1989.

7   Maisonsdieu were sometimes referred to by the name of the founder, sometimes by location; it is almost impossible to be sure whether different forms relate to the same maisondieu.

8   M. Rubin, *Charity and Community*, pp. 119–29.

9   J. Stow, *A Survey of London*, ed. C.L. Kingsford (Oxford, 1908), *passim*.

10 N. Tanner, *The Church in Late Medieval Norwich, 1370–1532* (Toronto, 1984), p. 134.

11 D. Keene, *Winchester in the Later Middle Ages* (Oxford, 1985), I, p. 248.

12 This study used material extracted from two sample groups of wills from the Probate Registers of the Exchequer Court of York now kept in the Borthwick Institute of Historical Research in York. These consisted of 200 wills from Probate Register 1 (1389–96), and 1004 from Probate Register 2 (1397–8, 1440–59); and a selection of wills from other probate registers, from the archbishops' registers, also in the Borthwick, and from Dean and Chapter Probate Register 1 (hereinafter D/C 1), now in York Minster Library. Prob. Reg. 1 fo. 98r (Steller); fo. 83v (Crosse).

13 Prob. Reg. 1 fo. 43r (Yhole); Prob. Reg. 2 fo. 103r (Grymmesby).

14 E.g. Prob. Reg. 2 fo. 231r, 1451, John Harpham of Hull left 20s. of coal to be distributed to six maisonsdieu in Hull. Prob. Reg. 2 fos 86–90v, 1444, John Brompton of Beverley left bequests of coal to various hospitals. Prob. Reg. 2 fo. 431v, 1460, Richard Croull left 100 bundles of firewood annually for three years to the Castlehill maisondieu in York. The relative commonness of these bequests in these towns was because coal was being shipped from Newcastle to the east coast ports, especially Hull, perhaps as ballast.

15 E.g. Prob. Reg. 2 fo. 369r, 1458, John Selby, tapster, left eight gallons of good ale to each maisonsdieu. D/C 1 fo. 312v, 1466, John Kirketon, bookbinder, left each maisondieu 4d. or its value in bread. Prob. Reg. 2 fo. 14r, 1398, Margaret de Knaresburgh, seamster, left 8d. in food to each of eight maisonsdieu.

16 Prob. Reg. 1 fos 13v–14r (Bridford); fo. 17v (Ledys); D/C 1 fo. 290v (Cotyngham).

17 Prob. Reg. 3 fo. 225r.

18 Prob. Reg. 5 fo. 270r.

19 Prob. Reg. 2 fo. 327v (Garton); fo. 158v (Hansforde); Prob. Reg. 6 fo. 272r.

20 Prob. Reg. 1 fo. 87r.

21 See n. 5. D/C 1 fo. 304v, 1461, Richard Parke, mason, left 4s. 4d. to distribute one pennyworth of bread each Friday at the door of his house for one year after his death.

22 Prob. Reg. 1 fo. 5v.

23 Archbishop's Register 16; Richard Scrope (1398–1405), fo. 173r.

24 Prob. Reg. 4 fo. 143r.

25 Prob. Reg. 2 fo. 2v.

26 Prob. Reg. 2 fo. 4r.

27 The varying nomenclature here indicates the problems of knowing how many maisonsdieu are being described. Amongst the varying descriptions are: the house of Thomas (sometimes Richard) Duffield; the maisondieu in St Andrewgate; the maisondieu in Little St Andrewgate; the house of Cecily Plater in St Andrewgate; and the maisondieu of John Bedford in Little St Andrewgate founded by Cecily Plater; another in Little St Andrewgate founded by 1353 by Thomas Duffield; and John Bedford may have founded a new maisondieu in Little St Andrewgate by 1486, or may have taken over the patronage of Duffield's maisondieu.

28 Prob. Reg. 2 fo. 432r.

29 Although Ysolda de Acaster (Prob. Reg. 1 fo. 81v, 1385) refers to it as her husband's, other testators seem to have regarded it as hers (Prob. Reg. 1 fo. 96v (Crome); fo. 101v (Holme). Joan Gregg refers to the maisondieu in her will (Prob. Reg. 3 fos. 555v–556v) as being of her recent foundation. *VCH Yorks.*, III, p. 312 refers to Gregg's maisondieu as being of John Gregg's foundation. A. Raine, *Medieval York* (London, 1955), p. 251 has John de Acaster as founder.

30 J. Leland, *The Itinerary* (London, 1964), I, p. 39.

31 Prob. Reg. 6 fo. 117r, 1502 (Armstrong); Prob. Reg. 3 fo. 254v, 1406 (Holme).

32 Prob. Reg. 2 fos 220r–221v, 1451.

33 P.J.P. Goldberg, 'Women in Fifteenth Century Town Life', in J.A.F. Thomson, ed., *Towns and Townspeople in the Fifteenth Century* (Gloucester, 1988), p. 119.

34 Prob. Reg. 3 fo. 275r.

35 Prob. Reg. 4 fo. 143r.

36 Prob. Reg. 4 fo. 96v, 1475.

37 C. Burgess, 'By Quick and by Dead', p. 848.

38 D. Keene, *Winchester*, I, pp. 236–7.

39 J. Stow, *Survey of London*, p. 128.

40 Prob. Reg. 1 fo. 100v (Holme); D/C Act Book H1/3 fo. 10r.

41 Prob. Reg. 3 fo. 606v (Craven); Prob. Reg. 3 fo. 268v (Vescy).

42 Prob. Reg. 1 fo. 15v (Gysburne); Prob. Reg. 3 fo. 254v (Holme).

43 Prob. Reg. 3 fo. 73v (Darthyngton); Prob. Reg. 1 fos 14v–15r (Moreton).

44 D/C Act Book H1/3 fo. 10r (Hibernia); Prob. Reg. 2 fo. 14r (Knaresburgh). But compare the even earlier foundation in 1344 by James de Kingston, king's clerk, of a maisondieu in Hull.

45 M. Rubin, *Charity and Community*, pp. 52, 175–6, 119, 127–9.

46 P. Slack, *Poverty and Policy in Tudor and Stuart England* (Harlow, 1988), p. 5.

47 See chap. 3 of P.H. Cullum, 'Hospitals and Charitable Provision'.

48 St Christopher's: first ref. in 1436, Prob. Reg. 3 fo. 487v (Bracebrig); A. Raine, *Med. York*, p. 135. Tanners': 1446, Prob. Reg. 2 fo. 134r (Tesedale). St Anthony's, Peaseholme Green: John Wyman's will of 1432 (Prob. Reg. 3 fo. 350r) leaves a bequest to the poor brothers and sisters in the hall of this guild, but otherwise it is only known to have had a hospital after it united with the Paternoster guild and received a royal licence in 1446 (*CPR, 1441–6*, p. 442). Marton's: 1436, Prob. Reg. 3 fo. 487v (Bracebrig). Stonebow: 1442, Prob. Reg. 2 fo. 45r (Close). It is possible that this clustering is an illusion caused by the loss of the Probate series covering 1409–25, but this is unlikely.

49 Prob. Reg. 6 fo. 117r.

50 Prob. Reg. 3 fo. 73v.

51 Prob. Reg. 1 fo. 100v.

52 Prob. Reg. 3 fo. 254v.

53 Prob. Reg. 3 fo. 606v.

54 *CPR, 1374–7*, pp. 167, 258.

55 Bequest to Monkgate maisondieu D/C 1 fo. 255v, 1444 (Kirkeby); A. Raine, *Med. York*, p. 283.

56 A. Raine, *Med. York*, p. 57.
57 Prob. Reg. 2 fo. 225r.
58 Prob. Reg. 1 fos 13v–14r (Bridford); Prob. Reg. 3 fo. 262v (Everton).
59 Female testators were a higher proportion of York-only testators, but by no means approached fifty per cent.
60 J. Tickell, *A History of Hull* (Hull, 1976), p. 756.
61 Prob. Reg. 5 fo. 269v.
62 Prob. Reg. 3 fo. 606v.
63 Prob. Reg. 1 fo. 100v.
64 *CPR, 1343–5*, p. 239.
65 Prob. Reg. 2 fo. 45r (Close). When testators refer to the poor lying (*iacenti*) as opposed to living (*existenti, moranti*), or where they use both terms as here, they are distinguishing the bedridden from other poor inhabitants.
66 Prob. Reg. 1 fo. 74v (Rigton); Prob. Reg. 2 fo. 37r (Lamley).
67 P.J.P. Goldberg, 'Female Labour, Service and Marriage in the Late Medieval Urban North', *Northern History*, 22 (1986), p. 35.
68 *York City Chamberlains' Account Rolls, 1396–1500*, Surtees Society, 192 (1978–9), pp. 14, 30. This may have happened at the same time as the kidcotes – the City prison on Ousebridge, which possibly lay under the maisondieu – was divided into a male and a female side.
69 Prob. Reg. 13 fo. 60v (Cape).
70 Prob. Reg. 5 fo. 106r.
71 Prob. Reg. 2 fo. 230v (Burgh); Abp Reg. 18 H. Bowet (1405–26) fo. 349r.
72 Prob. Reg. 6 fo. 64v–65r.
73 Prob. Reg. 1 fo. 50r.
74 Prob. Reg. 5 fo. 269v.
75 Prob. Reg. 5 fo. 327v.
76 *VCH Yorks, East Riding*, I (1969), pp. 334–5.
77 Prob. Reg. 2 fo. 356r.
78 *CPR, 1396–9*, p. 162.
79 Prob. Reg. 2 fo. 58v.
80 See n. 73.
81 Prob. Reg. 2 fo. 2v.
82 Prob. Reg. 3 fo. 606v.
83 Prob. Reg. 3 fo. 73v.
84 Prob. Reg. 2 fo. 583v.
85 *York City Records, Vol. II*, Yorks. Archaeol. and Architect. Soc. Record Ser., 103 (1941), pp. 120–1.
86 Prob. Reg. 1 fo. 103r (Holme); Prob. Reg. 3 fo. 73v (Darthyngton).
87 Prob. Reg. 3 fo. 254v.
88 Prob. Reg. 3 fo. 606v.
89 See n. 75.
90 See n. 73.
91 Prob. Reg. 5 fo. 327v.
92 Abp Reg. 23, Rotherham (1480–1500), pt. 1, fo. 14r.
93 Prob. Reg. 3 fo. 606v (Craven); fo. 254v.

4
The Datini Factors in London, 1380–1410

Helen Bradley

The Italians of the fifteenth century had a shocking reputation among their English contemporaries. At best they were regarded as usurers whose business methods were highly suspect. At worst, the case against them amounted to unsubstantiated abuse: for example, they were credited with the introduction into this country of '*un trop horrible vice q(ue) ne fait pas a nomer*', perhaps a less fortunate aspect of the spread of culture which accompanied Italian trading contacts.[1] As a consequence, they have hardly been likely to fare very well at the hands of English historians using primarily English sources. An alternative perspective on the Italians who lived in London would provide an interesting supplement to the existing understanding of their place in fifteenth-century trade. What, for instance, did the Italians themselves have to say about their business in England?

The Datini correspondence is a particularly rich unpublished Florentine source which covers the late fourteenth and early fifteenth centuries. Born in the small town of Prato near Florence, Francesco di Marco Datini made his early profits as an arms dealer in Avignon. Later, he organised an extensive trading network and became a Florentine citizen.[2] Despite the fact that Datini bought English goods over a long period of time, he did not set up a branch of his own in London.[3] Instead, he used resident Florentine businessmen as his agents. They kept in touch by a routine mailbag run from London through Bruges[4] to other European cities, which was carried on at some risk because the Italians were widely believed to betray state secrets.[5] For example, in 1402 their letters were intercepted on the way to Dover, and early the following year their courier was captured at sea by the Scots.[6] In fact, the content of the surviving letters was primarily commercial, much like the later published correspondence of the Celys and of the Venetian agent in Syria, Andrea Berengo;[7] but the Datini agents lived in rapidly changing times both in England and Italy.

In England, Richard II was deposed, and fewer Italians stayed on during the notorious anti-alien fervour which gained in momentum and violence throughout the Lancastrian period and peaked in the 1450s.[8] The London crafts were to the forefront of this movement and were especially hostile. The silkwomen protested against Italian imports that 'every wele disposed persone . . . wold rather that wymmen of their nation born and owen blode hadde the occupation thereof'.[9] Even the Grocers, who had counted Italians among their founder members in 1343, referred to 'our crafte of ynglishmen and fremen' and admitted the Venetian Giovanni di Marconuovo to wear their livery on condition that he wanted no more than 'gud maisterschipe Frendschipe and love'.[10] In Italy, there was as yet no state-owned galley fleet to support Florentine merchants trading abroad. The strategic position of Pisa, a nearby port situated at the mouth of the River Arno and much used by Florentine merchants, was vitally important to Anglo-Florentine trade. Both Pisa and Florence were directly in the path of Milanese expansion.[11] The Pisan alliance with Milan in 1397 was rapidly followed by occupation of the port by Milan's Visconti rulers. Subsequently, the Milanese effectively blocked Florentine access to other local ports, cut the overland route to Venice by the fall of Bologna in 1402,[12] and finally closed Pisa. After the short-lived Clarence match, two more Visconti marriages into the English royal family were planned: for Richard himself in the late 1370s and in 1399 for his cousin the duke of Lancaster, later Henry IV.[13] Moreover, the balance of business between the Italian nations within England was changing. Florentine commodity trade sank to third place, trailing that of Genoa and Venice; the Venetians were the principal Italian traders in London, the Genoese in Southampton.[14]

These were perhaps reasons enough for Datini to baulk at the idea of funding a branch in London. The circumstances were certainly inauspicious. Nevertheless, he took an active decision to trade in English goods, albeit on a basis which minimised the risks to his own investment by using London-based compatriots as his agents. Italian business arrangements of this period were conducted within a remarkably fluid structure of serial partnerships, and it was quite common for companies to dissolve and re-form in a slightly different way every few years. However, Datini dealt mainly with three leading Florentine firms: Domenico Caccini and Piero Cambini; the Mannini brothers, Alemanno and Antonio; and Giovanni Orlandini and Neri Vettori. Most of the Florentine community already knew each other or at least had mutual acquaintances, and had often worked together before whether as partners or otherwise. For instance, Cambini had previously worked for the Mannini, and some of their letters to the Datini company are in his hand. Very little is known about these agents from English sources and that largely as a result of their formal business requirements. Traces can be found of Caccini and Cambini's termination of business with another Florentine firm, and of Caccini's litigation in the mayor's court in London.[15] The Mannini, on the other hand, were heavily connected with Richard II. They provided his jewels, paid wages for the earl of Rutland's embassy to Paris to negotiate his marriage, and acted as his intermediaries with the papal curia.[16] Vettori advanced loans to the new king in the summer following Richard's deposition, and some of his licences for foreign exchange under Henry V have survived.[17] Partners in all three firms commonly appear in the customs records for London and Southampton, and in a more personal capacity they also feature as executors for Florentine merchants whose wills were proved in London.[18]

If solely English sources were available, this would be the totality of our knowledge of these firms. However, a very great deal of information is contained in the letters which they wrote to the various branches of the Datini company in Spain and Italy, and which are still kept in the Palazzo Datini at Prato.[19] From these it is possible to attempt a rather livelier and more personal reconstruction of their principal markets, their everyday working conditions, and their reactions to contemporary English politics.

There is a clear distinction in the correspondence between Datini's Italian branches which took English wool and cloth exports, and his Spanish branches which sent goods to this country. The Datini agents in London dealt with a strictly limited range of imports. The fine cloths, ivory combs and rare pets which featured prominently among Italian cargoes coming into London were not items in which they traded. Their attention was focused on spices. These, they said, were the goods from which most profit could be made in England.[20]

The commodities included under the heading of spices were grocery in the broad medieval sense. They dealt in the basic spices: pepper, ginger, cinnamon, cloves, nutmeg, mace, saffron and galingale. Sometimes several different kinds of the same spice were available. Ginger was often described as *'bellend'* or *'colombine'*, although the agents noticed that the type called *'mechin'* was not so much in demand.[21] All of these spices were ready garbelled except saffron, although there were complaints about the standard of Italian garbelling.[22] Grain, the most expensive of the dyestuffs, was also popular, and the agents imported it from Valencia, Portugal, Barbary and Provence as well as Seville. Other common imports were almonds, rice, tin and soap; these were priced by the hundredweight, whereas spices and grain were priced by the pound. On the whole, this reflected the division made by the City between goods weighed by avoirdupois measure and small wares.[23]

But, within this broad spectrum, the Florentine interest concentrated heavily in one area. The cargoes of oranges, lemons, dates and figs which the Italians usually brought into London, did not appear on their price lists. Nor did madder and woad.[24] Pepper was a regular and prominent item, usually the first to be quoted, and ginger and grain were also important. The Florentine eye was fixed firmly upon the more expensive goods in the range. It was here that prices were subject to the sudden short-term changes from which maximum profits could be made. For instance, spice values swung widely and rapidly in 1392 both in England and in Bruges.

Bellend and *colombine* ginger, bought at prices then payable in Genoa, were expected to make a considerable profit in England. From 1392 to 1394, there was a shortage of ginger in England and Flanders, and the Florentines took great interest in the possibility of filling this gap in the market.[25] The prices of other items such as cloves and galingale were also highly erratic. The types of grain were individually variable: Valencia usually attracted the highest price, Spanish held the middle place, and Barbary was the cheapest. In comparison with other spices, pepper was noticeably stable, although in 1411 the English complained that the Italians hoarded it to push up prices.[26] Where prices were given for different stages of the same year, they varied from month to month. But there was obviously a consensus that every commodity had its price, and many of the letters give general reflections on the state of the market. They simply say whether prices were normal, high or low.[27] Sometimes one particular item was in short supply and therefore expensive, while others were normal or slightly down in price.[28]

Whatever the problems in supplying a particular item, there were some acknowledged factors which affected the market as a whole. It was commonly observed that prices fell on the arrival of ships.[29] Although prices were at normal levels in May 1404, they were expected to fall when agreement was reached between Venice and Genoa because more ships would come north.[30] On the other hand, there was also a season for spices during July and August, and after the season prices were seen to drop.[31] So the Florentines observed a fall in values both when ships arrived and spices were abundant, and when the main season was over and demand dropped.

The agents in London, then, were mainly concerned with a narrow range of spice imports which made the best profit in a volatile market. However, it cannot be assumed that the import trade was an insignificant part of their business.[32] The information is not as abundant for the Spanish branches of the Datini company which sent imports to England as for the Italian ones which handled English exports. As one might expect, the bulk of extant correspondence concerns the export of wool to the Florence branch. The spice trade hinged on Spain and the Balearics, and centred on Barcelona;[33] comparatively few letters to these branches have survived. Although they give an indication of how this part of the business was conducted, it would be unreasonable to assume that they represent the totality of the Florentine grocery trade in London.

The export trade from England was the main reason for business between London and Datini's Italian branches, but it was not the lure of general English craftsmanship which proved so attractive. Although worked tin, candlesticks and caps were common Italian exports from London, they were not a regular or large part of Datini's trade. He rarely exported such goods from England; the quantities were very small and they were often packed in with other merchandise, a practice with which other aliens and the English were familiar.[34] The trade cannot have constituted adequate business for resale in Italy, and the goods were probably intended for personal use.[35] The expatriates in London occasionally asked for items such as treacle to be sent from Italy as a favour,[36] and the Florentines at home might also have wanted something special from London for themselves now and then. However, most of the letters were concerned with purchasing, packing and transporting wool or cloth to Italy, and wool was the real mainstay of the business.

The Datini company at Florence asked to be kept informed of wool and cloth prices in England on a regular basis, and they were especially interested in when to purchase wool.[37] The agents in London gave a simple and consistent answer. The time to buy was mid-June. It was at the summer shearing that new wools were coming onto the market at the fairs, and maximum profit could be made.[38] The Florentine interest was overwhelmingly in the fairs for Cotswolds wool, which started at the Nativity of St John the Baptist on 24 June.[39] Those which they mentioned most frequently were the fairs of *Borriforte* and *Norleccio*: Burford and Northleach.[40] The Burford fair was the first in the series to take place. The parish church there was dedicated to St John the Baptist, and the town was on the Oxford–Gloucester road, which provided a route to Northleach and the rest of the Cotswolds.[41] It was at Burford that the wool-buying season started, and prices were set for the other fairs which followed.[42] However, it was not only the fairs which took the Florentines to that part of the country, although that was their principal reason for going. They also negotiated for supplies of wool from other sources: from the abbeys, and from places which they called the *'pile'*. The Celys referred to having wool 'in pyle', and this is clearly an English word for storage rendered in Italian.[43] The *'pile'* were run by local English middlemen *'q(u)e del paexe che fano le pile.'*[44] Some were burgeoning gentry like Thomas Adynet of Northleach.[45] William Grevel of Chipping Campden ran two such storage centres, where he offered disadvantageous terms in 1401.[46] Adynet too was selling above the highest price payable at the fairs in 1402.[47] Wool bought at the *'pile'* was generally more expensive than the wool at the fairs,[48] but cheaper than that of the abbeys. The agents usually quoted overall prices for both the *'pile'* and the abbeys, but some abbeys were mentioned by name when wool was bought directly from them. These included Cirencester and Llanthony, which were on the Cotswolds circuit.[49]

Conversely, there is virtually nothing which might explain where the Florentines bought their cloth. There is no indication of a special time of year for buying, nor of cloth fairs.[50] There are several possible explanations. First, they could have bought local cloth at the wool fairs, but this is unlikely. Cotswolds cloth was occasionally mentioned, but most of their purchases were not of this type. Secondly, English cloth merchants from towns further afield could have brought stock or samples to sell at the wool fairs.[51] This is even less likely, because the fairs were firmly tied to the new season's wool production, and the discussions of them centred entirely upon the price and condition of wool. The men who attended them were experts in that particular line of commerce, not general traders.[52] Thirdly, the agents could have bought cloth on their way to and from the fairs. The difficulty with this solution is that they bought mainly Guildford and Essex cloth, produced in areas which would have involved some considerable detour from the Cotswolds route.[53] However, one obvious alternative remains: they could have been buying on a continuous basis throughout the year in London. This would readily explain why they did not mention travelling anywhere and why there was no season for buying. The probability of this being the case is increased by the ease with which both types of cloth could have been brought to market in London, and the evidence that the port of London was a substantial cloth exporting centre. Indeed by the 1320s London had already taken a large share of the cloth market away from the eastern town fairs, and the king was buying in London.[54] The majority of surviving advice notes issued by the agents also show that cloth was packed and invoiced in London, although wool was clearly packed in and sent from Southampton. It would seem very likely that the bulk of the Florentine cloth trade consisted of purchases made in London.

Wool was always sold at a rate of marks to the sack. Prices varied considerably, and many of the factors involved were regular features of the market.[55] There was a clear concept of an acceptable price, and anything much above 11 marks – £7 6s. 8d. – was reckoned expensive.[56] But the price of wool also depended upon less predictable factors. One of the major considerations was the health of the flocks, and the Florentines readily made rough calculations about the following year's market. They could freely observe the condition and numbers of the animals while touring the countryside on business,[57] and they would also have picked up local gossip from their suppliers. No doubt the striking of bargains involved considerable discussion of sheep-rearing and futures. The direction which wool prices took was no surprise to them, and they often anticipated market trends from what they had learned during the previous year's trading. The years 1401–3 were particularly difficult ones for the agents because of high mortality among sheep. Disease and flooding could hit flocks hard,[58] and in 1402 there were one-third fewer wools available than in the previous year.[59] The survival rate for sheep had been poor for the last twelve years, and it was noticed that there was a better market for the hides of the dead animals than for wool.[60] For the period covered by the correspondence, the range in price was from 9 marks – £6 – in 1395 to 15 marks – £10 – in 1404, a difference of £4 per sack, that is, just over half the value of the average-priced sack.

Cloth prices were more stable by comparison partly because the trade was not prone to natural disaster. But despite the fact that cloth was made throughout the year and there was no season for it, the agents did notice variations in price. The presence of ships meant a snap demand for cloth, and consequently higher prices.[61] It is interesting to see that the agents particularly linked cloth prices to shipping headed for Italy and not elsewhere on the Continent. They specifically associated the return of prices to normal levels with the departure of carracks and galleys, and not with other types of vessel.[62] As with wool, they had a clear idea of what was a reasonable price.[63] Guildford cloth was always priced by the ell, and Essex by the dozen consisting of twelve ells. They were prepared to pay 7¼d. an ell for Guildford, and 12s. a dozen (that is, 12d. per ell) for Essex. Prices did not usually vary by more than 1¼d. per ell.

Naturally, the Florentine buyers took a keen interest in the activities of their competitors. The major contenders in the wool market were their arch-rivals the Milanese, who were buying for the Lombard region of Italy. As a rule, they purchased their supplies in Lindsey while the Cotswolds were a Florentine preserve.[64] But the great shortages of 1401–3 caused them to venture out of their customary territory, and brought them into direct conflict with the Florentines in the Cotswolds.[65] In 1402 and 1403, the agents noticed a price rise in conjunction with the advent of the Milanese, although they did not accuse the Milanese of pushing up prices. The price level was largely a result of the shortages which had brought the Milanese to poach there in the first place. The Celys also complained of Lombard competition, but probably meant the Italians in general rather than the Milanese.[66] Venetian competitors were hardly mentioned, and the Genoese too were largely disregarded, although this may be because the Florentines and Genoese were able to cooperate to a certain degree.[67] The native English were also rarely considered, except when they interfered in some unexpected way with Florentine plans. Just such an event occurred in the summer of 1403, when the drapers of Bristol and London bought extensively and suddenly – much to Florentine surprise – in a concerted attack at the Burford fair: '*(i)l resto fu subito levato da drappieri di bristo & d(i) londra & altri & simile da paesani p(er) fare le pile*'.[68] This was something of a first strike by indigenous merchants starved of wool, which was the basis of their livelihood, after the severe shortages of 1402. It was a successful strategem, and was repeated at other fairs.[69]

Although the Milanese were the major rivals of the Florentines in supplying wool for the industries back at home, there was no suggestion that the Milanese were large-scale cloth buyers. Nor was there any reference to English mercers. The Florentines' main preoccupation in timing their cloth purchases was the movement of Italian shipping, and there were frequent mentions of rises in price and demand in association with the presence of Genoese carracks and Venetian galleys.[70] This does not necessarily imply that the Genoese and Venetians were their chief competitors, because merchants of other nations could load on their ships if there was sufficient extra space for them. Nevertheless, it is more than likely that this was the case. And on two occasions, they did make the link explicit. In 1405, the agents said that cloth prices had risen since the Genoese started to purchase for the carracks; '*i genovisi chominciera(nno) la investire p(er) le characche*',[71] and a rise in the price of Guildford cloth in 1392 was blamed upon the arrival of Venetians, buying for a galley '*e lla cagione ne viniziani venutici che gli an(n)o co(m)p(r)ati p(er) una galea d(i) veniziani*'.[72] This reference to the arrival of the Venetians, as well as the fact that the galleys were more often mentioned in connection with cloth than the carracks, fits well with the probability that the Florentines were buying their cloth in London, which was the principal port for the Venetian galleys. And while the Genoese carracks were simply linked with a general rise in cloth prices, the Venetians had a more specialised interest in English cloth. It was in conjunction with the Venetian presence that changes in the price of Guildford cloth in particular were noticed. On at least one occasion, the agents held over their purchases of Guildford until the galleys had sailed again.[73]

At this stage, the Datini agents had travelled around the local fairs, established current prices and market conditions for wool in the Cotswolds and for cloth in London, confronted their competitors and made the best purchases they could find. They had already worked hard, and had the satisfaction of having completed their commissions, but they had as yet done only half of their job. They still had to find a way of transporting the goods to Italy in the absence of Florentine shipping. This is where their letter-writing, which maintained a wide range of contacts and kept them one step ahead of common knowledge, really began to pay dividends.

It was extremely important for the agents to be able to pinpoint the position of individual ships. Their arrival and departure had a considerable impact on prices. Arrivals meant an influx of some goods, and a run on others as they were bought up by ships' crews and travelling merchants for the return sailing. This in turn meant fluctuations in the availability and price of credit. In Bruges, for example, money was dear in June and December before the galleys sailed.[74] Those who had the advantage of continuous residence expected to anticipate these market variations and reap maximum benefit. However, their interest in the whereabouts of shipping extended far beyond the imminent arrivals. The agents exchanged information about ships anywhere at sea. Once a ship left port, its position was reported at every stage of the voyage until it put in at its destination. A tight news network operated, involving Italians based in other cities. Information came in to London by letter from relatively nearby places like Southampton and Bruges, and from more distant cities.[75] Incoming ships' crews also relayed the current news from other ports, and sightings of vessels still at sea.[76] Ships were tracked all around the coasts of western Europe as a matter of routine.[77] Much of the detail was filled in at the last moment, and sometimes letters were sent with departure dates left blank.[78] Although arrival times and the risks of loss by bad weather were important, there were other reasons why the London agents were keen to have news of ships which were still cruising far away off Spain and Portugal. One was piracy, and another was war.

Although both presented a continuous hazard, the particular danger varied as ships passed through different coastal waters. Off north-west Italy and southern Spain, the most likely cause of catastrophe was attack by pirates on the lookout for rich cargoes. Many were Christian Europeans, sailing against the enemies of Church or state.[79] Some of them, such as Saragrus and Gherardo da Piombino, were known by name. The terror of the London agents was Francesco delle Schase, whose nephew followed him into the trade.[80] The Florentine attitude to this offshoot of Anglo-Italian commerce was decidedly uncharitable: they hoped that God would sink all pirate ships: '*che dio p(ro)fond lui & gl(i) altri corsali*'.[81] However, they were satisfied when delle Schase had to beach his ship in Spain and could not afford repairs. His nephew was captured shortly afterwards.[82]

The most likely source of danger in northern waters was trouble in the Channel stemming from hostilities between England and France.[83] However, the dividing line between independent piracy and act of war was barely distinguishable,[84] especially where West Country ship masters gave an informal boost to the war effort. This was a particular problem early in Henry IV's reign.[85] The net result for merchants was the same, and the theft of cargoes on the pretext that they were enemy goods was the basis of many Italian complaints to the Crown. It was therefore particularly unfortunate that the Genoese were often allied with the French. The English consequently eyed them with great suspicion: '*i genovesi ci stan(n)o pure co(n) sospetto e sonn(o) malveduti p(er)che sono franceschi*'.[86] In the 1390s, the Castilian Spaniards were in the same position.[87] During outbreaks of war, any alien ship could be physically stopped and forced into port on suspicion of being enemy-owned or carrying enemy goods. The situation was complicated by the fact that the Florentines usually used Genoese transport and the Genoese often shipped from Spain on local boats. Merchants also sometimes sent their goods in the name of someone of a different nation, to avoid reprisals or taxes.[88] Venetian ships could carry 80% Florentine or Milanese loads, and many Spaniards took work as sailors or pilots on Italian ships.[89] The result was that the English were unable or unwilling to distinguish between the Italian nations at sea, or for that matter between the Italians and the Spanish. For instance, in 1403 a Biscayan ship sailing from Catalonia laden with Alberti goods was taken at sea by the English. An enquiry headed by the mayor of Southampton found that a ship captained by Martin de Vaguisse Dartiaga had been captured off St Malo in May by Richard Spicer and his friends, and was forced to go to Guernsey where the cargo of salt, almonds and rice was divided and the salt sold off presumably with scant regard for the nationality of individual owners.[90]

However, the Anglo-French unpleasantness was not the only difficulty to be faced in the north. Endemic conflict among the Italian nations resulted in strikes against each other's shipping anywhere at sea, and war between Venice and Genoa meant that the safest forms of transport – Genoese carracks and Venetian galleys – were open to mutual attack.[91] The usual method of protection against both official and unofficial interception was the use of a convoy system with cargoes split between the ships.[92] These convoys were loose arrangements. Masters who were heading in broadly the same direction at the same time would travel together to minimise their risks. The agents set great store by this precaution, and the accidental break-up of convoys was a cause for anxiety.[93] Although undoubtedly the majority of journeys were completed in safety, a Florentine in London would not count upon the arrival of any ship, but would keep a careful eye on its progress until it came into port.

Once ships had arrived in the north, they were available for hire for the return trip.[94] Their condition, manning levels and likely convoy partners were a subject of intense interest to merchants seeking a safe passage for their goods. The Genoese carracks usually proved eminently satisfactory from this point of view. Often they were simply described by the agents as being noble and well-armed, an evocative but uninformative phrase.[95] Occasionally crew numbers were given, and these were sometimes separated out into sailors and marines, or extra crossbowmen were mentioned.[96] In the agents' opinion, fifty men constituted an adequate crew for a large ship.[97] The level of armament in particular was flexible enough to allow for sudden changes to suit varying levels of threat. While the same marines were often rehired for the return journey, plague and desertion ate heavily into crew numbers, and later Florentine state shipping sometimes hired English or north European manpower.[98] Extra crossbowmen could be taken on at intermediate stages if necessary.[99] With extra hands and sufficient defence, numbers often reached ninety or more. Although the Venetian galleys did not provoke adverse comments on this score, other Venetian ships came in for heavy criticism. They were often described as in bad condition and sailing short-handed, or travelling alone.[100] Certainly this was a deterrent to potential customers, but failure to take a full load was not always indicative of a poor ship. If there was a limited amount of merchandise for transport, only part of a convoy would be hired although no fault was found with the remaining ships.[101] This could also work in reverse. If there were more goods than expected, merchants based in England could be surprised to find the homebound ships fully laden from Sluys, and sometimes potential cargoes were left on the quayside for lack of space.[102]

The place of hire, and who exactly did the hiring, was in most cases unstated or uncertain. Nor was it usually made clear whether an entire ship was chartered, or whether space on board was booked.[103] These matters may have been considered perfectly obvious, or perhaps they were details which were the agents' private concern. The result was that very vague terminology was used, and it is almost impossible to pinpoint its meaning now. The Florentines used terms which conveyed that ships were being hired 'here', and described the hiring agency variously as 'ours of Bruges', 'we' or 'we with the others together'. This is of limited usefulness. 'Here' could mean England or Flanders, or perhaps both as the joint termini of the northern route. 'Ours of Bruges' could refer to the Bruges branch of the agents' company, the whole Florentine community in Bruges, or all of the Italians there. Similarly, 'we' could be just the agents' company, or the Florentines, the Italians in general, or even groups in England and Flanders acting as a united body. The evidence suggests that 'we' implied the Florentines,[104] as did 'we with the others together',[105] but it cannot be concluded that this was invariably the meaning of such phrases. It is seldom stated outright that the Florentines were taking a specific course of action, but on the whole, it seems very likely that decisions were usually made within the national community.[106] Even less is said about how these decisions were taken. The merchants might have gathered together at an appointed time, or the major dealers might have fixed the arrangements to suit themselves and expected the smaller fry to fall into line. The communities in England and Flanders may have conferred, but Flanders may have led the process, or England may have acted alone. The only certainty is that the arrangements to use the Sluys galleys must have involved some degree of cooperation with the Bruges Italians because loading levels were known in advance.[107] Possibly there was no single system by which these bargains were struck. Indeed, it is quite evident that matters were often settled very late in the day, or plans were changed at the last minute.[108] Individual merchants waited in agitation for a community agreement before going ahead with their own arrangements,[109] and occasionally the decision was left far too late. Then the merchants quite literally missed the boat, and had to make the best of the remaining alternatives.[110]

It has already been noticed that the better condition, manning and armaments of the Genoese ships, and their convoy arrangements, meant that the Florentines preferred them to other shipping. Moreover, they were plentiful; during the boom years of 1394–1401, two or three Genoese ships came to England and Flanders each year direct from the Middle East, and more from Genoa.[111] Their routes were also geographically ideal, as they normally put in at Southampton which was the natural outlet for the Cotswolds wool which the Florentines bought.[112] In addition, their home base was conveniently close to Florence,[113] and they offered the cheapest freight rates. The Venetian galleys were prohibitively expensive,[114] and called less conveniently at London and Sandwich; as we have seen, the smaller Venetian ships were not an acceptable alternative. However, this by no means exhausted the possibilities for an enterprising agent, as shipmasters of many other nationalities called at Southampton. Overall, the Florentines' second choice fell upon those of southern Spanish origin, but the exact nationality of shipmasters can be a perplexing business. Some, like Rafael Marabotto, were simply named after items of ships' equipment.[115] It was also probably in their own interest to blur the distinctions on occasions. The Savonese who joined Genoese convoys were sometimes labelled as Genoese themselves.[116] Other ships were described as Spanish or Biscayan, vague terms which in practice amounted to the same thing, and Catalan shipping may have subsumed Biscayans.[117] The Catalans too sometimes travelled with the Genoese,[118] and it may be that the Florentines' willingness to use other southern European shipping hinged upon the frequency with which they were accompanied by the Genoese. Of course, southern Spanish ships also had the major advantage of being engaged on the right routes for agents who were sending goods to Italy. Furthermore, the Italians had been instrumental in the commercial development of southern Spain, and their outward shipping completed its cargo there.[119] On the other hand, southern Spanish ships were rare on the cross-Channel run,[120] which was usually undertaken by northern European shipmasters. It was only under very special circumstances that northerners were hired to sail direct to Italy. In 1392, for instance, a firm of agents took a one-third share in a ship belonging to Sir Thomas Percy. It was chartered from Southampton to Pisa under an English captain.[121] However, the Florentines obviously favoured the Genoese ships above others whenever they could, and it was not simply a question of the excellence of their service. Southampton was very much a Genoese base, and their shipmasters virtually did as they pleased there. This included paying little attention to the king's customs officials. Genoese masters are known to have refused to cocket the goods which they had loaded. Their contempt extended to threatening to throw the searcher overboard, and once when he ordered them not to sail he was forcibly abducted '. . . I chargyd hym in (th)e kyng('s) name (tha)t he suld not saylle . . . untyll tyme (tha)t he hade hys coket & not w(i)t(h)stondyng he salyd forth hys way & lede me w(i)t(h) hym vii mylle into (th)e see & in (th)e ile of wyght (the)n I came oland'.[122]

This kind of freedom of action must have suited the Florentines very well, and they were sometimes alleged to be the prime movers behind the shipmasters' recalcitrance.[123] The later Florentine galley patrons knew the Southampton customs officials well, and were entertained privately by them.[124]

The loading of the ships was a complex business. Although formal insurance arrangements were available,[125] it was normal practice to split cargoes between the available ships to ensure that at least part of the consignment reached its destination. The instruction to split the load originated with the owner of the goods, but the practical decision was left to the agent on the spot, who had to do his best according to the circumstances.[126] Sometimes even he did not know exactly how the ships had been loaded until the boats which ferried the goods out to deeper water had returned.[127] If there were any problems during wet weather, boatloads of goods would have to be brought back to shore again to dry through before the whole process was started all over again.[128] Once he was sure what had been done with each individual sack of wool or bale of cloth, the agent sent a full list to the prospective recipient in Italy detailing the way in which the consignment was split. He gave the numbers and company markings on the wrappings, the identity of the merchants in whose name they were loaded, and the name of the owners who would supply further instructions.[129]

There was also a great curiosity about what else the ship was carrying, apart from the items for which the agents were directly responsible. It was part of their job to report on the make-up of ships' loads. It is particularly noticeable that such reports were made at different stages of loading. At first, reasonably accurate round numbers were given while goods were still being taken aboard, and precise figures were available later after the ships sailed.[130] But what interested the agents so intensely was not the ship's total capacity, but which parts of the cargo were going to which ports. Their correspondents at home were particularly anxious to know how much wool or cloth was on its way to north-west Italy, because this would affect local prices, credit, and ultimately their markets further afield. Early information would give them an edge over other companies. There was also another objective. Special attention was paid to the quantities of goods destined for Florence's most bitter enemy, the Lombardy region based on Milan. Estimates of her likely trading position had implications for politics and warfare. However, the agents' reports did not extend much beyond the destinations of immediate interest to correspondents in north-west Italy. More distant places were mentioned only with reference to stopovers in local Italian ports.[131] Although there must have been a good deal of information available in London concerning the Venetian galleys, their cargoes were spoken of only rarely by the Datini agents, in connection with the general profitability of the Flanders voyage. In 1401, for instance, the galleys would have done better to have stayed at home.[132]

One point which was often left in abeyance in the agreement between agent and shipmaster was the port of destination. It was obviously vital for both men to know where the ship was headed, but the exact port was regarded as a minor detail. The most important thing was arrival with cargo and crew intact, and the agents' network of correspondents could quickly respond to changes of plan. The master was consequently allowed considerable latitude to adapt his course to the weather, outbreaks of hostility and local piracy. Provisions were made for changes of destination according to circumstances on arrival.[133] Sometimes a whole string of permissible ports was agreed upon, and the master took his choice.[134] Masters also occasionally refused to stop at specified ports.[135] The uncertainty of destination applied to the outward journey too, and goods going north were addressed to either London or Bruges depending on where the ship went.[136] Decisions were often made quite late in the voyage, and the consultative process was an extensive one involving most of those aboard including the travelling merchants and crew.[137] However, the system was not foolproof. Even the Florentine state galleys were on one occasion disorientated as a result of bad weather in the Channel; the fleet's captain took advice from the Portuguese pilots and the crew, who thought they were in the approach to Plymouth, but on making enquiries with some local fishermen he found that they were in Mousehole Bay instead.[138] This was just the sort of unforeseen circumstance which formal contracts could not hope to cover. Ultimately, it must have been the decision at sea which counted. No master would have risked his ship, ninety or more lives and a profitable cargo for the sake of an agreement made back in England or Flanders. Florentine practice reflected this reality.

As we have seen, the Datini letters are packed with detailed information on trade and shipping, but what of the political aspects with which English historians have so often been absorbed? This was a period when the English were increasingly hostile to aliens, and especially Italians. Of course, minor harassments were normal enough, and even the Venetian galleys' patrons complained of malicious delay in customing their goods in London.[139] Officially, customs staff should not have been obstructive in their dealings with aliens, and in 1390 the Crown insisted that merchant strangers should be courteously and justly treated in order to encourage them to trade in this country.[140] It was a vain hope. In 1404 there were complaints both about the customers' treatment of the Italians, and the quality of justice available to them in the mayor's and sheriffs' courts in London.[141] At the same time, Italians were to be removed from the king's and queen's households, 'soient ils Scismatz ou noun'.[142] Yet the Datini agents seem to have mixed readily enough with the English and referred to their native business contacts by name.[143] There is no mention of violence against them, despite the fact that the capital was notorious for street crime after dark, and the country fairs were perennially rough.[144] Interestingly, the sole indication of any trouble was in relation to London, and provides an intriguing forerunner to the better-known Venetian proposal to withdraw from London in the mid-1450s.[145] The Florentines made an identical threat some fifty years earlier in October 1400 when they intended to enlist the king's help to change their base in England: *'noi fo(r)se dilibera(mo) mutare villa choll' aiuto de Re . . . e p(er) potello fare sanza troppo schoricio o dan(n)o'*.[146] This puts a rather different complexion on the Venetian threat in the 1450s. It was not a panic-stricken reaction to English violence, but an old Italian bargaining counter. If the situation did not suit them, they would take their business elsewhere, and a rival port could have the profitable spin-offs from their trade. The king's goodwill would be retained; customs revenue to the Crown would be unaffected.

The nature of contemporary domestic politics was such as to invite comment, and yet the progress of the Anglo-French war and the developing situation between Milan, Pisa and Florence were mentioned by the agents much more often than purely English events. It was international war which most affected the safety of the English Channel and access to the ports of western Italy, matters which were vital to merchants dependent for their livelihood upon long-distance shipping. Not even the greatest political upheavals within England were likely to disrupt the wool and cloth trades. Consequently the references to current internal crises are mostly cursory. The execution of Kent, Salisbury and Huntingdon in 1400 was mentioned, with a note that all traitors would meet the same end. *'Levoroncisy a q(ue)sti g(i)orni alchuni singnory contro a q(ue)sto Re . . . talgliato la testa al co(n)to di chonti & al co(n)to di salisbura e al co(n)to d'otindona . . . & cosy fara(nno) a tuti q(ue)lly tradictory . . . alla corona'*.[147] The two longest accounts both deal with the climax of the 1403 rebellion. Sir Harry and Sir Thomas Percy, two great English lords, had risen against the king with a large army; Harry had fallen on the field, and Thomas was captured. Harry's father, the earl of Northumberland, was holding out with a large force in his castle, and was expected to throw himself on the king's mercy.[148] The fuller version describes it as a hard and bitter battle, fought in the Welsh marches on 21 July; the king and his son were both wounded, and Sir Thomas was beheaded, although the others were pardoned except four or five ringleaders.[149] The Datini agents' connections with Richard II and the Percy family were common knowledge; Giovanni Orlandini's name appeared in an account of an inquisition at Newgate prison concerning a forged indictment, which implicated several Italians as conspirators in the Percy plot and which was intended to cause civil disturbances in London.[150] This special interest in the Percy rebellion, probably a result of earlier personal contacts made when the agents hired Sir Thomas's ship, contrasts with their stunning lack of concern over Richard II's deposition. The Florentines were more excited about prospective subsidy concessions to be wrung from the new incumbent than about the fate of hereditary kingship in England. They broke the news in mid-October 1399. The English had chosen the duke of Lancaster as king, and his predecessor was sentenced to life imprisonment: '*Anno costoro eleto p(er) loro Re il ducha di lanchastro e porta la cor(on)a di q(ue)sto Reame e q(uel)lo p(rim)a era Re e dispossto & condenato in p(er)petua inp(ri)gone*'.[151] In fact, Henry IV was unwittingly adopted by the agents. Within a short space of time, they referred to him as 'our king'.[152] This was perhaps somewhat odd for a staunchly republican nation, but neatly distinguished him from the French king. It was very different from their understandably venomous attitude to the duke of Milan, always labelled as 'the tyrant': *'(i)l teran(n)o che (Christo) lo distrugha'*.[153]

In conclusion, the Datini correspondence shows that Florentine trade occupied a special position in several respects when compared with the generality of Italian trade in the capital. This is very important, because the detailed information on the commodity trade in the customs particulars for London increasingly reflects Venetian arrivals and departures. As we have seen, the Florentines, although resident in London, were trading in the Cotswolds and exporting on Genoese vessels from Southampton. Consequently, the London sources tend to minimise the Florentine presence and activity here. The Datini letters redress the imbalance, and show us more fully what the Florentines were doing. Their imports were concentrated in a very narrow sector of the market compared with the range of goods which other Italians brought to the capital. Their exports, almost exclusively wool and cloth, differed again from the mixture of metalwork, cloth and small manufactures which the Italians as a whole exported from London.

The letters also draw an effective contrast between the twin trades of wool and cloth, associated in theory but so different in practice. Wool took up a disproportionate amount of the agents' time and attention, because of the importance of buying at one time of year, the necessity of travelling outside London to the fairs, the consequences of natural disaster for the yield, and the unpredictable competition which they faced on arrival. The cloth trade, on the other hand, was conducted continuously close by in the capital. The sole factor to be taken into account here was the presence of carracks and galleys, which temporarily pushed up prices. The correspondence also does much to confirm our existing knowledge of the wool trade in greater detail. Although the abbeys were no longer selling huge quantities on advance contract nor meeting the bulk of the Florentine export requirement,[154] they still made occasional sales to the Datini agents. English middlemen had found a secure niche of their own at the *'pile'*, and the wool fairs were already fully established in the Cotswolds. This system had clearly ousted the older cycle of fairs based on the eastern English towns, which had flourished until the early fourteenth century,[155] and went hand in hand with toll exemptions for the Cistercian houses in eastern England.[156] The letters also throw light on how voyages were organised and the hazards which the ships confronted. The Mediterranean coast was a perilous stretch, and the English Channel little better. Piracy and war posed a constant and real threat to business, and there was no point on the voyage at which the agents could relax and assume their cargoes were safe. As a result, they continuously exchanged snippets of news with their correspondents, and the exact movements of many ships carrying Italian goods have been preserved. Domestic political change, on the other hand, was not a determining factor but simply one of a number of variables.

Most of all, what the correspondence has to offer is a genuinely Italian perspective on Italian trade in England. The information which Datini wanted concerned current price levels, market trends, and the availability of transport. These are matters which the English government did not set out to record, and so there are no parallel English sources which give the same details. The agents may have lacked formal systems for buying and shipping their goods, but there were clear, flexible patterns in their choices which indicate dexterity in coping with a changing environment. The shifting markets, piracy and political upheaval with which they had to contend were not susceptible to rigid rules. Moreover, uncertainty was quite normal for the Datini agents, who conducted business under extraordinary circumstances in a very matter-of-fact way. In addition they usefully combined their job as expatriate merchants with keeping a dutiful covert eye on Milanese activities abroad. Ironically, although the English were beside themselves with anxiety about Italian espionage, the intended targets for Florentine observation in England were not the English but the Milanese. Had Gian Galeazzo Visconti not died when he did, had the Milanese held Pisa and consolidated their territorial gains in western Italy, and had Lucia Visconti married the future Henry IV, the Florentine trading position might have been very much jeopardised. But their merchants would certainly not have been caught ill-prepared.

Notes

1 I am indebted to Professor George A. Holmes for reading this paper, and for his valuable suggestions. *RP*, III, p. 554 dated 1404; R. Bernardini, 'Un Convegno Sulla Vita a Bordo delle Navi nel Mediterraneo nel Cinquecento e nel Seicento', *Archivio Storico Italiano*, 1987, 534 anno CXLV disp. 4, ottobre-dicembre, p. 678.

2 I. Origo, *The Merchant of Prato* (London, 1957, rev. edn New York, 1963, reprinted 1979), pp. 30–1, 35–7, 143–5; F. Melis, *Mercaderes Italianos en España (siglos XIV–XVI)*, (Seville, 1976), p. 3, n. 1.

3 The letters from London are dated between winter 1388 and spring 1405, a span of seventeen years; cf. Origo, *The Merchant of Prato*, p. 70.

4 Archivio di Stato di Firenze a Prato 777/416466 29 June 1401; ASFP 777/416352 16 July 1401 with postscript at Bruges dated 16 August. It was often convenient to add further information before forwarding to Italy, e.g. ASFP 777/313052 16 November 1398, postscripted 22nd at Bruges, with news of the death of the papal collector in England. Similarly letters from Italy to London bore postscripts from Bruges, e.g. ASFP 664/308913, 17 January 1402. Travellers on the overland route could arrive before the ships; M.E. Mallett, *The Florentine Galleys in the Fifteenth Century* (Oxford, 1967), p. 83, n. 3; see also Origo, *The Merchant of Prato*, pp. 106–7. For a definition of the bag or *scarsella* see F. Edler, *Glossary of Medieval Terms of Business (Italian series 1200–1600)*, (Cambridge, Massachusetts, 1934), p. 260. It was worn on the courier's belt: Origo, *The Merchant of Prato*, p. 106.

5 *RP*, II, p. 320 dated 1373.

6 ASFP 664/308919; 4 July 1402, ASFP 664/308923 and its copy 664/308924 4 January 1403. It was a common occurrence, and Datini told his factors to be careful about what they committed to paper: Origo, *The Merchant of Prato*, p. 107.

7 A. Hanham, ed., *The Cely Letters 1472–1488*, EETS, 273 (1975); U. Tucci, ed., *Lettres d'un Marchand Vénitien Andrea Berengo (1553–1556)* (Paris, 1957).

8 G.A. Holmes, 'Florentine Merchants in England 1346–1436', *EcHR*, series 2, 13 (1960–1), pp. 193–208, p. 198; R. Flenley, 'London and Foreign Merchants in the Reign of Henry VI', *EHR*, 25 (1910), pp. 644–55; M.S. Giuseppi, 'Alien Merchants in England in the Fifteenth Century', *TRHS*, 9 (1895), pp. 75–98; S.L. Thrupp, 'A Survey of the Alien Population of England in 1440', *Speculum*, 32 (1957), pp. 262–73.

9 *RP*, V, p. 325 dated 1455.

10 J.A. Kingdon, ed., *Facsimile of First Volume of MS Archives of the Worshipful Company of Grocers of the City of London, AD 1345–1463* (London, 1886), part 2 (1428–63), pp. 178, 180.

11 The Florentine galleys sailed 1422–80: Mallett, *Florentine Galleys*, p. 19; the first fleet to England and Flanders was in 1425 (p. 38). For Milanese expansion in the fourteenth century, see K.D. Ewart, 'Northern Italy in the Fourteenth and Fifteenth Centuries' section 67A and accompanying plate 67 in R.L. Poole, ed., *Historical Atlas of Modern Europe* (Oxford, 1902).

12 For news of the fall of Bologna, see ASFP 664/308920 and ASFP 664/308921, both dated 29 July 1402.

13 T. Rymer, ed., *Foedera, Conventiones, Literae, etc.*, 10 vols (The Hague, 1739–45), III part 3, p. 84, 18 March 1379; *CSP, Milan, I, 1385–1618*, pp. 1–2, 11 May 1399. The prospective bride, Lucia Visconti, later married Edmund Holland, earl of Kent, who was also related to Richard; see H.A. Doubleday and Lord Howard de Walden, eds, *The Complete Peerage* (London, 1929), VII, p. 161. Richard's uncle, Lionel duke of Clarence, had married Violante Visconti in 1368 and died shortly afterwards; V. Gibbs, ed., *The Complete Peerage of England, Scotland, Ireland, Great Britain and the United Kingdom Extant, Extinct or Dormant* (London, 1913), III, p. 258.

14 Holmes, 'Florentine Merchants', p. 208; E. Ashtor, *Levant Trade in the Later Middle Ages* (Princeton, 1983), pp. 107–8.

15 A.H. Thomas, ed., *Calendar of Select Pleas and Memoranda of the City of London 1381–1412* (Cambridge, 1932), pp. 294–6 dated 1408 and 1409; Corporation of London Record Office, Mayor's Court Bills 1/2/191, 1/2/196, 1/2/205, and Caccini as mainpernor in 1/2/221.

16 PRO E403/562 20 June 1399; E403/564 10 December 1399; E403/554 1 March 1396; Holmes, 'Florentine Merchants', p. 202, n. 7.

17 PRO E401/619 13 and 15 July 1400; E101/128/26 and E101/128/27.

18 PRO E122/71/13 (1390), E122/71/16 (1390–1), E122/71/17 (1392), E122/71/25 (1398), E122/72/4 (1400–1), E122/72/8 (1404), E122/161/1 (1423); E122/138/24

(1397), E122/139/4 (1403) and its controlment E122/139/9, E122/139/11 (1404–5), and a fine for an export licence from Southampton E401/593 18 November 1393; London Guildhall Library 9171/1/352, 9171/1/370v, 9171/1/422.

19 See G. Pampaloni and G. Nuti, *Storia di Prato* (2nd edn Prato, 1981), II secolo XIV–XVIII, plate 9.

20 ASFP 777/312995 25 October 1392.

21 ASFP 885/702767 7 September 1407. All three types are found in Kingdon, *Facsimile*, part 1, p. 111.

22 ASFP 885/702767 7 September 1407: '*tutte specierie si gha(r)bollano salvo zaff(erano) no(n) si gharbella*' – saffron was usually of the *bellighieri* type '*altro zaff(erano) no(n) ci vogliono*'. See also Kingdon, *Facsimile*, p. 191 dated 1429 and *RP*, V, p. 32 dated 1439.

23 By a City ordinance of 1309, avoirdupois weight of 112lb. to the hundredweight applied to wax, almonds, rice, copper and tin while small wares such as ginger, saffron, sugar and mace were sold by the pound, with 104lb. to the hundredweight: R.R. Sharpe, ed., *Calendar of Letter Books of the City of London, Letter Book D* (London, 1902), f. 97. Hence the four percent allowance for error in small wares, known to the Italians as *tratto di bilancia*: see Edler, *Glossary*, p. 47 with example which appears to come from ASFP 994/801733 4 March 1398.

24 These were more likely to be among Genoese cargoes landed at Southampton: O. Coleman, ed., *The Brokage Book of Southampton 1443–1444* (Southampton, 1960), I, p. xxx; A.A. Ruddock, *Italian Merchants and Shipping in Southampton 1270–1600* (Southampton, 1951), pp. 40, 44.

25 ASFP 777/312995 2 October 1392; 777/313003 11 July 1393; 777/313011 26 March 1394; 777/313013 1 July 1394.

26 *RP*, III, p. 662 dated 1411; the price of 20*d*. quoted in the king's response is double the price of between 10*d*. and 12½*d*. per lb. quoted in the Datini letters. Datini bought pepper for England in Venice: Ashtor, *Levant Trade*, p. 172.

27 E.g. ASFP 777/313022 28 December 1394; 664/407483 20 August 1392; 664/509986 1 November 1401.

28 ASFP 885/702767 7 September 1407; ginger was high in price while other spices had fallen.

29 ASFP 777/313018 14 November 1394; 777/313020 28 November 1394; 777/313021 14 December 1394; 777/313027 10 April 1395. See also F.C. Lane, 'Fleets and Fairs: the Functions of the Venetian Muda', pp. 651–63, pp. 655–60 in *Studi in Onore di Armando Sapori* (Milan, 1957).

30 ASFP 664/509950 14 May 1404.

31 ASFP 664/509883 26 March 1404: '*p(er)sino a luglio & aghosto poi chominciera loro stagione*'.

32 Cf. Mallett, *Florentine Galleys*, who argues that apart from pepper and ginger the Florentine galleys in their trade with the eastern Mediterranean were mainly concerned with the supply of dyes and tanning agents for home industries; cf. also W.B. Watson, 'The Structure of the Florentine Galley Trade with Flanders and England in the Fifteenth Century', *Revue Belge de Philologie et d'Histoire*, 39, part 2 (1961), pp. 1073–91, and see p. 1089: 'the Florentines themselves were not interested in England as a market for their satin cloths and oriental spices'. While both are undoubtedly correct about Italian-based branches, the Datini correspondence shows that Spanish-based branches of Italian companies were keen to sell spices to England.

33 For Barcelona as a source of products previously brought from the Levant, see Melis, *Mercaderes Italianos en España*, p. 185.

34 The practice is confirmed by the definition of *fardello*: Edler, *Glossary*, p. 116. See also *RP*, III, pp. 625–6 dated 1409–10; and ASFP 664/407488 dated 1399; 664/407487 27 May 1399; 664/9995 13 November 1404.

35 ASFP 664/407468 6 November 1398. Items were ordered for Francesco and Manno, presumably Datini himself and his partner Manno d'Albizzi degli Agli.

36 E.g. ASFP 777/313003 11 July 1393.

37 ASFP 664/407469 4 January 1392.

38 E.g. ASFP 664/509939 14 April 1403, 664/9996 7 March 1404.

39 ASFP 664/407470 4 January 1392: 'alla San Gi(ov)an(n)i cio e ad 24 d(i) guingnio i(m)p(er)oche a q(ue)l tempo sono le fiere i(n) codsgualdo e allora se ne co(n)viene fornire chi vole avere buona roba'. See also ASFP 664/407470 8 February 1392; 664/407472 28 February 1392; 664/308912 27 December 1401; 664/308913 17 January 1402. It is obviously the Nativity which is intended rather than the other dedication on 29 August; see C.R. Cheney, ed., Handbook of Dates for Students of English History (London, 1948), p. 53. March wools were more expensive and the Celys did not deal in them; A. Hanham, The Celys and their World (Cambridge, 1985), p. 112. They formed only a very small part of Datini's business. The fairs in the Welsh marches were held about a month after those in the Cotswolds; ASFP 664/407469 4 January 1392. Cotswolds wool was particularly suitable for high-grade Italian woollens and was standard staple quality in the late fifteenth century; Hanham, The Celys and their World, pp. 112–13. See also BL Add. MS 48082 'Sommario di Merca(tan)tie in Ingliterra' (1553) fo. 126: 'lana quotisgualda . . . e quella che ordinarime(n)te si manda a Venecia & Fiorenza'. I am grateful to Miss Joan Henderson for knowledge of this latter document.

40 Norleccio is particularly close in pronunciation to the contemporary English 'Norlache' found in Hanham, Cely Letters, no. 67, pp. 60–1, ll. 11–12.

41 R.H. Gretton, The Burford Records, a Study in Minor Town Government (Oxford, 1920), ch. 8. Gretton finds little evidence of the wholesale wool trade in the local records (p. 165), although the fair of St John the Baptist was still in existence until 1861 as a livestock market held on 5 July, p. 230.

42 ASFP 664/308927 21 June 1403: '(Borri)fortte alla fiera che danno il suono a tutto chontisghualdo'; according to 664/509972 25 July 1400, wools were expensive at Burford and similarly valued throughout the Cotswolds; see also 664/509982 19 June 1401.

43 Hanham, Cely Letters, no. 67, pp. 60–1, ll. 11–12; and no. 104, pp. 90–2, l. 37; Hanham, The Celys and their World, p. 115.

44 ASFP 664/9994 30 June 1404; see also 664/308920 29 July 1402; 664/407469 4 January 1392; 664/407485 8 March 1393; 664/308926 22 April 1403.

45 ASFP 664/308922 20 September 1402: 'alla pila d(i) Tomaso Adinetto'. I am grateful to Dr Nigel Saul for the identification of Adynet; see N.E. Saul, Knights and Esquires: the Gloucestershire Gentry in the Fourteenth Century (Oxford, 1981), pp. 231–2.

46 ASFP 664/700708 12 October 1401: 'le ii pile di Grivello a mar(chi) xi ½ & chattivo peso.'

47 ASFP 664/308922 20 September 1402.

48 ASFP 664/509988 12 April 1402. The fairs offered a better quality and gave better weight.

49 Sirisestri, ASFP 664/9998 10 May 1404. It was rated the second-best wool-producing abbey in the Cotswolds; ASFP 664/308922 20 September 1402, 'lle lane della badia del'antonea', ASFP 664/509943 2 July 1403, which must refer to Llanthony Secunda – Llanthony Prima was dedicated to St John the Baptist, but the subsequent foundation was richer and its possessions included the manor of Turkdean and Northleach; VCH Gloucs, II, pp. 87–91.

50 The sole reference to a season for cloth refers to Italy, not England; ASFP 664/407482 6 August 1392.

51 Non-local cloth was offered for sale in the Cotswolds, see the paviage grant of 1321 for Cirencester in Rev. E.A. Fuller, 'Cirencester: the Manor and the Town', Transactions of the Bristol and Gloucestershire Archaeological Society, 9 (1884–5), pp. 298–344, p. 338, n. 4. The list is very similar to the Burford bridge tolls for 1322; see Gretton, The Burford

Records, p. 166. However, the cloths mentioned are mostly luxury imports rather than English manufactures.

52 Domenico Caccini's knowledge of the wool trade was second to none; ASFP 664/700710 1 December 1401. This was skilled work; Hanham, *The Celys and their World*, p. 115.

53 Guildford cloth was produced in Surrey, Sussex and Hampshire: *RP*, III, p. 294. Essex, Suffolk and Norfolk were also grouped together for cloth production: *RP*, III, p. 320. For the popularity of Guildford and Essex cloth see Melis, *Mercaderes Italianos en España*, p. 51.

54 E. Wedemeyer Moore, *The Fairs of Medieval England* (Toronto, 1985), pp. 43, 218, 220.

55 The price differed between the abbeys, '*pile*' and fairs; new wools were always cheaper than old, possibly because of the water content which would be lost in transit; see Hanham, *The Celys and their World*, pp. 125, 127. Cotswold and March differed in price; better quality cost more, e.g. ASFP 664/9994 30 June 1404, when Northleach was selling at a mark dearer than Burford, but the quality was better.

56 E.g. ASFP 664/407472 28 February 1392, prices were normal at 9½ to 10½ marks and possibly 11 marks.

57 *RP*, V, pp. 334–5. Freedom of movement in the Cotswolds was later restricted, BL Add. MS 48082 '*Sommario*' fo. 126.

58 The priory of Llanthony attributed its poverty in the 1320s to floods and murrains; *VCH Gloucs*, II, p. 89.

59 ASFP 664/308918 13 June 1402. Wool was expected to be in short supply and expensive the following year; ASFP 664/509988 12 April 1402.

60 ASFP 664/509987 29 December 1401. Similarly Hanham, *The Cely Letters*, no. 111, pp. 99–100, ll. 38–9: 'Ther ys lyke to be many fellys, for scheype begynys to dy faste in diverys contrey'.

61 ASFP 664/509986 1 November 1401; 664/509988 12 April 1402; 664/509946 21 September 1403.

62 ASFP 664/509886 5 March 1405; 664/308922 20 September 1402.

63 ASFP 664/509980 27 March 1401.

64 'Lindsea'; ASFP 664/308918 13 June 1402.

65 ASFP 664/700708 12 October 1401; 664/308918 13 June 1402; 664/308919 4 July 1402; 664/509992 13 November 1402; 664/509993 31 January 1403; 664/308929 9 August 1403. The Milanese were not expected in 1404; ASFP 664/9993 20 March 1404.

66 '. . .nor I have not bogwyt thys zere a loke of woll, for the woll of Cottyswold ys bogwyt be Lombardys'; Hanham, *The Cely Letters*, no. 107, pp. 94–5, ll. 22–4.

67 ASFP 664/509950 14 May 1404; 664/308924 4 January 1403; 664/9995 13 November 1404.

68 ASFP 664/308927 21 June 1403.

69 ASFP 664/308928 9 July 1403.

70 ASFP 664/509887 26 March 1405; 664/509947 3 November 1403; 664/509973 18 August 1400; 664/509984 6 August 1401; 664/509985 24 September 1401; 664/509991 10 October 1402.

71 ASFP 664/509888 10 May 1405, copied in 664/509889 10 May 1405, continued on 21 June.

72 ASFP 664/407480 11 May 1392.

73 Ibid.; 664/509973 18 August 1400; 664/509961 15 October 1399.

74 R. de Roover, *Money, Banking and Credit in Medieval Bruges* (Cambridge, Massachusetts, 1948), p. 67. The Datini letters often mention the concepts of *stretteza* and *larghezza*, e.g. ASFP 1072/1101668 5 October 1399 and 664/509883 26 March 1404; also '*ristretto a d(enari)*' 664/308919 13 June 1402 or '*carestia d(i) d(enari)*' 664/308919 4 July 1402.

See also de Roover, p. 76. The captain of the Florentine galleys on the northern voyage in 1429–30 mentioned a *carestia* of men when hiring for the return trip; Mallett, *Florentine Galleys*, p. 263.

75 News from Southampton, e.g. ASFP 664/407474 25 March 1392; 664/509989 13 May 1402; 528/6365 1 July 1395. News from Bruges, e.g. ASFP 664/308922 20 September 1402, continued 21 October, and 664/509991 10 October 1402. News from Beirut via Venice, ASFP 777/313003 11 July 1393.

76 ASFP 885/517786 10 December 1405; 664/308919 4 July 1402.

77 E.g. ASFP 885/702766 18 June 1407. The London agents had heard from Barcelona that a ship from England had reached Majorca and subsequently Pisa, but there was no news from Genoa where it was scheduled to unload.

78 E.g. ASFP 664/407475 and 664/407479, both dated 1392. The details were completed in 664/407481 16 July 1392 and 664/407482 6 August 1392.

79 E.H. Byrne, *Genoese Shipping in the Twelfth and Thirteenth Centuries* (Cambridge, Massachusetts, 1930), pp. 62–3; Mallett, *Florentine Galleys*, pp. 149–50.

80 For Saragrus, see ASFP 994/1102198 29 December 1400 and 994/1102186 29 January 1401. For da Piombino, ASFP 1072/603884 8 August 1400, 1072/603885 30 August 1400 and 1072/603887 31 October 1400. For delle Schase, ASFP 777/313013 1 July 1394 and 777/313020 28 November 1394.

81 ASFP 994/1102198 29 December 1400, with reference to Saragrus.

82 ASFP 777/313021 14 December 1394; ASFP 777/313028 22 May 1395.

83 E.g. ASFP 664/308926 22 April 1403 and 664/509945 5 September 1403.

84 Mallett, *Florentine Galleys*, p. 58: 'accredited warships were more discriminating but often just as dangerous'.

85 W.R. Childs, *Anglo-Castilian Trade in the Later Middle Ages* (Manchester, 1978), p. 43.

86 ASFP 664/10038 29 March 1407. See also 885/703147 3 May 1404.

87 Childs, *Anglo-Castilian Trade*, p. 43.

88 The Datini agents used Genoese or Venetians based in London, e.g. ASFP 528/506174 19 April 1396 and 528/506175 25 May 1396. The Venetian Senate expected alien goods to travel under the correct identification; *CSP, Venice, I 1202–1509*, p. 53, 4 April 1412.

89 Melis, *Mercaderes Italianos en España*, p. 191; Childs, *Anglo-Castilian Trade*, pp. 167–8.

90 ASFP 664/509942 13 June 1403; *CPR, 1401–5*, p. 283, 16 July 1403. I am grateful to Dr Carole Rawcliffe for identifying Spicer as M.P. for Portsmouth in 1402.

91 ASFP 664/9991 16 November 1403; 664/9992 31 December 1403; 664/9996 7 March 1404; 885/703146 24 March corrected to 26 March 1404; 664/509950 14 May 1404.

92 By the fourteenth century, Genoese vessels were obliged by law to sail in convoy; Byrne, *Genoese Shipping*, p. 50.

93 ASFP 664/509978 29 December 1400; 664/509979 23 January 1401.

94 It was common practice for the Genoese to charter in one direction only; Byrne, *Genoese Shipping*, p. 35.

95 ASFP 664/509945 5 September 1403; 664/509946 21 September 1403; 664/509948 4 January 1404.

96 E.g. Novello Larcharo's ship carried 70 men, ASFP 664/308922 20 September 1402 and 664/509993 31 January 1403, but these must have been sailors only, because ASFP 664/308924 4 January 1403, continued on 29 January, shows a total of 90–100 men, sailors and others. ASFP 528/6365 1 July 1395 shows two Savonese ships carrying 23 crossbowmen each.

97 ASFP 664/509978 29 December 1400; cf. Mallett, *Florentine Galleys*, pp. 29, 58–60, 201–2. The figures given by the Datini agents are closer to those in Byrne, *Genoese Shipping*, pp. 9–11, 36–7.

98 Mallett, *Florentine Galleys*, pp. 54–7. By Genoese sea law, shareholders in a voyage were

individually responsible for mariners who had to be kept in service while the shareholder retained his interest; Byrne, *Genoese Shipping*, p. 16.

99 ASFP 664/407471 16 March 1392.

100 ASFP 664/308924 4 January 1403, continued 29 January; 664/509987 29 December 1401.

101 ASFP 664/308912 27 December 1401 and 664/509987 29 December 1401; the Florentines hired only two of a convoy of five Genoese while the third was hired by the Genoese in England for the Levant. If all five had been hired, none could have had a full load; ASFP 664/700710 1 December 1401.

102 ASFP 664/407469 4 January 1392; cf. the paucity of Florentine exports from Sluys in Watson, 'The Structure of the Florentine Galley Trade with Flanders and England in the Fifteenth Century', see pp. 1089–91; ASFP 664/509973 18 August 1400; 664/509975 15 September 1400. Excess cargo was often a problem in the case of the Venetian galleys at London; *CSP, Venice, I*, p. 54, 24 January 1413, p. 61, 11 January 1421.

103 For a discussion of charter parties, see Byrne, *Genoese Shipping*, section 7. It was rare to charter a whole vessel for long-distance trade in the thirteenth century; see p. 30.

104 ASFP 664/509958 14 March 1402.

105 ASFP 664/308912 27 December 1401. The ships were in Flanders according to ASFP 664/509987 29 December 1401, so the 'others' may be the Bruges Florentines. However, ASFP 664/509993 31 January 1403 includes the Genoese as 'others'.

106 ASFP 664/407472 28 February 1392; 664/407471 16 March 1392.

107 ASFP 664/509985 24 September 1401. All five Venetian galleys were hired for Venice via Mutrone. Two loaded in England, but small boats took extra goods out to the three Flanders galleys. Contact between Bruges and London was undoubtedly close; see de Roover, *Money, Banking and Credit*, Appendix 2, where London Italians appear in the books kept by the Bruges money-changer Collard de Marke; also Mallett, *Florentine Galleys*, pp. 132–3, and W.B. Watson, 'The Structure of the Florentine Galley Trade with Flanders and England in the Fifteenth Century', *Revue Belge*, 40, part 1 (1962), pp. 317–47, see pp. 317–26.

108 ASFP 664/509961 15 October 1399; 664/509992 13 November 1402; 664/407471 16 March 1392.

109 ASFP 664/308918 13 June 1402.

110 ASFP 664/800629 5 December 1388.

111 Ashtor, *Levant Trade in the Later Middle Ages*, pp. 191–2. Freight was expected to be cheap in 1400 because there were nine Genoese in northern waters; ASFP 664/509971 4 June 1400.

112 Ruddock, *Italian Merchants and Shipping in Southampton 1270–1600*, p. 28.

113 By the end of the fourteenth century Genoa was a Florentine market; Mallett, *Florentine Galleys*, p. 7.

114 ASFP 777/313003 11 July 1393; see also Mallett, *Florentine Galleys*, p. 148.

115 ASFP 777/313004 4 August 1393; 777/313006 22 August 1393; 777/313008 25 January 1394; 777/313009 and its copy 777/313010 13 March 1394; 777/313011 26 March 1394. The *marabotto* or *terzaruolo* was about one third the size of a mainsail; Mallett, *Florentine Galleys*, p. 208, n. 6.

116 E.g. Piero Scorzuto ASFP 528/6365 1 July 1395, continued 15 July; 777/313047 7 November 1397; 777/313053 6 April 1399.

117 Three Spanish ships in ASFP 528/6366 and 528/6367, both dated 18 February 1396, were described as Biscayan in 528/506173, 17 February 1396; see also note 90 above, a Biscayan from Catalonia.

118 ASFP 885/702766 18 June 1407.

119 Childs, *Anglo-Castilian Trade*, pp. 93–4, 152, 155; Melis, *Mercaderes Italianos en España*, p. 58; Mallett, *Florentine Galleys*, pp. 32–3, 133–5; Watson, 'The Structure of the

Florentine Galley Trade with Flanders and England in the Fifteenth Century', see pp. 1078–80. The last port of call was Lisbon; Childs p. 152. For the Italian presence in Portugal, see C. Verlinden, 'La Colonie Italienne de Lisbonne et le Développement de l'Economie Metropolitaine et Coloniale Portugaise', pp. 617–28, and V. Rau, 'A Family of Italian Merchants in Portugal in the Fifteenth Century: the Lomellini', pp. 717–26 in *Studi in Onore di Armando Sapori*.

120 Childs, *Anglo-Castilian Trade*, p. 154.

121 ASFP 664/407482 6 August 1392; 664/407483 20 August 1392; 777/312994 2 October 1392; 664/407486 dated 1392 lists the contents of a bale of Essex streits loaded aboard. Cf. Origo, *The Merchant of Prato*, pp. 73–4, Sir Thomas Duplessis.

122 PRO E122/184/3 fos 19v–20, 12 June 1423, the searcher John Pole confronting the Genoese shipmaster Leonard Savenon.

123 PRO E122/184/3 fo. 21, 5 October 1423.

124 Mallett, *Florentine Galleys*, pp. 258–60.

125 The only detailed example in the Datini correspondence is ASFP 664/308916 13 April 1402.

126 When it was impossible to split the load, the whole was sent on one ship: ASFP 664/800627 17 July 1388; 777/416352 16 July 1401.

127 ASFP 777/416352 16 July 1401. The details are in the postscript dated 16 August in Bruges.

128 Mallett, *Florentine Galleys*, pp. 256–7.

129 E.g. ASFP 777/312993 15 July 1392. Such a letter travelling overland by courier would arrive before the ship carrying the merchandise; see note 4 above.

130 E.g. ASFP 777/416352 16 July 1401 gives an estimate for which the exact figures follow in 664/509984 6 August 1401.

131 E.g. ASFP 777/416352 16 July 1401 mentions a cargo of cloth. Half was for Spain, Ghaeta and Chios, half for Genoa and Pisa. Prices were expected to hold in Florence.

132 ASFP 777/416352 16 July 1401.

133 ASFP 1072/800888 8 April 1397. Sir Pauolo Biancho's ship was booked for Pisa, but was to take Florentine goods to Venice if there were no settlement in the meantime between Florence and Pisa.

134 ASFP 777/602939 17 November 1399; 664/509963 20 December 1399.

135 ASFP 664/308916 13 April 1402.

136 ASFP 885/517786 10 December 1405.

137 Mallett, *Florentine Galleys*, p. 53; Byrne, *Genoese Shipping*, pp. 35–6; *CSP, Venice, I*, p. 30, 3 August 1384, 10 January 1385 and 8 May 1386; ASFP 664/308916 13 April 1402.

138 Mallett, *Florentine Galleys*, pp. 235–7.

139 *RP*, II, p. 251 (1353). See also *CSP, Venice, I*, pp. 46–7 no. 165, 29 November 1408.

140 *RP*, II, p. 262 (1354); III, p. 281 (1390).

141 *RP*, III, pp. 553–4 (1404). The Sluys customers could also be difficult; see *CSP, Venice, I*, p. 45, 22 July 1408.

142 *RP*, III, p. 527 (1403–4).

143 ASFP 664/407471 16 March 1392 continued 22 March: '*Manno n(ost)ro amico drappiere*'; 664/308922 20 September 1402 mentions Thomas Adynet, while 664/700708 12 October 1401 mentions William Grevel, both Cotswolds-based wool dealers.

144 C.A. Sneyd, trans., *A Relation, or Rather a True Account of the Island of England*, Camden Society, 37 (1847), p. 34; T. Wright, ed. and trans., *The Political Songs of England*, Camden Society, 6 (1839), pp. 319–20.

145 *CSP, Venice, I*, pp. 84–5, 23 August 1457.

146 ASFP 664/509977 18 October 1400.

147 ASFP 777/602941 14 January 1400. This refers to the Christmas plot by Thomas Holland, third earl of Kent, John Montagu, third earl of Salisbury, and John Holland,

earl of Huntingdon. See Sir Bernard Burke, *A Genealogical History of the Dormant, Abeyant, Forfeited and Extinct Peerages of the British Empire* (London, 1883, facsimile edition 1962), pp. 279, 280, 372 and R.R. Sharpe, ed., *Calendar of Letter Books, Letter Book I, AD 1400–1422* (London, 1909), pp. I–II.

148 ASFP 664/509944 28 July 1403.
149 ASFP 664/308929 9 August 1403. The battle is dated the eve of Mary Magdalene. The feast falls on 22 July; see Cheney, *Handbook of Dates*, p. 55. See also C.W. Previté-Orton and Z.N. Brooke, eds, *Cambridge Medieval History* (Cambridge, 1936), VIII, pp. 366–7 (Northumberland submitted on 11 August and was promised a pardon); and Burke, *Genealogical History*, pp. 423–4, 425–6. Both place the battle near Shrewsbury. Burke confirms the date.
150 Sharpe, *Letter Book I*, pp. 227–31, 25 July 1419.
151 ASFP 664/509961 15 October 1399, closed on 20 October.
152 ASFP 664/509977 18 October 1400; 664/509978 29 December 1400.
153 ASFP 777/313049 5 March 1398.
154 R.A. Donkin, 'The Disposal of Cistercian Wool in England and Wales during the Twelfth and Thirteenth Centuries', reprinted from *Cîteaux in der Nederlanden*, VIII, (1957), pp. 114, 190–3.
155 For the earlier fairs, see E. Wedemeyer Moore, *The Fairs of Medieval England*.
156 Donkin, 'The Disposal of Cistercian Wool', p. 119.

5
The English Enterprise in France, 1412–13*

John D. Milner

On 20 April 1415 a mandate from the bishop of London was issued to the bishop of Bath and Wells which contained letters of the archbishop of Canterbury of 9 April ordaining litanies, special collects, celebrations of the mass and processions every Wednesday and Friday for the peace of the Church, for the king and for fine weather. There seem to have been no attempts to encourage popular devotions in support of the expedition to France in the year of Harfleur and Agincourt. It had been very different in the summer of 1412.[1] On 26 August 1412, for example, a letter was sent by the bishop of London, following a mandate of 14 August from Thomas Arundel as archbishop of Canterbury, to Bishop Repingdon of Lincoln for prayers and processions for the peace of the realm and for the success of the expedition for the recovery of Aquitaine. Repingdon certified to the archbishop on 9 September 1412 that his wishes had been carried out.[2] Similar letters were sent by the bishop of London to the other bishops of the province. Throughout that autumn, in the dioceses of Canterbury province, on Sundays, Wednesdays and Fridays (but only on Sundays when the exigencies of the harvest outweighed even the need to pray for the success of a royal campaign) prayers were offered up, with the seven penitential psalms and sermons. Those who participated, with the promise of forty days' indulgence to spur them on, were seeking divine assistance in the regaining for Henry IV of the duchy of Aquitaine, his by right, or at least by the terms of the treaty of Brétigny, as well as the safe progress and happy return of Thomas, duke of Clarence, the king's second son, and his army.[3]

It was not surprising, perhaps, that efforts were made to bring this major royal enterprise to the attention of the people. This expedition marked a shift in English policy in France, reflecting the removal from power at the end of 1411 of Henry, prince of Wales and his party and the resumption by Henry IV and Archbishop Arundel, of the control of policy. The prince of Wales, ever an advocate of the Burgundian alliance, had agreed in 1411 to a request for armed assistance from John the Fearless, duke of Burgundy. Under the command of Thomas, earl of Arundel, a force of 800 men-at-arms and 2,000 archers was sent to join Burgundy at Arras on 2 October 1411. This assistance helped Burgundy to defeat the Orléanists at St Cloud and thus to enter Paris on 22 October. Further English assistance was given to the Burgundians in their recovery of Etampes and Daudon. As this expedition took place, developments in England included speculation that Henry IV was to abdicate, and the king's subsequent reassertion of authority. The shock of St Cloud and related events had been sufficient to provoke the Orléanists into seeking an alliance with England. On 18 May 1412, by the Treaty of London, the leading Orléanists (the dukes of Berry, Bourbon and Orléans, the count of Armagnac and the seigneur d'Albret) agreed to assist Henry IV to regain the duchy of Aquitaine in return for his military assistance against the Burgundians.

The Orléanists offered their relatives in marriage, at the full disposal of Henry IV. They offered castles, towns, treasure and goods, friends and supporters from the nobility, clergy and citizenry of France. They offered the whole duchy of Aquitaine, to be held as Henry IV's predecessors had held it, with nothing excepted from its appurtenances. Unlikely in the extreme as it must have seemed to Henry IV that all the terms of this agreement would ever have been honoured, and whatever was in the minds of the Orléanists in authorising their ambassadors to swear to uphold the terms of the treaty, he none the less hurried to honour his obligations under it. To have been invited to France, and with such a comprehensive and solemn undertaking, convinced Henry IV that it was worth committing substantial resources, and reversing the policy of support for Burgundy so recently demonstrated by the prince of Wales in the 1411 expedition. The treaty, with an attention to detail which gave it an impression of great diplomatic stature, was soon to be proved worthless. Henry IV had, however, re-established his authority, and was involved in making policy and directing events. Whatever the divisions in the royal family, all four of Henry IV's sons swore on 20 May 1412 to observe the treaty. This new departure in English policy was marked, therefore, by efforts to demonstrate its importance and to make men aware of what was happening. The Church thus had an important rôle to play.[4]

Nor was it just spiritual aid which was sought from the Church. Very considerable resources were put into an expedition that saw a resumption on a large scale of the Hundred Years War and which committed England to a major excursion in which the king himself displayed a great interest. Henry IV had, after all, agreed to pay the army's wages for the first two months, with £1,565 being paid to Clarence immediately and a similar sum after the muster had been taken. Daily rates of pay for the army were raised for the occasion to those associated with campaigns in Aquitaine – 1s. 6d. for mounted men-at-arms, 9d. for archers.[5] The army was large, too. Clarence, as the leader of the English expedition, entered into an indenture with his father on 8 June 1412 to take 1,000 men-at-arms and 3,000 archers to France. Of this number, 500 men-at-arms, including three earls, eight barons and bannerets and twenty-one knights, as well as 1,500

archers, were to be in Thomas's retinue. The rest were to be divided
between the company of Edward, duke of York and that of Thomas
Beaufort, the king's half-brother.[6] York's retinue, agreed on 9 June, was
260 men-at-arms and 800 archers, while the following day Thomas
Beaufort undertook to serve with 240 men-at-arms and 700 archers.[7] A
month later, on 9 July 1412, with the agreement of the king's council,
steps began to be taken to meet the costs. The bishops were major
contributors: Lincoln was asked to give 100 marks, Norwich to give £600,
Ely, and Coventry and Lichfield, to give £200 each, London to give 500
marks, Worcester to give 200 marks. The prior of St John of Jerusalem was
also asked for a gift of 500 marks. Others lending money on surety for its
eventual return included the archbishop of Canterbury (100 marks), the
bishop of Bath and Wells (400 marks), the keeper of the privy seal (£200)
and the Florentine and Venetian communities in London (£200).[8] It was
all needed. The costs of shipping the expedition to France, estimated
initially at 3,000 marks, would, the council noted, in fact cost 7,000.[9] With
such a large army and ambitious purpose, even the charges for equipment
were considerable. By a writ of 15 November 1412, orders were made for
payment for 500 bows (£31 5s.), 1700 sheaves of arrows (£148 15s.) and
forty gross of bow strings (£12), with £32 for carriage, for the use of the
duke of Clarence and others in his retinue 'resisting the king's enemies in
Aquitaine', a total of £224.[10]

By the time John Benet's *Chronicle* was written in the first Yorkist
decade, this expensive, large-scale and much-heralded campaign could be
dismissed with a passing reference to Clarence's crossing into Gascony and
France and the observation '*et nihil profuit*'.[11] The earlier English
chroniclers had been scarcely more encouraging. Their verdict is, in the
main, one of silence. The *Eulogium* is perhaps the most negative. Clarence
crossed to Aquitaine, wintered at Bordeaux and, after Easter 1413,
returned home '*cum exercitu satis parvo, sine honore*'.[12] John Capgrave simply
observes that, after Clarence and Charles, duke of Orléans had met, the
English army spent the winter in Guienne, and Clarence subsequently
returned home.[13] Thomas Otterbourne merely records the return of the
new king's brother from Gascony and the fact that, after reaching an
agreement with Orléans, Clarence had spent the winter in Aquitaine.[14]
The *Polychronicon* has much the same comment, but at least adds that the
English, while at Bordeaux, 'set the country in peace and rest' before
coming home.[15] From St Albans little is said of the outcome beyond a
mention of the truce with Orléans, winter spent at Bordeaux and the
return to England in the spring of 1413.[16] The *Brut* makes reference to the
country being set in order while Clarence wintered at Bordeaux and
rejoices that Clarence and his men returned in safety to England when the
vintage was ready to be transported.[17] The London chroniclers make

similar brief observations about the departure and some refer very briefly to the upshot of the campaign. They show no real interest in the outcome.[18] Hardyng, in the Lancastrian version of his chronicle, observes that

> In to Guyen he (Clarence) rode with grete honoure
> To kepe that londe and be thayr gouernoure

while the Yorkist version, acknowledging that Clarence rode through France into Guienne 'with hoste then full royall', comments that, on his return to England, he 'came to the kyng with ioye and great pleasaunce'. At least there is some enthusiasm here.[19]

Some of the later English chronicles are rather more positive. One concludes that only in 1417 at the siege of Caen was Clarence's 'manhod provid' and ignores any reference to his role in 1412 in a brief mention of that expedition, but this is unusual. Fabyan, for example, refers to the English taking an abbot as prisoner and bringing him into England.[20] Hall, doubtless relying on French sources, is the only English chronicler to refer to the count of Angoulême being taken hostage, and he adds that Clarence and York came to Bordeaux 'with great prey, rich prisoners and wealthy hostages' and made war on the frontiers of France to their great gain and 'profitable lucre'.[21] Stow, in his *Annales*, merely records the return of Clarence to England after his brother's coronation.[22] It must be emphasised that the English chroniclers were not entirely ignorant of the events in France. The St Albans chronicles, for example, give brief yet vivid accounts of the landing in Normandy, the burning and pillaging which ensued when Orléans failed to meet Clarence, and the eventual meeting between the two after which hostilities ceased. By 1413 Thomas Walsingham, so full of detail as he is about the Treaty of London, observes quite baldly that Thomas returned from Gascony where he had been sent to help the duke of Orléans against the duke of Burgundy, with no allusion at all to the scheme to regain Aquitaine.[23] Other English chronicles give similar summaries of the events in France. The brevity of treatment in the London chronicles is in marked contrast with their often quite extensive accounts of the sieges and terms of surrender of towns in Henry V's second French expedition.[24] There are no precursors of the *Gesta Henrici Quinti*. That one of the most significant expeditions into France of the Hundred Years War, and the first major enterprise of the Lancastrian period, should be so summarily treated is surely remarkable.

It is the public documents that are, on this occasion, more expressive of the sense of urgency and importance attached to the campaign, suggesting the royal impetus behind it. Within days of the agreement with the Orléanists, a commission was issued for Geoffrey Pampyng of Great

Yarmouth to be ready to take his ship *La Grace Dieu* to France with Clarence's men.[25] On 9 June 1412, an order was issued to the treasurer and chamberlain of the exchequer for the payment of the wages of Thomas and his retinue. From 12 June letters of protection were being issued in great number to those indenting to serve in France.[26] On 11 July, Thomas was appointed lieutenant of Aquitaine in readiness for the expedition, the document giving details of his powers appearing on 12 July.[27] On 14 July Clarence appointed his attorneys.[28] Furthermore on 11 July a commission, headed by Sir John Pelham, had been appointed to supervise the muster of Clarence's retinue, with powers of arrest and punishment.[29] The relative silence, by contrast, of the chroniclers is perhaps suggestive of the confusion and uncertainty, not to say unreality, surrounding the enterprise.

Thomas Walsingham, remarking that by the time Clarence, York and Thomas Beaufort were sent to help Orléans against Burgundy not all of those sent under Arundel to assist Burgundy had yet returned, draws attention to that shift in policy stemming from difference in view, even conflict, between Henry IV and his eldest son which was, in one sense, at the heart of the expedition of 1412–13.[30] Otterbourne comments on the amazement which this change of policy created '*ut sub temporis tantilli spacio contingeret Anglos velut duo contraria manutenere*'.[31] The return of Clarence had, of course, been overshadowed by Henry IV's death in March 1413 and the coronation of Henry V which followed so rapidly. Clarence and his fellow captains had left England at the head of a great army, resolved to win back the king's rightful inheritances in Aquitaine. It was believed, also, that Clarence was substituting as head of the army for the king who, it was said, would himself have led the expedition had the strength of his body corresponded to the determination of his spirit.[32] Whether or not Henry IV really would have left his country when his heir apparent was creating not inconsiderable political dissension is arguable. It is important to recognise that contemporaries believed that he might. By the spring of 1413, when the disaffected prince of Wales had been metamorphosed into Henry V of England, the great army under his brother was at best an embarrassment and at worst a nuisance. Henry, ever an advocate of the Burgundian alliance, remained convinced of the appropriateness of this position: that Thomas appears to have continued to support the Orléanist cause after his father's death and as late as 1414 proved in practice to be of no political moment.[33]

Yet if to the English the enterprise was of little significance, to the French it was an embarrassment, in some ways a humiliation. Whilst Jean Juvenal des Ursins could rail against both Arundel and Clarence for desecration of church property and the destruction of the people's goods, adding dark comments about grave and dishonourable abuses of vestments and other ornaments, it is not so much the English as the French themselves who emerge badly from native accounts of the expedition.[34] K.B. McFarlane's conclusion that the invasion of 1412 only drove the opposing French princes together and into a temporary peace amongst themselves is obviously correct.[35] That this could happen was the result of an invitation to France by some of the most senior of the French nobility – Orléans, Berry, Bourbon and Alençon – of a large English army, the bait being Aquitaine but the motive, as clearly explained in the requests they made of Henry IV, being assistance against Burgundy.[36] It may have been that the information brought to Charles VI by Carmin, the Breton spy, about the size of the English army and the imminence of its departure hastened the reconciliation at the besieged city of Bourges which brought a temporary and artificial peace to the warring noble factions.[37] The cost of inviting the English was extremely high.

Just as the English chroniclers are at best restrained and, on occasion, even silent about events in France, so the French, even those writing much later, are united in depicting a horrific experience for their country. The English utterly devastated the Cotentin and began hostilities in the lands of the count of Alençon.[38] Entering Anjou and '*rapinas et incendia exercentes*', they did not even spare parish churches. Crossing the Loire, the English burnt both town and abbey at Beaulieu, taking the abbot prisoner, and then destroyed Buzançais.[39] The English '*pradeas magnas conducebant*'.[40] Not receiving the payments due to them from the French, the English '*firent depuis grans maulx en France*'.[41] Even chronicles which give a very brief treatment of the period make mention of Clarence's expedition: the short, even terse, *Chronique du Mont-Saint-Michel* speaks of the expedition and remarks that Clarence crossed France into Aquitaine. Its next reference is to the Agincourt landing.[42] Almost all the French chroniclers emphasise the size of the English army: even though figures differ, they are all large. The vulnerability of the French is thus emphasised in all that their own chroniclers say. No English chronicler ventures any comment on the size of the expeditionary force.

Perhaps even more significant than the almost inevitable first flurry of dramatic military activity after the invasion landing was the threat which the English under Clarence continued to pose after Buzançais and the agreement over the payments due to them. The French court was disturbed by news brought in late autumn by spies that, after a quiet winter in Bordeaux, the English would return into the heart of Guienne, renewing their efforts against the towns and castles of the province.[43] That these reports had some basis in fact is suggested by the authorisation to William Alyngton, one of Clarence's attorneys, on 14 October 1412, to spend £500 on the purchase of military stores to be taken to Bordeaux for the duke's use.[44] The area bordering Aquitaine and other parts of France was seen as particularly vulnerable to English encroachment. By the end of

January 1413, when the ill-fated Assembly General met in Paris, those attending were told of the cruel ravages which the English were already again perpetrating in Guienne. The duke of Bourbon had been sent by Charles VI and his council into the Languedoc, with the count of Armagnac and the seigneur d'Albret, to resist Clarence and his supporters who were already causing serious harassment on the frontiers of Aquitaine.[45] The Sire de Hely, commissioned to head a small force to confront the English, had been quite frank in his appraisal. Only a powerful army would defeat the English: send a small force, and the English would win and thus consolidate their position.[46]

The worst indignity suffered by the French was in the agreement reached, by the will of Charles VI and his council, at Buzançais on 14 November 1412 between Berry, Orléans, Bourbon and Alençon on the one hand, and Clarence, York and Dorset on the other. As early as 15 October 1412, the Orléanists had attempted to take an initiative to reach a settlement, in appointing commissioners, headed by Guillaume de Tigonville, to treat with Clarence and the English lords. By the treaty of Buzançais the Orléanist lords promised 210,000 *écus d'or* to the English with the count of Angoulême, younger brother of Orléans, and six other gentlemen, as hostages, to stand as sureties against the payment of the full amount owing.[47] Not only were a significant number of Orléanists thus consigned to custody in English hands for an unspecified period because of the 'service' undertaken by Clarence on behalf of Orléans, but the impoverished state of French finances was made clear to all, including the English, by the fact that such a settlement had to be made. It has been argued also that merely by agreeing to such considerable sums in settlement, the French showed their own weakness.[48] Orléans may have attempted to appeal to Clarence's chivalric sensibilities by the brotherhood in arms agreement made between them on the same day as Buzançais, when Thomas undertook to be 'a true and good kinsman, brother, companion-in-arms and friend' to Orléans, and to 'serve, aid, console and comfort him'. [49] Orléans may have tried to maintain good relations on a personal level with the captors of his younger brother by expending 21 *livres tournois* on a decorated headdress of white satin in a jewelled case as a present for the duchess of Clarence.[50] None the less, once the Treaty of Buzançais was made, it was kept to the last *écu d'or*.[51] The chronicler Mathieu d'Escouchy was obliged, in describing Angoulême's eventual release three decades later, to give a résumé of the circumstances in which the count had been taken prisoner.[52] Perhaps helped by the 60,000 florins Charles VI allowed him to raise in tax following his restoration to him of the town of Channy, Orléans was able to make some payments to Clarence.[53] For example, on 10 April 1413, John Fastolf, then constable of Bordeaux, received 1,365 *écus d'or* (£227 10s. sterling) towards the outstanding debt.[54] Following his return to England, Clarence, on 4 July 1413, issued a letter of attorney to Sir William Marnie, his chamberlain, authorising him to receive such sums of money as Orléans might pay him.[55] Clarence might have learnt by then that, on 5 April 1413, Charles VI had granted permission to Orléans to raise 40,000 *livres tournois* for the ransom of the count of Angoulême on the lands which he held from the Crown.[56]

In addition to the great financial burden imposed on Orléans, and the prestige that came from taking a number of French hostages, the inability of the Orléanists to pay the full costs of the English enterprise led to the duke of Berry being obliged to give a number of treasures to both Clarence and York. Amongst other valuables, York was given a set of gold rosary beads: fourteen of the twenty-eight studs were of gold thread. York was also given a great diamond, for which Berry had paid 1,250 *écus d'or* when he had bought it in November 1406. Clarence's share of Berry's treasures included a plaited collar of gold thread, decorated with gold studs, each of which contained a rosette with a small diamond. On 22 December 1412, Clarence received from Berry a gold ring containing two diamonds as well as two books with silver-gilt clasps and scarlet hide covers. The most remarkable of the treasures acquired by Clarence was, however, the magnificent and richly jewelled gold cross, originally a gift from Berry to his private chapel at Bourges. Within a gold casing, the cross contained what was believed to be a nail from Christ's Cross. The cross which Berry gave to Clarence was adorned with large numbers of precious stones. The upper arm alone bore a great ruby, a large emerald, nine other rubies, six small emeralds, six sapphires and fifty-one small pearls.[57] Clarence had, then, with his army, from landing at La Hougue in mid-August, made a significant impact on France.[58] It should, of course, be recalled that he was not a complete stranger to this part of France, for in 1405 when, as admiral of England, he had been on a naval expedition in the Channel, he had landed at La Hougue and had advanced some thirty miles into Normandy, the population fleeing before him as he burned towns and villages.[59] He had demonstrated both English strength and French weakness, had reached a satisfactory financial solution in all the circumstances and had, as lieutenant of Aquitaine, given the people of Bordeaux a taste of an English royal presence and authority.[60] He had also the prospect, in the spring of 1413, of an adventure in Navarre in support of the count of Urgel, then engaged in a struggle against Ferdinand of Aragon.[61] It is known that, in late November 1412, Clarence's chancellor, Jean Seurmaistre, was travelling to Rome on the duke's affairs: it is at least possible that Clarence was speculating on the possibility of pursuing papal service.[62] It was, after all, only in the previous year (9 November 1411) that the clerk of the papal camera had been given a faculty to take Clarence into the pay or service of

John XXIII. On his visit to England in 1412, the papal nuncio, Anthony de Pireto, minister-general of the Friars Minor, had tried to persuade Henry IV to send Thomas to Rome as captain of the papal army against the king of Naples and the antipope, Gregory XI. Although the king refused, Clarence, who throughout his career demonstrated a willingness, even eagerness, for military adventure, was perhaps keen to pursue this interest.[63]

Amidst some undeniable military success, with a threat to France clearly demonstrated and further pressure on the French still to be exerted, with the hint of military adventure in Spain and perhaps beyond, but always with the practical considerations of an army to pay and feed, the English enterprise in France reached its end.[64] Involvement with the count of Urgel would doubtless have done little to serve longer-term English interests:[65] it would certainly have detracted from the possibility, even probability, of further weakening France had the English army remained. There was a hint of that flamboyance and impracticality that was to bring Clarence to his death at Baugé in 1421. There had, however, been positive achievements and there was room for consolidation, even though the abandonment of the English alliance by the Orléanists had robbed the expedition of its *raison d'être* and made its progress lacking in structure.

It would be difficult to sustain the view that the 1412–13 expedition had either lived up to the expectations which Henry IV clearly had for it or been worth the investment of such very considerable quantities of money, of which he was always so acutely short. The sudden shifts in English policy in 1411–12 were expensive, even though, thanks to the success of the English army under Clarence, York and Dorset, the reputation of the English was enhanced rather than diminished. Yet the reversal of policy by Henry V in abandoning the expedition and not seeking to pursue his own claims in France immediately on his accession was sensible, both politically and militarily. The new king did not attempt to capitalise on the investment of men and money made by his father even though in the spring of 1413 Thomas's army was well established in France and had already created significant problems for the French.

Perhaps Henry V concluded that the whole affair had been a delusion, a great mistake on the part of a sick father apparently given an opportunity to make a mark in France and secure the advancement of the Lancastrian cause in the French wars in a positive way. The opportunity had come when the prince of Wales was at loggerheads with the king, and it would seem, with Clarence as well. The offer from the Orléanist lords, however unrealistic it was likely to prove, had been possible only because of the shift in policy which had resulted from Henry IV's resumption of power and the end of the prince of Wales's period of dominance. If Clarence's absence abroad, in company with Thomas Beaufort, chancellor of the realm during the prince's recent period as head of the council, took out of the country protagonists in the internal political conflict, the fact that such an expedition was sent at all, and that Clarence and not Prince Henry led it, seriously aggravated the difficulties.[66] After all, *The First English Life* records an alleged discussion at the end of Henry IV's reign between the king and the prince in which Henry IV revealed his fears that, after his death, 'some discord shall gourd and arise betwixt thee and Thomas thie brother . . . whereby the realme may be brought to destruction and miserie'. Although the prince could reassure his dying father that, as long as his brothers were loyal to him, he would 'honnor and love (them) aboue all men', the king and the prince had 'fell at distance' in 1412 while Thomas appears to have been advanced in royal circles, without ever being formally a member of the council.[67] The prince had appeared in London, at the end of June 1412, with a great number of his friends and such a crowd of supporters as had not been seen before, staying at the bishop of Durham's inn from 30 June until 10 July.[68] The creation of Thomas as earl of Albemarle and duke of Clarence on 9 July 1412 with an annual grant of £40 per annum might only have exacerbated the prince's feeling of isolation, even if, as seems probable, the elevation was largely designed to enable the leader of the impending expedition to have a title to match that of the French lords then expected to be his allies. The possibility of Thomas's advancement further alienating the prince was perhaps lessened by Henry IV's masterly stroke of diplomacy in creating Thomas Beaufort, chancellor during Prince Henry's ascendancy, earl of Dorset four days earlier on 5 July 1412. None the less, despite the gross neglect of his Irish responsibilities which had led the royal council, when headed by his brother, to threaten to reduce his salary as lieutenant of Ireland, Thomas had been granted, on 2 February 1412, the reversion of the castles and lordships of Hawarden and Flint in North Wales, worth 400 marks a year.[69]

If Henry IV conveniently forgot his apparent undertaking to the prince of Wales to ensure measures were taken to arrest and punish such conspirators against him as could be identified, the departure of the great English force to France removed some of the protagonists from the immediate scene of conflict.[70] Its progress must have remained a cause of great speculation and interest in England. If Clarence had been successful, the prince of Wales's position at home would surely have been jeopardised. If he had faced a humiliating defeat, Henry IV's position would have been extremely difficult. The abandonment of the alliance by the Orléanists cannot have helped convince opponents of its wisdom and, on 23 September 1412, the prince returned to London 'with a huge people'. At least following this episode a lasting reconciliation appears to have been achieved between the king and his heir apparent.[71]

On becoming king, on 21 March 1413, Henry V ensured that his coronation was as little delayed as possible, and he was crowned on Passion

Sunday, 9 April 1413.[72] For whatever reason, whether contrived or not, Clarence and the other peers abroad with him were not ordered to return for the coronation. The chronicles are unanimous in dating Thomas's return from Gascony after Easter (23 April 1413)[73] and, in any case, well after the summons on 22 March 1413 of Henry V's first parliament, called to meet at Westminster on 14 May 1413. The parliament lasted until 9 June 1413.[74] Because of his absence abroad, no summons was issued to Clarence.[75] During the proceedings, however, a petition was presented by a London merchant, Richard Merlowe, and other merchants. Sailing to Bordeaux in the course of their normal mercantile activities, their ships had been arrested on the orders of Clarence for the conveyance back to England of some of the duke's men and goods. Sir John Colville, governor and captain for the voyage, captured two Prussian hulks during the crossing and the merchants laid claim to these.[76] Clearly, then, steps were in hand for the expedition's return by late April or early May 1413, although the formal replacement of Clarence as lieutenant of Aquitaine by Thomas Beaufort, earl of Dorset did not occur until 22 July 1413.[77]

As late as 18 April 1413, the collectors of customs and subsidies in London had been ordered to allow the master of the French ship *La Katerine*, then in London, to load his ship with 100 quarters of wine to the use and profit of Clarence and, after the payment of customs and subsidies, to transport his cargo to Aquitaine.[78] On 7 April 1413, letters patent had been issued at Bordeaux in the name of Henry IV, and it would seem, therefore, that seventeen days after his father's death the new heir presumptive to the English throne was unaware of what had happened.[79] Although steward of England, and thus with an official rôle to perform at a monarch's coronation, Clarence was absent and the earl of Warwick carried out the duties in his stead.[80] It should, however, be noted that, because of his absence on the Scottish border, a deputy was also found for Henry V's brother John as constable of England. By the time that Clarence returned, and many of his troops with him, Henry IV had been firmly replaced by his pro-Burgundian son. A poem written at Easter 1413 had the line 'God save the kyng and kepe the crown'.[81] Henry V had ensured that, for his coronation and the crucial first weeks of his reign, no possibility of family disagreements and renewal of earlier tensions could cloud events or hinder the smooth transition of power.

On 19 April 1415, William Hokhyrst received the considerable sum of £23 12s. 1½d. for the costs and expenses incurred by him in organising a meal within the Palace of Westminster for the duke of Clarence and other lords dining there for their advice to the king about his forthcoming voyage to Harfleur and Normandy.[82] Expensive as this meal was, the cost was doubtless regarded as small enough for the benefit which Henry V could gain before his own departure from those with relatively recent first-hand experience of French terrain and people. As has been observed recently, Clarence had at least proved that to march from Normandy to Bordeaux was possible, and the value of that was obvious enough when Henry V decided, independently of any promises made by a French faction, to pursue his claims in France.[83]

It is difficult to discover any other long-term gain of the expedition although, as has been argued, the change of policy with the accession of the new king effectively meant that practical short- or medium-term advantages were impossible. Historians, with the almost inevitable tendency to be constrained by the chronological divisions of reigns, have emphasised insufficiently the really quite significant abandon with which Henry IV had embarked on the expedition or, indeed, the dramatic waste of resources which stemmed from the decision of Henry V, however predictable, not to continue with Clarence's campaign. Given the difficulties which it faced, as well as its abandonment at the moment when consolidation would have seemed possible, not least because of the renewed factional strife in France, the campaign had had successes which the enterprise almost certainly did not warrant.

The fact that the expedition happened at all tends to obscure how remarkable it was that it should have been allowed to sail. On 16 September 1412, Clarence, in accordance with the terms of the Treaty of London, was in the plain before Blois. He was faced with replying to a letter from the duke of Berry and the other Orléanist lords in which they renounced the alliance made scarcely four months earlier: his tone of righteous indignation seems genuine but naïve. The fascinating and remarkable feature is that Henry IV, who by no stretch of the imagination could be called politically unaware, had given such a wholehearted commitment to this cause. Clarence, the single-minded soldier, with few political pretensions and with experience limited very largely to Ireland, seemed to convey a genuine frustration, anger and bewilderment when he wrote to the Orléanists *'que croire ne povons bonement que nulles tielles lettres procedent de consentement de tielx princes et de si haut sank comme vous estez'*. Indeed, his lack of political guile was borne out in the same letter when he said that, had it not been for the alliance with the Orléanists, to which he felt bound, he would have been compelled to give careful consideration to concluding an agreement with Burgundy.[84]

Almost as if belief had been suspended and reality overtaken by fancy, Henry IV had allowed himself to be drawn into an agreement which depended on the reliability and cooperation of French lords interested only in their own vendetta. Of the French chroniclers only Jean le Févre gives any credence to the letter of the Treaty of London, writing of the Orléanists offering towns, treasures, fortresses and all their goods to help Henry IV in his quarrels and the restitution of the duchy of Guienne.[85]

When the Orléanists' ambassadors had been commissioned in January 1412 to conclude an alliance with Henry IV and his sons, within less than a week of his issuing safe conducts to them (6 February 1412)[86] Henry IV had appointed ambassadors (10 February), headed by Thomas Langley, the bishop of Durham, to treat for marriage between the prince of Wales and the Lady Anna, Burgundy's daughter.[87] This was the typical, cautious Henry IV. Such political good sense was abandoned with the London treaty and by the speed with which the king met the obligations it placed on him. It can be argued that the Orléanist lords soon fell victim to their own political skill in persuading Henry IV to cooperate with them against Burgundy in exchange for aid in securing Aquitaine. They faced considerable embarrassment as well as unexpectedly heavy expenses when they were held to their word. They had perhaps gambled on an English duplicity or delay that did not materialise. None the less, in terms of real gains, certainly compared with those which by the strict letter of the agreement could reasonably have been anticipated, the English also lost heavily. On 16 May 1412, Henry IV had written to the advocates, burgomasters and assessors of Ghent, Bruges and Ypres, informing them of the assistance which Berry, Orléans and the others had offered and that he had determined to proceed in his own person to Aquitaine to win back his duchy of Guienne. He asked them not to support either the king of France or the duke of Burgundy, who he knew would attempt to hinder him.[88] It has been argued that Henry IV believed that, by threatening the rupture of Flemish mercantile truces, he might prevent Burgundy from undermining his great scheme to reclaim Aquitaine.[89]

The reality was to be starkly different. The indiscretion of the duke of Berry's proctor had revealed the details of the Treaty of London to Charles VI in one of his sane moments.[90] Thus, on 21 July 1412, at least three weeks before the expedition sailed, Charles VI ordered his nobles to revoke the alliance, declaring it null and void.[91] On 22 July 1412 Berry and his allies wrote to Henry IV explaining that, because the alliance lately made with England had displeased their king, revoking it was the only option open to them.[92] Whether the expedition left at St Lawrencetide (10 August) or the Assumption (15 August), (the chronicles are divided on the point), the French nobles had achieved a sufficient degree of reconciliation to make the alliance of no avail before an English soldier had left to fulfil the terms of the treaty.[93] The situation at the siege of Bourges, where a *'fort marveilleuse'* outbreak of dysentery had increased the willingness of the French factions at least to pretend to an agreement, did not help the English chances. As early as 15 July, Berry, Bourbon and several other lords had emerged from Bourges and gone for discussions with the Dauphin, who himself bore the title of duke of Aquitaine.[94] The sealing of the reconciliation came on 22 August in the church of St Germain at

Auxerre.[95] As the English arrived their military services were no longer required and so they had committed themselves unnecessarily to an impressive display of strength. Had the expedition been gathered together more rapidly, and had Clarence with his company been in time to offer some assistance to the Orléanists at the siege of Bourges, more might have come out of it. Given that the siege was over and immediate help no longer needed, the very military success of Clarence on his landing – the defeat of the lord Hambe and 700 French killed – made it much less likely that the Orléanists would seek to do other than buy off their erstwhile friends.[96] A strong and successful English force would have been much more likely to be able to seize the initiative if the Orléanists had not attempted to patch up an understanding with it, and at the heart of the planning by the French nobles for the English intervention was the assumption that they would not be allowed to take any lead. The English were to be the instruments of Orléanist ambition against Burgundy. Forces within France prevented the realisation of this hope. It is, however, difficult to imagine how a radically different outcome could have been achieved and to calculate how far the Orléanists would have gone in delivering to Henry IV what they had promised in so much elaborate detail in the terms of the Treaty of London.

The lesson of 1412–13 for the English was that they must never again become embroiled in other people's conflicts. Henry V waged his own war on his own terms: being dictated to by a foreign faction or ending as its puppet, while at the same time having a large army to support, was grossly unsatisfactory. It is a tribute to the leadership of Clarence and his fellow generals that the English, in many ways, gained so much. From the longer-term perspective of Henry V's reign, the enterprise could be seen, in Stubbs's words, as 'neither honourable nor fortunate'.[97] The random burning and looting might have offended Victorian susceptibilities, and might be more difficult to explain than some of Henry V's actions, justified as they were by the prevailing laws of war.[98] Yet Clarence had shown, quite convincingly, that an English army, abandoned by its allies, would neither quietly go home with honour so offended nor be defeated by defaulting allies. In exacting what Professor Contamine has called a 'danegeld' of 210,000 *écus d'or* Clarence took another of those ransoms which were specific to the Hundred Years War and which had a serious effect on French society.[99] Weakened, divided yet again, with their finances further undermined, the French must have been far more apprehensive and demoralised than they otherwise would have been at the prospect of a further English incursion when Henry V came to France in 1415, a little over two years after Clarence's return.

Although the financial settlement at Buzançais was met in full only painfully slowly, none the less the achievement of reaching such an agreement was an indication to the very many who participated in the campaign that foreign war could be advantageous. Booty and ransoms were useful supplements and symbols of prestige.[100] That a change of king and a shift in policy led to the abandonment of the enterprise should not lead to its being dismissed merely as an expensive and idiosyncratic exercise by a dying king. Foolish it might have been, but it was not without benefits. When M.R. Powicke discusses length of service by Lancastrian captains in France, he begins his reckoning with 1415. There were many on that and subsequent expeditions of Henry V who knew something of the country – there had been considerable fighting in Normandy – as well as something of the French from 1412–13. They were men who had tasted the scent of victory and whose leader had come home with a clutch of quite eminent prisoners and a chest full of jewels. Henry V overshadows, and outshines, what happened in 1412–13, but that does not mean that it should be ignored: it set the scene for a further and better-organised invasion in his reign. The very dread with which the Normans anticipated the 1417 invasion, and the folk-memory of ruthless atrocities committed by the English was, at least in part, another legacy from 1412.[101]

Apart from Clarence himself, who played a considerable part in the siege of Harfleur before having to return home through illness, both Dorset and York returned to France in 1415. Although York is mainly noted for being almost the only English peer to die at Agincourt, Dorset made a major contribution to Henry V's work in France, as did Clarence until his fatal misjudgement at Baugé.[102] There were those, too, who were starting on eminent careers in 1412: Ralph Cromwell, for example, who is found in France in that year, then in 1415 and again in 1419 and 1421, and the ubiquitous John Fastolf.[103] Walter Intebergh, esquire, with Clarence in 1412, was in the duke's retinue again in 1415, whilst Thomas Halle of Norfolk, having been in the duke's retinue in 1412, appears in his service in 1417.[104] The army of 1412 was large enough to be widely representative of England and English society: the experience of fighting in that war could not have been discouraging for the participants – other than the leaders whose opportunity for regaining for the Crown one of its sizeable lost portions had vanished before Bourges. For the rest on their return home, the vigour of the campaign and their participation in seriously inconveniencing the French must have been paramount. A sample of the people who participated helps to demonstrate the impact that this expedition had on England in 1412. Examples taken from those who indented to serve with Clarence include a merchant of Winchester, London citizens and fishmongers and men of various social ranks from Bedfordshire, Cheshire, Cornwall, Devon, Gloucestershire, Kent, Leicestershire, Staffordshire and Sussex.[105] There were those, too, who seem to have prospered by being close to the leaders. The opportunities of foreign service gave men of ambition and ability a chance to be noticed and to serve those in command. Sir William Marnie of Essex, a Clarence man since the 1405 naval expedition who had later served under him in Ireland, became his chamberlain and served in that capacity in France. Such offices were doubtless of more importance when the person served was abroad and not subsumed in court or country activity at home. Although William Marnie's death in 1414 precluded further service in France, it is interesting to note that his son, Thomas, was retained by the duke in December 1419, and may have died at Baugé.[106] Clarence's secretary, John Dupont, was granted 225 *écus d'or* under the terms of the Treaty of Buzançais and in February 1413 two houses in Bordeaux.[107]

The effect of the expedition on the two royal brothers who appear to have been at odds with each other before its departure, and had had moments of difficulty before (the clash between Prince Thomas and Henry Beaufort over the John Beaufort inheritance;[108] Prince Henry's insistence that his brother should serve in Ireland or receive reduced payments),[109] is important. There had been, in Clarence's absence abroad, an opportunity for tempers to cool. Clarence had had to exercise generalship and authority, and, in all the circumstances, had acquitted himself satisfactorily. He came back neither so humiliated as to face derision nor so triumphant as to pose a challenge to the new king. Like the expedition itself, he faded into obscurity for some time, although he was with Henry V and his other brothers at Eltham at Christmas 1413.[110] Henry V could be vindicated in his refusal to support the Orléanists and in his preference for Burgundy. Thomas could, at least, claim that, although treated dishonourably by the Orléanists, he had preserved his and the Crown's dignity, and had a healthy ransom as a tangible sign of his achievement.

The expedition of 1412–13 should probably never have taken place. Embarking on it soon proved to be misguided, even if there were advantages in the undertaking, both short- and long-term, and even though it served a quite useful domestic purpose. For Henry IV it must have seemed that here was the possibility of having a successful foreign expedition and bringing military glory and distinction to him and his house. That its success relied on Orléanist nobles keeping their word at a time when they were under military pressure appears to have escaped him or been dismissed. While he was king, England was to invest France again. The scale of the exercise was considerable and the vigour of the royal commitment to it great. The personal involvement of the king in the arrangements is beyond question. Obviously the decision to elevate Thomas as duke of Clarence was the king's and was inextricably linked to the expedition. The charter was warranted '*per ipsum Regem et per breve de privato sigillo*', a form of words clearly indicating Henry's personal involvement.[111] In the Leicester parliament of 1414, after Henry V raised his brothers John and Humphrey to the dukedoms of Bedford and Gloucester respectively, the king took the very curious step of confirming his father's bestowal of titles on both Dorset and Clarence.[112] Henry IV's actions had been for a war of which his eldest son had then disapproved and at a time when he was alienated from his father. This disapproval was shown when as king Henry V rapidly reversed the policy his father had pursued in 1412–13. In confirming these titles in an unprecedented way in parliament, Henry V was perhaps not only expressing disapproval retrospectively of his father's decisions in the context of the 1412 expedition but also, by as it were overtaking them, closing the door on that enterprise. Dorset and Clarence were, it could be said, no longer holding titles granted by a dying monarch prior to his embarking on a doomed attempt at the fulfilment of a dream; they were given not for a vision which had turned into an expensive delusion but confirmed for a future to be governed by pragmatism. No honours, no grants, no recognition came from Henry V for participation in the enterprise of 1412–13. Those were to come for service under him in his own campaigns; there was no room there for floundering and foundering on the rock of Orléanist deceit. He did not live to see that, in the end, a pragmatist might have opted for Buzançais rather than for Troyes.

Notes

*I am indebted to my supervisor, Professor C.T. Allmand, University of Liverpool, and Dr Peter McNiven, John Rylands University Library, Manchester, for their encouragement, help and advice at so many times, and for their extremely helpful comments on an earlier draft of this paper. I am very grateful to my colleagues, Mrs Karen Pannett and Mrs Carol Rothwell, Northern Examinations and Assessment Board, Manchester, for typing the paper from an uncongenial manuscript.

1 T.S. Holmes, ed., *The Register of Nicholas Bubwith, Bishop of Bath and Wells, 1407–1424, from the original in the Registry at Wells*, I, Somerset Record Society, 29 (1914), pp. 208–9.

2 M. Archer, ed., *The Register of Philip Repingdon, 1405–1419*, II (*Memoranda 1411–1414*), Lincoln Record Society, 58 (1963), pp. 270–2.

3 J.M. Horn, ed., *The Register of Robert Hallum, Bishop of Salisbury 1407–1417*, Canterbury and York Society, 72, Part 145 (1977–8, 1978–9) (1982), no. 1012; J.H. Parry, transcribed, *Registrum Roberti Mascall, Episcopi Herefordensis AD MCCCCIV – MCCCCXVI*, Canterbury and York Society, 21, Part 54 (1917), p. 114; Holmes, ed., *Register of Nicholas Bubwith*, I, pp. 126–7; F.C. Hingeston, ed., *R(oyal and) H(istorical) L(etters during the Reign of Henry the Fourth King of England and Lord of Ireland)*, II (with corrections), RS (London, 1965), pp. 333–8. Thomas, Henry IV's second son, was created duke of Clarence on 9 July 1412, after his appointment as leader of the expedition to France. To avoid confusion he is referred to as 'Clarence' throughout this paper.

4 E.F. Jacob, *The Fifteenth Century 1399–1485* (London, 1961), pp. 111–13; J.L. Kirby, *Henry IV of England: a Biography* (London, 1970), p. 237; A. Tuck, *Crown and Nobility*

1272–1461 (London, 1985), pp. 237–9; P. McNiven, 'Prince Henry and the English Political Crisis of 1412', *History*, 65 (1980), pp. 4–5; T. Rymer, ed., *Foedera*, 20 vols (London, 1704–35), VIII, pp. 738–43; V.H. Galbraith, ed., *The St Albans Chronicle 1406–1420* (Oxford, 1937), p. 64.

5 *Foedera*, VIII, pp. 745–6; J.H. Ramsay, *Lancaster and York, a Century of English History* (Oxford, 1892), I, p. 136.

6 *Foedera*, VIII, pp. 741, 745–6.

7 Ibid., pp. 749–50.

8 *POPC*, II, pp. 31–2.

9 Ibid., pp. 121–2.

10 F. Devon, ed., *Issues of the Exchequer* (London, 1837), p. 318.

11 G.L. Harriss and M.A. Harriss, eds, 'John Benet's Chronicle for the Years 1400 to 1462', in *Camden Miscellany*, 24, Camden Society, 4th series (1972), p. 176; for the date of authorship, see p. 153.

12 F.S. Haydon, ed., *Eulogium (Historiarum sive Temporis): Chronicon . . . a Monacho Quodam Malmesburiensi*, III, RS (1863), p. 420.

13 P.J. Lucas, ed., *John Capgrave's Abbreuiacion of Cronicles*, EETS, 285 (1983), pp. 237–8; F.C. Hingeston, *The Chronicle of England by John Capgrave*, RS (1858), p. 302.

14 T. Hearne, ed., 'Chronica Rerum Angliae per Thomam Otterbourne', in *Duo Rerum Anglicarum Scriptores Veteres* (Oxford, 1732), I, p. 272.

15 J.R. Lumby, ed., *Polychronicon Ranulphi Higden Monachi Cestrensis Together with the English Translations of John Trevisa and of an Unknown Writer of the Fifteenth Century*, VIII, RS (London, 1882), p. 547.

16 T. Walsingham, *Historia Anglicana*, ed. H.T. Riley, II, RS (London, 1864), pp. 288–90; Galbraith, ed., *The St Albans Chronicle*, pp. 67–9; see also J.A. Giles, ed., *Incerti Scriptoris Chronicon Angliae de Regnis Trium Lancastrensium, Henrici IV, Henrici V, et Henrici VI* (London, 1848), p. 62, for a reference to Clarence's return *'cum vintagio'*.

17 F.W.D. Brie, ed., *The Brut or the Chronicles of England*, Part II, EETS, 136 (1908), p. 372.

18 C.L. Kingsford, ed., *Chronicles of London with Introduction and Notes* (Oxford, 1905), p. 68; A.H. Thomas and I.D. Thornley, eds, *The Great Chronicle of London* (London, 1938), p. 90; [N.H. Nicolas and E. Tyrrel, eds,] *A Chronicle of London from 1089–1483* (London, 1827), pp. 94–5; 'William Gregory's Chronicle of London', in J. Gairdner, ed., *The Historical Collections of a Citizen of London in the Fifteenth Century*, Camden Society, new series, 17 (1876), p. 106; J.S. Davies, ed., *An English Chronicle in the Reigns of Henry IV, Henry V and Henry VI*, Camden Society, 64 (1856), p. 37; J. Gairdner, ed., *Three Fifteenth Century Chronicles*, Camden Society, new series, 28 (1880), p. 54.

19 C.L. Kingsford, ed., *The First English Life of King Henry the Fifth Written in 1513 by an Anonymous Author Known Commonly as 'The Translator of Livius'* (Oxford, 1911), p. xxiii; H. Ellis, ed., *The Chronicle of John Hardyng* (London, 1812), p. 369; see also C.L. Kingsford, 'The First Version of Hardyng's Chronicle', *EHR*, 28 (1912), p. 462.

20 J. Leland, 'Owte of a Booke of Chroniques in Peter College Library', in *De Rebus Britannicis Collectaneorum*, I (ii) (Oxford, 1715), pp. 486, 488; H. Ellis, ed., *The New Chronicles of England and France, in Two Parts; by Robert Fabyan: Named by Himself the Concordance of Histories* (London, 1811), pp. 562–3, 576.

21 *Hall's Chronicle; Containing the History of England during the Reign of Henry the Fourth and the Succeeding Monarchs, to the End of the Reign of Henry the Eighth . . .* (London, 1809), pp. 42–5. For Hall's reliability as a chronicler in Henry V's reign, and the use he made of early fifteenth-century writers, see B.J.H. Rowe, 'A Contemporary Account of the Hundred Years' War', *EHR*, 41 (1926), e.g. pp. 510–11.

22 J. Stow, *Annales or a Generall Chronicle of England*, I (London, 1631), pp. 339(b), 340(a).

23 Walsingham, *Historia Anglicana*, II, pp. 288, 290; Galbraith, ed., *St Albans Chronicle*, pp. 68–9.

24 See e.g. Thomas and Thornley, ed., *Great Chronicle of London*, pp. 100–3 for details of the surrender of Falaise in 1417.
25 *CPR, 1408–13*, p. 373.
26 *Foedera*, VIII, pp. 745, 751–2; T. Carte, ed., *Catalogue des Rolles Gascons, Normans et François Conservés dans les Archives de la Tour de Londres* (London and Paris, 1743), II, p. 206.
27 *Foedera*, VIII, p. 758; Carte, ed., *Catalogue des Rolles Gascons, Normans et François*, I, p. 195.
28 *Foedera*, VIII, p. 762.
29 Ibid., p. 757; *CPR, 1408–13*, p. 431; *POPC*, II, p. 33.
30 Walsingham, *Historia Anglicana*, II, p. 268.
31 Hearne, ed., 'Otterbourne', p. 271.
32 Galbraith, ed., *St Albans Chronicle*, p. 64; Hearne, ed., 'Otterbourne', p. 270; see also P. McNiven, 'The Problem of Henry IV's Health', *EHR*, 100 (1985), pp. 764–5.
33 J.F. Michaud and J.J.F. Poujoulat, 'Histoire de Charles VI, Roy de France . . . depuis 1380 jusques à 1422; par Jean Juvenal des Ursins, Archévêque de Rheims', in *Nouvelle Collection des Mémoires pour Servir L'Histoire de France, depuis le XIIIe Siècle jusqu'à la Fin du XVIIIe*, II (Paris, 1836), p. 500(a) – s.a. 1414.
34 P.S. Lewis, ed., *Écrits Politiques de Jean Juvenal des Ursins*, S(ociété de l') H(istoire de) F(rance) (Paris, 1978), I, p. 309.
35 K.B. McFarlane, *Lancastrian Kings and Lollard Knights* (Oxford 1972), p. 125: perhaps, in making this comment, McFarlane revises his earlier judgement that this was an 'insignificant expedition', *The Nobility of Later Medieval England* (Oxford, 1973), p. 37.
36 Galbraith, ed., *St Albans Chronicle*, p. 64; L. Douët d' Arcq, ed., *La Chronique Enguerran de Monstrelet . . . 1400–44*, I, SHF (Paris, 1858), p. 257.
37 M.L. Bellaguet, ed., *C(hronique du) R(eligieux de) S(aint-Denys)*, Coll. de Documents Inédits sur l'Histoire de France, IV (Paris, 1842), pp. 656–9.
38 Ibid., pp. 706–7; H. Moranvillé, ed., *Chroniques de Perceval de Cagny*, SHF (Paris, 1902), p. 71: for estimates of numbers in the English army see, for example, ibid., p. 76; A. le Vavasseur, *Chronique d'Arthur de Richemont, Connétable de France, Duc de Bretagne (1393–1458), par Guillaume Gruel*, SHF (Paris, 1890), p. 10; C. de Robillard de Beaurepaire, *Chronique Normande de Pierre Cochon*, Soc. de l'Histoire de Normandie (Rouen, 1870), p. 263.
39 V. de Viriville, ed., *Chronique de la Pucelle ou Chronique de Cousinot* (Paris, 1859), p. 144.
40 Baron Kervyn de Lettenhove, ed., 'Chronique de Jean Brandon' in *Chroniques Relatives à l'Histoire de la Belgique sous la Domination des Ducs de Bourgogne* (Brussels, 1870), p. 159.
41 F. Morand, ed., *Chronique de Jean le Févre Seigneur de Saint-Remy*, I, SHF (Paris, 1876), p. 69; see also W. and E.L.C.P. Hardy, ed. and trans., *A Collection of the Chronicles and Ancient Histories of Great Britain, now called England, by John de Waurin, from AD 1399 to AD 1422*, RS (London, 1887), IV, p. 160.
42 S. Luce, ed., *Chronique du Mont-Saint-Michel (1343–1468) Publiée avec Notes et Pièces Diverses*, Soc. des Anciens Textes Françaises, I (Paris, 1879), p. 19.
43 *CRS*, IV, pp. 732–3.
44 PRO, Exchequer Warrants for Issue E404/28/98.
45 *CRS*, IV, pp. 736–7; see also J.H. Wylie, *The Reign of Henry the Fifth*, I (1413–15) (reprinted New York, 1968), p. 167; Douët d'Arcq, ed., *Chronique de Monstrelet*, II, p. 305; Moranvillé, ed., *Chroniques de Perceval de Cagny*, p. 71.
46 *CRS*, IV, pp. 734–5; Walsingham, *Historia Anglicana*, II, p. 289; 'Histoire . . . par Jean Juvenal des Ursins', p. 484(a) and (b).
47 BN, K 57 no. 28, Treaty of Buzançais; de Viriville, ed., *Chronique de la Pucelle*, p. 144; J. Tardif, *Monuments Historiques (Inventaires et Documents publiés par ordre de l'Empereur)* (Paris, 1866), no. 1882; C.P. Cooper, ed., *Appendices to a Report on Rymer's 'Foedera'*, Appendix D (London, 1869), p. 147.

48 M.H. Keen, *England in the Later Middle Ages* (London, 1973), p. 321.
49 L. Douët d'Arcq, ed., *Choix de Pièces Inédites Relatives au Règne de Charles VI*, I, SHF (Paris, 1863), p. 359; for the fragility of such agreements see P.S. Lewis, 'Decayed and Non-feudalism in Later Medieval France', *Essays in Later Medieval French History* (London and Ronceverte, 1985), p. 60; see also M.H. Keen, 'Brotherhood in Arms', *History*, 47 (1962), p. 5. For a comment on the emphasis which Clarence placed on reserving his allegiance to his father, see M.H. Keen, *The Laws of War in the Late Middle Ages* (London and Toronto, 1965), p. 87, n. 4. For Clarence's future interest in heraldry and laws of arms, see his 1417 'Ordinances and Statutes . . . for Reformation and Good Government in the Office of Arms', in A.R. Wagner, *Heralds and Heraldry in the Middle Ages, an Inquiry into the Growth of the Armorial Function of Heralds*, 2nd edn (Oxford, 1956), pp. 60–1, 136–8. Clarence was also a knight of the Garter, see G.F. Beltz, *Memorials of the Order of the Garter* (London, 1841), pp. xiv, clv.
50 BL Add. Ch. 60 – 28 March 1413; see also BL Add. Ch. 56.
51 See, for example, M. Jones, 'Henry VII, Lady Margaret Beaufort and the Orléans Ransom', in R.A. Griffiths and J. Sherborne, eds, *Kings and Nobles in the Late Middle Ages: a Tribute to Charles Ross* (Gloucester and New York, 1986), pp. 254, 257: on Angoulême's release, sums were still owed to the executors of Edward, duke of York and Thomas, duke of Exeter who were both parties to the Buzançais agreement.
52 G. du Fresne de Beaucourt, ed., *Chronique de Mathieu d'Escouchy*, I, SHF (Paris, 1863), pp. 82–3.
53 Douët d'Arcq, ed., *Chronique de Monstrelet*, II, p. 303.
54 BL Add. Ch. 1403.
55 *Appendices to Rymer's 'Foedera'*, Appendix D, p. 148; Tardif, *Monuments Historiques*, no. 1910.
56 V. de Viriville, 'État des Sommes Envoyées à Jean, Comte d' Angoulême, en Angleterre, Pendant sa Captivité, de 1413 à 1436', *Bibliothèque de l'École des Chartes*, 16 (1855), p. 560, n. 1.
57 J. Guiffrey, ed., *Inventaires de Jean Duc de Berry (1401–1416)*, I (Paris, 1894), pp. 32, 49, 128, 132, 226, 339 (note on p. 226 art. 860); II (Paris, 1896), pp. 405 and 5, n. 1.; C.T. Allmand, ed., *Power, Culture, and Religion in France c. 1350 – c. 1550* (Woodbridge, Suffolk and Wolfeboro, N.H., 1988), p. 96 – illustration from AN, J185, no. 6 of Charles V presenting his brother, John, duke of Berry, with a portion of the relic of the True Cross; 'Histoire . . . par Jean Juvenal des Ursins', p. 478(b); J.H. Wylie, *History of England under Henry the Fourth*, IV (1411–13) (London, 1898), pp. 83–5; G.P. Cuttino, *English Medieval Diplomacy* (Bloomington, Indiana, 1985), p. 106; Jacob, *The Fifteenth Century*, p. 115.
58 M.G.A. Vale, *English Gascony, 1399–1453* (Oxford, 1970), p. 74; C.T. Allmand, *Lancastrian Normandy 1415–1450: the History of a Medieval Occupation* (Oxford, 1983), p. 2.
59 H.T. Riley, ed., 'Annales Ricardi Secundi et Henrici Quarti Regum Angliae', in *Johannis de Trokelowe et Henrici de Blaneforde . . . Chronica et Annales*, RS (London, 1866), pp. 401–2; Hearne, ed., 'Otterbourne', pp. 253–4.
60 *Registres de la Jurade, Délibérations de 1406 à 1409; 1414 à 1416 et de 1420 à 1422*, IV (Bordeaux, 1873), p. 28 for financial regulations introduced by Clarence; pp. 9, 12, 24 for enquiries into damage caused by the English army in Bordeaux.
61 T. Goodwin, *The History of the Reign of Henry the Fifth, King of England, etc* (London, 1704), p. 9; Wylie, *Henry V*, I, p. 88; R. Altamira, 'Spain 1412–1516', in *Cambridge Medieval History*, VIII, p. 482; J. Ferguson, *English Diplomacy, 1422–1461* (Oxford, 1972), pp. 38–9.
62 BL Add. Ch. 56.
63 Haydon, ed., *Eulogium*, III, pp. 419–20; Davies, ed., *An English Chronicle*, p. 37; *Cal. of*

Entries in the Papal Registers relating to Great Britain and Ireland, Papal Letters, VI (London, 1904), pp. 170, 212–13, 249.

64 See Vale, *English Gascony*, p. 63.

65 Wylie, *Henry V*, I, p. 89; Ferguson, *English Diplomacy*, pp. 38–9.

66 For tensions and disagreements between Clarence and Prince Henry, see, for example, Giles, ed., *Chronicon Angliae*, p. 62.

67 C.L. Kingsford, ed., *First English Life*, p. 14; see also Stow, *Annales*, I, p. 341(a). J.F. Baldwin, *The King's Council in England during the Middle Ages* (Oxford, 1913), p. 156 states that Prince Thomas was appointed a councillor in 1406 – based on an incorrect interpretation of 'steward of the household' in *RP*, III, p. 573: on p. 164 he states that Thomas 'returned' to the council in 1411, but gives no references. Although attendance records are scant, there is no evidence that Thomas was formally a member of Henry IV's council at any time – see A.L. Brown, 'The Commons and the Council in the Reign of Henry IV', *EHR*, 79 (1964), pp. 1–30; J.L. Kirby, 'Councils and Councillors of Henry IV, 1399–1413', *TRHS*, 5th series, 14 (1964), pp. 35–65.

68 *A Chronicle of London, 1089–1483*, pp. 94–5; Hearne, ed., 'Otterbourne', p. 271.

69 *Lords Reports touching the Dignity of a Peer of the Realm* (London, 1829), V, Appendix, pp. 168–9; *Foedera*, VIII, p. 757; *Calendar of Charter Rolls, 1341–1417* (London, 1916), p. 447 – omits a reference to Clarence's creation as earl of Albemarle; PRO, Exchequer Warrants for Issue, E404/33/89; *CPR, 1408–13*, p. 407; see also (*Annual Report of the) D(eputy) K(eeper of the Public) R(ecords)*, 36 (Calendar of Recognisance Rolls, Chester), Appendix, p. 109; 37 (Welsh Records, Calendar of Recognisance Rolls, Chester), Appendix, p. 150.

70 Hearne, ed., 'Otterbourne', p. 271.

71 *Chronicle of London, 1089–1483*, p. 95.

72 Hearne, ed., 'Otterbourne', p. 272, for the death of Henry IV; Galbraith, ed., *St Albans Chronicle*, p. 69.

73 E.g. ibid., p. 69; Walsingham, *Historia Anglicana*, II, p. 290; Hearne, ed., 'Otterbourne', p. 273.

74 *Dignity of a Peer of the Realm*, IV, Appendix, pp. 816–17: these lords were also not summoned to Henry IV's last parliament (summonses issued on 21 December 1412), ibid., p. 812.

75 Wylie, *Henry V*, I, p. 118 appears incorrect in stating that Clarence left Bordeaux on 6 April 1413.

76 *RP*, IV, p. 12(b).

77 Carte, ed., *Catalogue des Rolles Gascons, Normans et François*, I, p. 197.

78 *CCR, 1413–19*, p.11.

79 P. Chaplais, 'The Chancery of Guyenne 1289–1453', in J. Conway Davies, ed., *Studies Presented to Sir Hilary Jenkinson* (London, 1957), p. 88 (facing), Plate II(iii).

80 *Foedera*, IX, p. 2 – order made on 2 April 1413.

81 J. Kail, ed., *Twenty-six Political and Other Poems*, Part I, EETS, original series, 124 (1904), p. 50.

82 Devon, ed., *Issues of the Exchequer*, p. 340.

83 Allmand, *Lancastrian Normandy*, p. 2.

84 *RHL*, II, pp. 328–32; M. Champollion-Figeac, ed., *Lettres de Rois, Reines et Autres Personnages des Cours de France et d'Angleterre*, II, Coll. de Documents Inédits sur l'Histoire de France, ler ser. (Paris, 1847), pp. 330–2 – where the letter is given as dated 6 September; *Foedera*, VIII, pp. 745–6; Moranvillé, ed., *Chroniques de Perceval de Cagny*, p. 77.

85 Morand, ed., *Chronique de Jean le Févre*, I, p. 60.

86 *Foedera*, VIII, pp. 718–19.

87 Ibid., VIII, p. 721.

88 *RHL*, II, pp. 314–17.

89 Vale, *English Gascony*, p. 61.

90 Cuttino, *English Medieval Diplomacy*, p. 106.

91 H. Courteault and L. Celier, eds, *Les Chroniques du Roi Charles VII par Gilles le Bouvier*

dit le Héraut Berry, SHF (Paris, 1979), p. 51; Douët d'Arcq, ed., Chronique de Monstrelet, II, p. 287; RHL, II, pp. 323–4; Champollion-Figeac, ed., Lettres de Rois, II, p.329; CRS, IV, pp. 716–17; Morand, ed., Chronique de Jean le Févre, I, pp. 73–4; see also G. du Fresne de Beaucourt, Histoire de Charles VII, I (Paris, 1881), pp. 73–4.
92   RHL, II, pp. 332–3; Champollion-Figeac, ed., Lettres de Rois, II, p. 328.
93   For Assumption see e.g. Lucas, ed., John Capgrave's Abbreuiacion of Cronicles, p. 239; for St Lawrence tide see e.g. Kingsford, ed., Chronicles of London, p. 68.
94   'Histoire . . . par Jean Juvenal des Ursins', p. 478(a); de Viriville, ed., Chronique de la Pucelle, p. 143; Douët d'Arcq, ed., Chronique de Monstrelet, II, p. 287 – dates agreement as 15 July 1412.
95   CRS, IV, pp. 708–9.
96   'Chronique de Jean Brandon', p. 160; Polychronicon, VIII, p. 547; Davies, ed., English Chronicle, p. 37; Brie, ed., Brut, p. 372.
97   W. Stubbs, The Constitutional History of England in its Origins and Development, 2nd edn, III (Oxford, 1878), p. 69.
98   Keen, Laws of War, p. 123.
99   P. Contamine, La France au XIVe et XVe Siècles: Hommes, Mentalités, Guerre et Paix (London, 1981), p. 139.
100 M. Powicke, 'The English Aristocracy and the War', in K. Fowler, ed., The Hundred Years' War (London, 1971), p. 131.
101 M. Powicke, 'Lancastrian Captains', in T.A. Sandquist and M. Powicke, eds, Essays in Medieval History Presented to Bertie Wilkinson (Toronto, 1969), p. 376; R.A. Newhall, 'Henry V's Policy of Conciliation in Normandy, 1417–1422', in C.H. Taylor, ed., Anniversary Essays in Medieval History by Students of Charles Homer Haskins (Boston and New York, 1929), p. 207; Tuck, Crown and Nobility, p. 241.
102 See, for example, J.H. Wylie (and W.T. Waugh), Henry the Fifth, II and III, passim.
103 Foedera, VIII, p. 752; DKR 44 (French Rolls), Appendix, p. 570; DKR 41 (Norman Rolls), Appendix, p. 398.
104 Foedera, VIII, p. 752; DKR 44, Appendix, pp. 560, 587; Carte, ed., Catalogues des Rolles Gascons, Normans et François, II, p. 206; for Intebergh in 1415 see PRO E101/45/4, mm. 2 and 12v (Clarence's Muster Roll).
105 Foedera, VIII, p. 752; Carte, ed., Catalogues des Rolles Gascons, Normans et François, II, p. 206; Wylie, Henry the Fourth, IV, p. 74, n. 2; CCR, 1409–13, pp. 283, 287, 289–90; J.S. Roskell, The Commons in the Parliament of 1422: English Society and Parliamentary Representation under the Lancastrians (Manchester, 1954), p. 173.
106 Foedera, VIII, pp. 390, 752; Carte, ed., Catalogues des Rolles Gascons, Normans et François, II, pp. 189, 206; CPR, 1405–8, p. 444; CFR, 1413–22, pp. 63, 377; DKR 42, Appendix, p. 808; for Thomas Marnie in 1415, see PRO E101/45/4, m. 2v (Clarence's Muster Roll).
107 BL Add. MSS 21, 359, fo. 2v; BL Add. Ch. 1399; Foedera, VIII, p. 774.
108 Giles, ed., Chronicon Angliae, p. 62; B. Williams, ed., 'Extract from MS Regius 13 c.l., fo. 1296 and MS Sloane, 1776', in Henrici Quinti, Angliae Regis, Gesta (London, 1850), pp. 281–2.
109 POPC, I, pp. 318, 340–1.
110 Galbraith, ed., St Albans Chronicle, p. 77.
111 H.C. Maxwell-Lyte, Historical Notes on the Use of the Great Seal of England (London, 1926), pp. 228–9.
112 RP, IV, p. 17(a) – the king 'de sa tres benigne grace et tres gracious volunte', and with the assent of the lords spiritual and temporal and the commons assembled, declares that Thomas and Thomas Beaufort might have and enjoy the names, styles and titles previously granted them by letters patent. It should, however, be remembered that, even before this confirmation, payment had been authorised by Henry V of the £40 annually granted by Henry IV at the time of Thomas's elevation: see, for example, a warrant for issue dated 1 October 1413, PRO E404/29/8.

6

The Recruitment of Northerners for Service in English Armies in France, 1415–50

Neil Jamieson

The re-opening of the war with France by Henry V in 1415 was to commit the country to a period of continuous warfare which was to last, with only a short truce from 1444 to 1449, until the final expulsion of the English from Bordeaux in 1453. This period of constant warfare was to place almost intolerable burdens on the resources of the Crown. The manpower required for the conquest and retention of the Lancastrian domains in France was considerable. How were the men needed for service in the army provided, and was there any regional bias displayed in the recruitment of soldiers? This essay seeks to examine the manpower contribution of the North to the English war effort in France.[1]

The selection of this subject immediately raises a series of problems regarding definitions. The most obvious of these is the precise definition of the North, for without such a definition it would be impossible to decide who was and who was not a northerner. Often the only information we have on the geographical origins of an individual is his county of origin; we are indeed lucky to have that, so what is needed is a list of northern counties upon which a decision can be based. Clearly such a list should be based as closely as possible on the medieval idea of what constituted the North. The problem is to find out exactly what that definition was, for although there clearly was an idea in the medieval mind that the North formed a recognisable geographical area, there seems to have been little consensus as to what that area was. Consequently it is difficult to ascribe precise boundaries to the region, although for this study the provision of such boundaries is essential.

The northern region can be identified by a number of features which gave it a distinctive character. Population in the region was less dense than it was in some of the other, more favoured, parts of the country. There was a different pattern of social organisation here than in the South; large areas of the North were dominated by the power of a few mighty families such as those of Neville and Percy. Fewer people meant fewer towns and less commerce. The great city of York was the pre-eminent urban centre of the North and had few rivals. In general it was the highland area of England, with much of its land being of a marginal nature, which had a deadening effect on the economic prosperity of the region. The combination of these factors meant that the North formed a compact and distinctive unit in the geography of England.

However, the problem of establishing the precise boundaries of the region still remains. The northern limits of the region are easy to define, resting as they do on the frontier of what was then still foreign territory, Scotland. It is the southern boundary of the area that is difficult to find; at what point does the North end and the South begin? For the purposes of this study the limits chosen run, with a few modifications, along the line of the River Trent, the modifications being the inclusion in the northern region of Lincolnshire and Cheshire. The choice of this line does reflect to some extent medieval practices and opinions. For administrative purposes England was often divided along the line of the Trent; there was, for example, an escheator for the land to the north of the Trent and one for the land to the south. The additions of Lincolnshire and Cheshire also reflect to a degree medieval opinion. Lincolnshire troops were summoned to defend the northern border against the Scots on numerous occasions; indeed Lincolnshire seems to have been about as far south as troops came from.[2] Cheshire is included because of its strong links with Lancashire; the two counties clearly formed a cohesive unit that was a part of the north of England. True, Cheshire also had strong links with Wales and was to some extent a marcher county, but these links were almost colonial in nature and did not alter the fact that Cheshire was at heart a northern county.[3]

Having attempted to define the North, it is now time to move on and consider the methods used by the Crown to raise troops in the first half of the fifteenth century. There were three basic ways of raising soldiers for service in the wars. Forces could be raised using commissions of array; through the use of indentures; or by calling upon the services owed by those in possession of fees or annuities from the Crown. Each method had its own advantages and disadvantages which affected its suitability for certain types of military action.

Of the three methods, the use of commissions of array probably represented the most traditional source of manpower. Long centuries of use had meant that a wide series of customary limitations on the use of the militia had been developed. Consequently, although large numbers of men could be raised using the system, there were severe limitations on how these men could be used. In particular there were restrictions placed on the use of such troops abroad which meant that, in practice, the militia was usually only deployed in domestic conflicts, especially the suppression of revolt.

The provision of troops by retainers and annuitants was a way of providing large forces quickly. In times of emergency the Crown could simply summon all those who owed it service to attend with as many men as they could raise. The soldiers who appeared would then be paid wages by the Crown. The system was a simple one and had much to recommend it, but it had several disadvantages. Quite apart from the fact that the payment of fees tied up large sums of money, it would have been impossible to predict how many soldiers each summons would produce. It is also likely that enthusiasm to serve would decrease if retainers were called out too often. This particular system was best used in response to a sudden domestic crisis, and was not of any great value in sustaining a major foreign war.

The problems of providing troops for long periods of service overseas were met by the use of the indenture system. Here captains contracted to serve with specific numbers of men for a specified period of time, thus eliminating the problems encountered in the two previous systems. Indeed indentured troops provided the mainstay of English armies in France; there was a voluntary element in such service which was necessary to sustain a long war abroad. If men were compelled to serve, there was likely to be large-scale avoidance and desertion. Using the indenture system, provided the Crown could find the money there were usually enough volunteers to be found. It was only towards the end of the war that difficulties were experienced in recruiting troops of sufficient quality in the numbers required. With this system, too, there were problems, principally the speed with which the system operated. It could take months for a planned expedition to depart; while this did not matter in the years when the English held the initiative in the war, it was to do so after 1429 when the French took the offensive. The slowness of the system meant that the response of the English to any crisis was sluggish, relief from England only arriving in Normandy after the crisis was over and the damage done.

Using a combination of the three methods outlined above, the Crown attempted to provide enough men to meet the needs of its armies in France. We should now consider examples of how each system was used in practice with special reference to recruitment in the north of England.

Commissions of array were of severely limited use in providing troops for service abroad. The fact that the Crown had to pay for the services of the militia overseas removed one of the chief attractions of the system, its cheapness. This, coupled with the fact that the use of pressed men tended to invite desertion, meant that the system was used less and less to provide men for foreign service, until by the fifteenth century its use had almost died out. However, the use of such troops abroad did enjoy a brief revival during the reign of Henry V, who used them on a large scale, reflecting, perhaps, the determination of the king to use his resources to the full to prosecute the French war. It is significant that soldiers raised in this fashion came exclusively from the north of England, such troops coming only from Lancashire, Cheshire and Derbyshire. Perhaps the fact that troops were levied here, and nowhere else, reflects the palatine status of Lancashire and

Cheshire, as presumably the restrictions imposed on militia service at Westminster did not apply there. Such recruitment certainly reflects the dominating influence of the Crown in the area and perhaps also the martial reputation of the men of the north-west.

The scale of the contribution made by the militia of the north-west in the years between 1415 and 1422 was substantial. It has been estimated that Lancashire and Cheshire men constituted between a fifth and a quarter of the army which Henry V led to France in 1415.[4] Cheshire alone raised a force of some 700 men-at-arms and archers, whilst Lancashire provided 500 archers.[5] In addition to these men there was a body of 400 Cheshire and Lancashire archers attached to the royal household, presumably as a sort of bodyguard unit.[6] Of these troops it is perhaps the unit from Lancashire that is most interesting, as it is well documented in a series of accounts rendered by both the sheriff of Lancashire and several individual captains which enable, at times, the service records of individual companies to be assessed.

The Lancashire contingent of 1415 consisted of 500 archers, the total force being divided into ten companies of fifty men each. Each company was commanded by a member of the local gentry, in the majority of cases a knight. All the captains were duchy of Lancaster annuitants and all had probably been among the commissioners responsible for the raising of the troops. It is interesting that most of the captains appear to have led, in addition to the archers, their own personal retinue for which they had sealed indentures in the usual fashion.[7] The troops had certainly been raised before 16 June, as on that date an instruction was issued to move the men to Warrington by 24 June ready to move south to join the king. These archers served throughout the 1415 campaign, and it is fortunate that the account presented by one of the captains details precisely what happened to the men under his command. The executors of Sir Richard Kyghley gave account for the money he had received from the sheriff of Lancashire for his men. From this account it can be seen that, of the original forty-nine men, six had died during the siege of Harfleur, ten, ill at the conclusion of the siege, had left for home, nine had remained to garrison the captured town, and seven were somehow captured the day before Agincourt, which left only eighteen men who actually fought at the battle. The company does not seem to have sustained any casualties at Agincourt, as all eighteen men are recorded as returning to London through Calais with seven horses.[8] Unfortunately this sort of detail is not repeated in any of the other accounts for the Lancashire archers that we possess. However, if it reflects a common experience, then fewer than half the soldiers who set out in June would have returned home.

There was further large-scale recruiting of Lancashire and Cheshire archers in 1417 as part of the preparations for the invasion of Normandy.

The muster roll of the army at Southampton in 1417, although incomplete, contains a list of 400 Cheshire archers, not as many as in 1415 but still a substantial contingent.[9] Sir James Harrington was commissioned to raise 400 Lancashire archers, two-thirds of whom were to be provided with horses.[10] However, it seems that those recruited at this time remained in service for a considerable period of time; a series of musters taken in April 1419 contain ample evidence of the continued existence of these county contingents some two years after they had first been raised. All the musters seem to have been taken about 1 April 1419, when most of the Cheshire contingent was at Evreux. There were some sixty-eight Cheshire archers there along with fifty-six from Lancashire. A more specific reference is made to seventy-one archers from Macclesfield hundred, presumably all that were left of the 105 men who set out in 1417. Similar losses seem to have taken place in the contingents of the other hundreds; Broxton had sent thirty-three archers in 1417, of whom seventeen were left in 1419, whilst only seven of an original eighteen men from the Wirral remained. Thirty-four archers from Amounderness hundred in Lancashire also appear at Evreux as do seventeen archers from Derbyshire. Certain garrisons in Normandy at this time appear to have had detachments of Cheshire or Lancashire archers attached to them, such as the eighteen archers of Eddisbury hundred at Dieppe.[11]

As the war in Normandy dragged on, however, these county contingents decreased in numbers still further until they eventually disappeared altogether about the time of Henry V's death. The troops must either have died, gone home or else been recruited into the indentured retinues that now came to dominate the military scene in Normandy. The last few references to these Lancashire and Cheshire archers come in the accounts of William Phillip, Henry's treasurer of wars in 1421–2, in which John Stanley is recorded as leading twenty-one Cheshire and thirty-five Lancashire archers.[12] There was also a company of men at Paris under Richard Pickering, William Harrison, James Barne, John Lovelace, Robert Prestwich and Richard Berningell on 26 August 1422. This seems to be the last time such troops are mentioned.[13]

The use of these levies died out at a time when the character of the war in France was changing from being a war of conquest to one in which the defence of what was already held was the primary consideration. Consequently what was needed was an army geared towards the long-term occupation of territory. This need could be best supplied using contract troops, which removed the need to recruit men by commissions of array. There was probably always some element of compulsion involved when county contingents were raised, and some men were probably not volunteers. It is possible that the commissioners and local officials responsible for organising the units took the opportunity to rid the locality of some of the more undesirable elements. This in turn may have led to problems with discipline and desertion. It is impossible to tell whether these problems were more prevalent in the county contingents than in the indentured retinues, but if this was so it may help to explain why their use was abandoned. Interestingly, a mandate to arrest deserters issued to Henry de Bothe in 1419 specifically mentions those absconding from the Cheshire contingents of Bucklow and Macclesfield, as well as Derbyshire archers, men of the king's unit of archers and Cheshire archers with the retinue of Philip Leche.[14] Clearly such men were not completely reliable.

Another source of manpower which could be used was the service owed by the annuitants and retainers of the Crown. Anyone who was in receipt of such a gift was bound to render military service with an appropriate retinue when required. This system was of most use in domestic conflict when there was, at times, a need for rapid action which made the usual system of signing contracts impractical. This did not, however, mean that the Crown did not bring pressure to bear on its annuitants to serve overseas. There were many precedents for such service being demanded although, typically, in this period it was during the reign of Henry V that most requests for this type of service were made.

Several requests that duchy of Lancaster annuitants serve in Gascony were made during the reign of Henry IV, but there is no evidence to suggest that they ever embarked on the trip.[15] Henry V not only asked for service but made sure that it was actually performed by as many people as possible. In 1415 the list of Crown annuitants in Lancashire and Cheshire was examined for those who had failed to follow the king to France. Of eighty-six annuitants in Lancashire thirty-four were at Harfleur with Henry; of the absentees some were noted as sick or infirm but others appear to have had no good reason for non-attendance. Presumably they experienced difficulties drawing their annuities that year.[16] Certainly in 1416 there was a summons for duchy annuitants to cross to France, and on this occasion the receiver in Lancashire was instructed not to pay the annuity unless the recipient could prove he had served in person or had been excused.[17]

Henry seems to have used the payment of fees and annuities as a means of putting pressure on individuals to serve in his wars, but with only mixed success. Many seem to have remained at home despite the threat of non-payment; if thirty-four annuitants went with Henry to the siege of Harfleur, fifty-two clearly did not. Some of these would have been officials whose presence at home was essential, while some could have been sick or infirm; but there would seem to have been many who were not afraid to lose their annuities if the alternative was a campaign in France. Those who did go to serve with the king seem to have sealed indentures for the forces they would bring, as did all the other captains. Once again the best documented of the companies provided by annuitants are those belonging to the captains of Lancashire archers in 1415. These men were all duchy of Lancaster annuitants and, in addition to leading a company of fifty archers, they all indented for a smaller private retinue, probably connected with their obligations as annuitants. The size of these smaller companies varied widely. Sir James Harrington contracted for a company of ten men-at-arms and thirty archers; of these, eight men-at-arms and twenty-six archers eventually returned to England, light casualties which contrast sharply with the heavy losses sustained by Sir Richard de Kyghley's archers. Sir James was still trying to obtain payment for his company in 1425.[18] Sir Richard de Kyghley himself indented for a company of six men-at-arms and eighteen archers on 15 May 1415. Once again it is possible to trace what happened to these men; one man-at-arms died at Harfleur and another left with the king's licence, while one knight, presumably Sir Richard, and four archers were killed at Agincourt.[19]

The direct summoning of Crown annuitants for military service in France died away in the later years of Henry V and no longer seems to have taken place under the regency council or in the reign of Henry VI. The reasons for this are probably much the same as they were for the decline in the use of commissions to raise troops. The nature of the war had changed and the demands made for manpower could best be met with the use of indentured troops. As the war dragged on it would not have been reasonable to expect those in receipt of fees to continue to serve for an almost unlimited period of time. It is thus to the study of the rôle of northerners in contract forces that we must now turn.

From what has been said above it will be clear that soldiers raised by means of a contract with a captain provided the mainstay of the armies of the period. This was the primary way of raising troops for service in France under Henry V and virtually the only way used in the time of Henry VI. From the point of view of this study, which is concerned with the geographical origins of the troops, the large-scale use of contract soldiers raises considerable difficulties. The simple fact is that there is usually little indication given in the sources as to where these men actually came from. Nevertheless, there are certain ways in which rough estimates of the geographical origins of troops can be made. These involve the use of account rolls, musters, sub-contracts and letters of protection.There are of course pitfalls involved in using all these methods. Account rolls usually furnish only the name of the individual to whom money was owed, the captain; even this limited amount of information can be valuable, however, if we can make some guess as to what the make-up of his company was. This can be done by making use of the large quantity of muster rolls which survive for the indentured companies of this period. These give long lists of names of soldiers serving in France, and while geographical origins of men are seldom given, it is possible, through the study of the surnames in the roll, to make a reasonable guess at where some of the soldiers came from. The study of muster rolls can be backed up by the use of sub-contracts and letters of protection. Sub-contracts can sometimes indicate where a captain was recruiting, whilst protections issued to men on the retinues of captains frequently state the place of origin of the recipient. There are problems with the use of letters of protection in this way, however, for not everyone bothered to apply for one and probably not all those that did were soldiers, some being household servants, craftsmen, or merchants engaged in victualling operations. Consequently any conclusions drawn from the study of letters of protection must be tentative. Nevertheless their use is essential in the face of the lack of other sources of evidence on this subject.

The first point which can be made about recruitment into indentured retinues is that the geographical origins of the captain had a profound effect on the make-up of his company. If the captain was a northerner then it is likely that many of his men would be so too. Consequently it is possible for a rough guess at the composition of an army to be made by studying the list of the captains in that army. The fact that recruiting was, to a certain extent, localised is confirmed by the study of muster rolls and by some existing sub-contracts. On 2 May 1443 John Standish of Duxbury in Lancashire sealed indentures with two local men to help fulfil his military obligations to the duke of Somerset, whom he had undertaken to serve on the duke's ill-fated expedition to France. Laurence Longworth of Sharples and Adam de Lever of Haigh each indented to serve for one year for the sum of £40, Longworth agreeing to supply a man-at-arms and three archers.[20] This sort of recruiting would obviously lead to retinues having a regional character and it is easy to see why it should be so, since many of the men would have been known to the captain, thus easing the problems of recruiting and perhaps introducing an element of trust into the relationship. It is often possible to trace members of the same county community in each other's retinues. The musters of Edward Weaver, captain of the garrison of St Lô in 1429, record the presence among the men-at-arms of John Savage, a neighbour of his from Cheshire.[21] Two years later back in Cheshire, Weaver undertook a recognisance of £100 for Savage to keep the peace, an example perhaps of friendship formed in France being maintained at home.[22]

As well as recruiting from their immediate locality, those looking for soldiers also seem to have obtained considerable numbers of men from their families. Once again this is hardly surprising, as it would reduce the numbers of men the captain would have had to find from other sources as well as helping to create a trustworthy core for the company. Consequently it is common to find men in the company with the same surname as the captain; furthermore, study of the lists of names of men-at-arms and archers frequently reveals common surnames, indicating perhaps that some of those who indented to serve as men-at-arms may have brought along a junior member of the family as an archer. This phenomenon is reflected to a most pronounced degree in the musters of retinues of members of the Standish family of Lancashire. One muster for the garrison of Pontoise taken in 1437 shows that in the company of Henry Standish, the captain of the town, seven of the thirty-two men-at-arms and three of the seventy archers bore the surname of Standish.[23] This is, of course, an extreme example, but it is by no means an isolated one, most retinues displaying the same characteristic to some degree.

This combination of recruiting family members and local men tended to give retinues a regional character, at least when they were first recruited. However, once the company had been overseas for some time it seems that its composition lost some of its regional identity. This probably occurred as soldiers recruited in England for six months' or a year's service either died or left, to be replaced by soldiers recruited on the spot in Normandy. These men usually had no connection with the captain other than that they were professional soldiers recruited to serve in the company. Perhaps the most startling example of this process occurred in the retinue of Griffith Don, which garrisoned Tancarville in 1438. This was a Welsh retinue and when it first appeared in the garrison it had a strong regional character, fifty-two of the 101 archers being Welsh as were twenty-five of the thirty-three men-at-arms.[24] Musters taken later in the year, however, show that these Welsh troops had to a large extent drifted away, presumably as their contracts had expired, to be replaced by English and Normans who were more willing to undertake longer periods of service.

The fact that retinues which served for a long period in Normandy tended to recruit replacements locally highlights the existence of a pool of more or less professional soldiers who could be taken into service as the need arose. The numbers of men required in garrisons was never particularly large, and to a great degree it seems as though the garrison soldiers required could be recruited within the duchy. The presence of such soldiers available for service is indicated by the short space of time needed to fill vacancies in garrisons, often only a day or so.[25] There are also frequent references to soldiers living off the land, usually connected with the disorder they created. On 17 March 1434, for example, John Salvain, *bailli* of Rouen, was informed that various Welsh, Norman, English and Picard troops were living off the land and disturbing the peace in his jurisdiction. He was authorised to muster any English troops he could find into royal pay in an attempt to ease the problem.[26] It is, of course, impossible to establish the English origins of any of these troops; indeed the soldiers who served in the Norman garrisons during the later years of the English occupation are generally very difficult to identify. Many undoubtedly served in Normandy for a considerable period of time, whilst others seem to have drifted back and forwards between England and the continent. Indeed it would be fair to say that most probably lost their regional roots in the process, to the extent that it would no longer be possible to speak of them as being northerners or as belonging to any other part of England at all. The long drawn out nature of the war created a class of rootless professional soldiers.

If there was a pool of soldiers in Normandy it would seem that there was a similar gathering of soldiers for hire in London. It appears that as the war dragged on through the 1430s and 1440s London increasingly became a place where professional soldiers could be recruited. The reason for this is not hard to see; London was the capital of the realm where all important decisions about sending troops to France were made, a convenient place for a captain who had just sealed an indenture to do some recruiting; while it possessed a large surplus population which made such recruiting easier. In 1450 Sir John Fastolf had no difficulty recruiting old soldiers of Normandy in London to defend his house in Southwark against Cade's rebels.[27] The evidence of the letters of protection also indicates that London was an important centre of recruiting for Normandy. Most captains, even those with no apparent connection with the city, seem to have done some recruiting there. Some ninety-one protections were issued to men in the retinue of the duke of York during his various terms of office in Normandy. Of these, some seventy men can be given definite geographical origins and of these a group of thirteen men claim to have come from London. Such figures are repeated time and again. The retinue of Sir Thomas Kyriell, which admittedly has a marked bias towards London and the south-east, is even more striking; out of a total of eighty-four men who received protections some sixty-five could be given geographical origins, and of these twenty-three were Londoners. The retinue of the earl of Huntingdon has fifty-nine recorded protections, of whom fourteen had London origins.[28] Not everyone bothered to apply for a protection, so what we are dealing with is only a sample of the total number of men who went to France. The figures should not be completely disregarded, however, for this is a substantial sample and may be of value in attempting to estimate any geographical bias in recruitment. After all, there would seem to be no reason why a man from the North would be less likely to apply for a protection than someone from London. Finally, on this topic, it is possible that not all the men who said they came from London on their letters of protection actually did so. A considerable number may only have been giving the place where they had been recruited.

The use of letters of protection can also give us some indication as to the proportion of northerners who served in France in indentured retinues. Once again these figures should only be taken as a rough indication of the percentage of northerners in the army, and precise numbers can never be established. The information contained in the letters of protection would seem to indicate that northerners were in a substantial minority. For example, in the retinue of the duke of York, of the total of ninety-one enrolled protections, only fourteen came from the group of northern counties. The retinue of the earl of Salisbury had some forty protections enrolled, of which some thirty-two gave the origins of the recipient, only four of whom came from the North, all from 1428 and three of them Lancashire men. Nine protections are recorded for the retinue which Henry Standish took to France in 1436; yet of these only one came from his native Lancashire, whilst five gave London as their origin.[29] It may be that the service of many northerners is hidden from us by the fact that there may have been a tendency to give a London origin as an alias. This, however, is impossible to establish, and the question must be asked as to why northerners were apparently not serving in larger numbers.

Perhaps one of the most interesting documents in this respect is one which contains the responses of the gentry of Yorkshire to a request for service made during the later years of Henry V. This reveals a profound lack of enthusiasm for Henry's cause, for although there were eighty-seven responses, forty-six failed to reply at all, while most pleaded illness, poverty or age, some a combination of all three. One seems to have been claiming to be some sort of academic and asked to be excused, like other learned men. Another patriotically offered to send his brother, whilst another volunteered his son-in-law; yet another declined on the grounds that he was not a gentleman, and so was not obliged to serve. Others gave more interesting, if less comic answers. One man, Roger Silton of Bridforth in the West Riding, refused on the grounds that he had already served with the earl of Northumberland in Scotland and would not serve twice. Others agreed with him, and some voiced their feelings even more strongly. Walter of Flynton and William Twyer, both of Holderness, flatly told the commissioners that they were not prepared to serve outside England. Here at least Henry's appeal fell on stony ground.[30] The reasons seem to be fairly obvious: to men in the north of England it was the Scots who were the real enemy, who could descend at any time on the very homes of the northerners. It is certainly significant that the three northernmost counties of England seem to have provided, with some exceptions, very few men for the French wars. Perhaps this lack of commitment also reflected the attitude of the great magnates of the region. The war record in France of the great northern families of Neville and Percy is, with certain exceptions, not a particularly impressive one. In an area of the country where the lordship of these two families was so influential the effect could have been to damp down any enthusiasm there may have been to serve in the wars in France.

Nevertheless, northerners did serve in France in quite considerable numbers. Why did they do so? The most obvious reason was for financial gain; some did, indeed, make substantial profits out of the war. William Bowes was a Durham man who served in France for seventeen years, serving for a time as chamberlain to the duke of Bedford. He grew rich in France and, on his return home, used his profits to augment his lands and build a manor house at Streatham.[31] Here was the kind of success story that all those who went to serve in France must have been hoping to repeat, yet such stories must have been all too rare. For most, their only remuneration would have been their wages, generous by the standards of the day, but often in arrears. There was also the hope that a profitable ransom might make a fortune or a valuable piece of plunder might be obtained. Henry Standish removed a valuable church cross from Normandy in 1449, and it was from sources such as this that many soldiers hoped to profit.[32] Although few made their fortunes in the wars, most must have hoped to do so.

Traditional notions of service probably also aided recruitment considerably. Serving the king in his wars was regarded as prestigious and could even confer nobility on those who distinguished themselves.[33] Those who followed the king to war could expect to share in the rewards won and receive favours as a result of their actions. Compulsion also seems to have played a considerable part in the raising of forces. The majority of northerners who served in France came from Lancashire and Cheshire, the very areas where Crown influence was strongest. It has already been demonstrated how the Crown could put pressure on its retainers in that part of England to serve abroad. It is also interesting that in areas where the leading nobles did not take an interest in the French war, such as Yorkshire and the northern counties of England, few recruits seem to have been forthcoming. The vigorous exercise of lordship was undoubtedly a strong encouragement to recruitment.

It is impossible to quantify precisely the numbers of northerners who served in France in the years between 1415 and 1450; however, it seems that the proportion of northerners in the army varied through the years. It is probable that the reign of Henry V saw the greatest commitment of northerners to the war in France. Not only were large county contingents recruited in the north at this time, which boosted numbers considerably, but it was also the time when indentured retinues displayed most regional character. A glance at the musters for the companies of the earl of Northumberland, Henry, Lord Fitzhugh and John Neville in 1417 confirms their strongly northern character.[34] Compare these with the retinue of William Neville, Lord Fauconberg in 1442, in which there seem to have been few northerners, probably most being professional soldiers recruited in Normandy.[35] Of course many northerners did serve in France during the reign of Henry VI; men such as Henry Standish, John Salvain and John Handford all gave distinguished service. The connection between Lancashire and Cheshire was important throughout the period, and captains from the region were prominent in the army; yet their influence was by no means overwhelming and, as has been said above, they were always in a minority. In any case, after the early 1420s, it may be misleading to talk of northerners, or men from any English region, serving in France. After that date the war in France was conducted largely by men who had, to a certain extent, settled in the duchy, and by professional soldiers who made a living out of the war. John Salvain and John Handford both spent long years in Normandy and must have felt out of place when forced to return to England. Northern soldiers played an important rôle in the conquest of Normandy for the English Crown, but it was largely through the efforts of those within the duchy that it was retained for so long.

Notes

1   I would like to thank Professor C.T. Allmand, my Ph.D. supervisor at the University of Liverpool, for reading and commenting on an earlier draft of this paper.
2   *CPR, 1401–5*, pp. 138–40.
3   For a fuller discussion on the north of England see J. Le Patourel, 'Is Northern History a Subject?', *Northern History*, 12 (1976), pp. 1–15.
4   M.J. Bennett, *Community, Class and Careerism: Cheshire and Lancashire Society in the Age of Sir Gawain and the Green Knight* (Cambridge, 1983), p. 171.
5   PRO E101/46/35.
6   N.H. Nicolas, *History of the Battle of Agincourt and the Expedition of Henry the Fifth into France* (London, 1832), p. 358.
7   PRO E101/46/35.
8   PRO E101/44/29.
9   PRO E101/51/2.
10   PRO DL 42/17, fo. 112.
11   BL Add. MS 38525, fo. 77.
12   PRO E101/50/10.
13   PRO E101/50/13.
14   *DKR* 42 (1881), p. 321.
15   PRO E101/42/16.
16   PRO DL 28/27/6.
17   PRO DL 42/17, fos 113–15.
18   PRO E101/47/32.
19   PRO E101/44/29.
20   *HMC, 10th Report, Appendix IV* (1885), p. 227. See also C.T. Allmand, *Lancastrian Normandy 1415–1450: the History of a Medieval Occupation* (Oxford, 1983), pp. 64–6.
21   BN MS Fr.25769, no 513.
22   PRO CHES 2/103, m. 6, no. 2.
23   BN MS Fr.25774, no. 1289.

24   Ibid., no. 1320. See R.A. Griffiths, *The Principality of Wales in the Later Middle Ages: the Structure and Personnel of Government 1 – South Wales* (Cardiff, 1972), pp. 201–2.
25   On this subject see A.J. Pollard, *John Talbot and the War in France 1427–53* (London, 1983), p. 87 ff.; also A. Curry, 'The First English Standing Army? Military Organisation in Lancastrian Normandy, 1420–1450', *Patronage, Pedigree, and Power in Later Medieval England*, ed. C.D. Ross (Gloucester and Totowa, 1979), pp. 193–214.
26   BN PO 2623 Salvain 32.
27   N. Davis, ed., *Paston Letters and Papers of the Fifteenth Century* (Oxford, 1971–6), II, p. 314.
28   Information derived from many references in *DKR* 41, 42, 44, and 48.
29   Ibid.
30   PRO E101/55/13.
31   *Leyland's Itinerary in England and Wales*, ed. L. Toulmin-Smith (London, 1907–10), II, p. 9.
32   BL Harleian MS 2042, fo. 239.
33   See M.H. Keen, *Chivalry* (Yale, 1984), pp. 162–78.
34   PRO E101/51/2.
35   BN NAF.8606, no. 86.

7
When Did Henry VI's Minority End?[1]

J.L. Watts

'In the large emerald room at the top of the tallest tower of the castle, four travellers watched as the great screen in front of the throne tottered this way and that.

As it fell with a crash, they looked that way, and the next moment all of them were filled with wonder. For they saw, standing in just the spot the screen had hidden, a little old man with a bald head and a wrinkled face, who seemed to be as much surprised as they were. The Tin Woodman, raising his axe, rushed towards the little man and cried out, "Who are you?"

"I am Oz, the Great and Terrible" said the little man in a trembling voice, "but don't strike me – please don't – and I'll do anything you want me to".

Our friends looked at him in surprise and dismay. "I thought Oz was a great head," said Dorothy.

"And I thought Oz was a lovely lady," said the Scarecrow.

"And I thought Oz was a terrible beast," said the Tin Woodman.

"And I thought Oz was a ball of fire," exclaimed the Lion.

"No, you are all wrong," said the little man meekly. "I have been making believe."

"Making believe!" cried Dorothy. "Are you not a great wizard?"

"Not a bit of it, my dear; I'm just a common man."

"You're more than that," said the Scarecrow, in a grieved tone; "you're a humbug."

"Exactly so!" declared the little man.

"Doesn't anyone else know you're a humbug?" asked Dorothy.

"No one knows it but you four – and myself," replied Oz. "I have fooled everyone for so long that I thought I should never be found out".'[2]

The magic spell of the Wizard of Oz was not at all unlike the power exercised by the late medieval English kings. Just as the lion looked to Oz for courage and the tin man sought a heart, so the king was the final resort of all earthly hopes. Like Oz, he derived his power to meet these needs, or some of them, from his place at the pinnacle of national endeavour. This university of need was the basis of a national community defined by the king's rule and, in turn, feeding it. The king's good was the common good: optimal peace and justice achieved and maintained by the labour of his people, a labour shaped – indeed, governed – by the security his rule afforded. Like Oz, the king was held aloft, a great shining mirror of the realm, and when the glass was broken by the anarchy of the later 1450s the insubstantiality of kingship was just as dramatically revealed. The king had no power beyond what was freely, if habitually, conceded to him. When this concession was withdrawn, at first individually, later corporately, he was powerless – his claims to be 'great and terrible' shown to be based on nothing more than a willing suspension of disbelief.

There is perhaps no better object for a study of the insubstantiality of royal power than the reign of Henry VI. This 'shadow on the wall . . . submissive and mute, like a crowned calf'[3] was, in his meek and feeble person, the perfect antithesis of the English royal *persona*, yet he reigned for a grand total of thirty-nine years. It is generally agreed that for over half of them, the king played no – or almost no – personal rôle in politics. Until the mid-1430s, it is argued, he was a child. After 1453, he was mad, or ill, or both. Analysis of the politics of the reign consequently focuses on the king's character and thus on the period *c.* 1435–53 when he is held to have been capable of having one. Most historians have followed the tradition that the king was passive and monkish, a man whose kingdom was not of this world.[4] His interest in politics did not extend beyond the issue of peace in the Church. The 'primer notable workes' of his reign were the colleges at Eton and Cambridge.[5] From this tradition, B.P. Wolffe was the most famous dissenter. Turning to the records of government, he found a king very much at the centre of affairs, a second Edward II, partisan, unpredictable and vicious.[6] Wolffe's doubts were stimulated by the improbability that Henry's ministers had been a 'unique pack of self-seeking knaves, fools or incompetents': the king himself had to take responsibility for the disasters of his reign.[7] At the heart of Wolffe's thesis was the belief that the appearance of the king's name at the head of all the issues of his government made it impossible to argue that he was not associated with them. Politics and the king's will were inseparable. There is, of course, plenty to suggest that Henry VI, the man, was barely behind many of the acts of Henry VI, the king. But Wolffe's point was an important one, especially as it is now widely accepted that Henry was actually involved in the peace policy, in the founding of the colleges and in the judicial activity of the early 1450s primarily on the basis of the same evidence which shows him to have run the government in his adult years. If we are going to examine the personal rule of Henry VI, we need to know what was the constitutional rôle of the royal *persona* – a phenomenon both private and public.[8]

Behind every action of the king's *persona publica* lay three main components, of which one was broadly public (counsel), one included both public and private elements (will), and one was broadly private (the king's own character). Counsel represented input: drawing the king's attention to a particular problem; supplying information and advice concerning it. It was public because it mostly came from outside the king, in a variety of forms and locations – a word or two at court or in council, by petition or demonstration.[9] Will, on the other hand, might be said to be output: it was the king's will which was the necessary authority behind every act of government.[10] This was public in as much as it invited universal participation through counsel.[11] Yet it also had a private aspect, in that the formal public will of the king drew part of its force from being irreducibly his private wish.[12]

Such wishes came from the king's individual and independent character. Scholastic concepts of (adult) personality posited a contest between 'rationality', composed of the four cardinal virtues – prudence, justice, temperance and fortitude – and the baser forces of the body.[13] At stake in this contest was the character of the man, the internal predispositions governing his will and, hence, his behaviour. This is the philosophy underlying advice-literature, which sought to inculcate in its princely readers the moral virtues of the Christian polity, thereby effecting a higher quality of rule in the common interest. It was the king's most private self which received counsel and expressed will: virtue made good the links between his private and public *personae*. How counsel was transformed into action depended on the king's prudence, his sense of justice, his temper and so on.

These three elements – counsel, will and character – constituted the basic paradigm of monarchical politics. It is not difficult to see what flexibility this model permitted in practice. As was patently the intention of the advice books, the king who possessed the political virtues was less in need of counsel: his innate prudence enabled him to perceive the common good, whatever the counsel he received.[14] Where prudence and other virtues were deficient in the king, more counsel was necessary. Meanwhile, will remained a constant: whatever the king's character, whatever the quality of counsel, royal will remained the mainspring of the polity, and defiance of it was rebellion. This structure of expectations allowed a wise and vigorous man, like Henry V, to fulfil, in large measure, his private wishes in his public acts. It seems safe to assume that a substantial part of the initiative behind his royal policy was his own. Meanwhile, the same structure enabled less remarkable men to govern sufficiently well for some sort of public peace to be preserved. There were limits, even so. Kings whose nature was strong, wrong and resistant to counsel – King John, Edward II, Richard II – could not be borne. Like his *persona publica*, the king's will was ultimately separable from his private person only by death or deposition. Because the essence of this private person could not be made by counsel to amend itself, these dire solutions became unavoidable. But what of a king whose virtue was insufficient to discriminate between the counsels offered him, who, in fact, handed over the weighty approbation of the royal will to whoever was close at hand? Before considering this question, it will be necessary to look briefly at the forms taken by counsel in the later medieval polity.

The most important thing to understand about royal counsel is its informality: it was, and had to be, free. I would argue, and I have elsewhere,[15] that there was no place in the conventions of the late medieval polity for a royal council, if by that term we mean a definite body of men who met regularly to advise the king on important matters of state and to execute the policies which resulted. The royal councils which seem to dominate the period 1377 to 1437 were a series of separate responses to crises, sometimes ongoing, in the relations between the king and his greater subjects. I do not have time here to go into detailed arguments to support this claim, but I think it can be justified on the grounds of constitutional principle. The sovereign power wielded by the king's *persona publica* and its inseparability from his body natural made it essential for all his subjects to have access to the man himself. For most, this would be through some form of mediation – whether seigneurial or parliamentary. For the nobility – the king's *consiliarii nati,* as even Fortescue calls them – it was face to face. Any fixed body which monopolised counsel over a long period would frustrate this need. Counsel was supposed to provide for participation in government, but formal councils restricted this.[16] Meanwhile, the executive functions attributed to councils were usually adequately covered by the officers of state and household. Above all, counsel had to be representative. This was achieved on a day-to-day basis by the sense that the king, in his prudence, was responsive to the common weal, that he was surrounded by the right sort of people and that anyone might have access to him – even if only by petition – if he needed it. From time to time, the king took counsel more formally: in great councils and parliaments, where representation was more direct, but less free. In general, though, it was through informal access to the king that the representation and reconciliation of interests was achieved. The preservation of this informality depended largely on the virtuous character of the king: counsel could not be satisfactorily imposed.

Returning to the problem of Henry VI's personal rule, we can immediately see that it is a more complex question than it first appeared. In a public sense, the king's personal rule began with his reign, even if he was a baby and had no 'personality': if there was no *persona publica,* there could be no body politic. The greater lords of 1422 not only provided counsel, but also established an artificial royal person as a basis for the royal will which they needed to be able to exercise. In fact, the effective operation of this contrivance depended on the absence of alternative claimants to the execution of royal power. The claims of the king's uncles could be defeated by political pressure, but what was far less resistible was the claim of Henry VI himself, first advanced in 1432, though implicit even before then. The predicament of the lords in the 1430s stemmed from a general fear that the independent capacity asserted, by Gloucester and others, on behalf of the king in person was no less manufactured and a good deal less representative than that exercised by the councillors themselves. This I believe to have been the central political problem of the reign. It was to emerge time and again. What I would like to do in this paper is to examine the events of the later minority, when it was still ideologically and politically acceptable to doubt the king's possession of an independent character, and to compare them with the later experience of the reign, when this could no longer be done. Perhaps in this way it will prove possible to unravel the mystery of Henry VI's personal rule.

The basic principle of Henry VI's minority − that the rule of Henry VI had already begun − was made clear at almost every opportunity. At nine months, Henry received the great seal from his father's last chancellor.[17] At three, he presided over the opening of parliament and so removed the need for a parliamentary lieutenant.[18] When he was five, the lords of the council recognised that, in Henry VI, they had a king 'whom and noone other they knowe' and declared,

> How be it that the king as now be of tendre eage nevere the lesse the same autoritee resteth and is at this day in his persone that shal be in him at eny tyme hereafter whan he shal come withe Goddes grace to yeers of discrecion.[19]

As I have suggested, the blandness of this concept masked a considerable complexity. The assertion of a model closely resembling normal government − royal authority, representative counsel − was accompanied by a number of artificial expedients designed to take account of the inescapable fact that the king was a small child and unable to wield his authority in the normal way. Characteristic of this was the appointment of the king's uncles to attend to the protection and defence of realm and Church in the king's stead and also to be chief of his counsel.[20] In a sense, the two appointments were different in kind. The former reflected an aspect of kingship which Henry was in no way able to fulfil − later defined as 'a personell duetee of entendance to the actuell defense of the land'.[21] It invited the dukes to replace, or represent, the king. The latter, on the other hand, made them the king's servants: the post of counsellor, even chief counsellor, presupposes a figure of authority to whom counsel is offered.

This ambivalence was reflected in the other arrangements for government made in 1422. Various men were named '*pur Conseillers assistentz a la governance*'.[22] They were to counsel the king as if he were an adult, but because he was not, they were also to assist in government.[23] This convention was by no means entirely problematic. The normal model for acts of government – counsel plus royal will – was more or less upheld. The councillors provided for the king's inability to direct his will in various ways. They were a fixed, named group: the king could not take counsel from just anybody.[24] A sufficient number of them had to attend before acts could be considered 'doon by Counseill'.[25] Decisions were made not in accordance with abstract merit, but with majority support.[26] Most importantly, the councillors were held responsible for what they advised, which is to say that while formal authority for their actions lay with the king, their practical authority was recognised.[27] These measures took account of the fact that the king could not be presented with different counsels, as was usual, and left to decide, in his prudence, whom to ask and what was best; that he could not, in fact, release his advisers from responsibility. Royal will was usurped corporately by the council, the king's own stake in his *persona publica* being merely ceremonial. This is what the lords meant in 1427 when they declared that 'the . . . counsail, the king being in suche tendrenesse of age, represente his persone as toward execucion of the saide pollitique rule and governaille'.[28]

Such was the difficult paradox which characterised the minority. Bedford, Gloucester and the lords of the council both represented and served the infant sovereign. He ruled, but the lords executed his rule. They counselled him, but, equally, they, not he, were the recipients of this counsel. If this seems needlessly complicated, it is worth recalling that this was the only feasible solution to a grave situation. The only source of legitimate authority was the will of the king, rooted in his private character. This was absent in 1422. The lords could be guided by the dead king's testament, by the principles of inheritance and by the counsel of the realm in parliament, but they could only act in the context of a vigorous assertion of Henry VI's rule if they were to prevent division, the terror of the age and the enemy of monarchy.[29] Under these circumstances, it is not hard to see that the attribution of authority to the infant king was the obvious, indeed inescapable, solution.[30]

King and counsel, then, was the nature of the minority settlement, defended systematically by the lords against the assaults of Gloucester in 1422, 1425 and 1428.[31] The paramountcy of the king's authority was upheld on a daily basis by the council, given practical assistance by the lords in parliament, from whom it was a delegation.[32] Hobbesian oaths not to act upon grievances or maintain peacebreakers helped to realise royal authority and the common interest which it protected. Only after Beaufort and Gloucester took up arms in the autumn of 1425 did the conciliar principle waver. The lords appealed to the duke of Bedford, as they were to do again in 1433. The duke's authority was apparently intrinsic, rather than delegated, and certainly more considerable than any enjoyed by Gloucester.[34] Although it was parliament which brought Beaufort and Gloucester to terms, it was Bedford's superior status which made this possible: the forces of counsel gathered temporarily about him, rather than the king.[35] Even so, this was not a distinction which Bedford, or anyone else, would have cared to make. Before his departure, the duke was explicitly asked to recognise the king's authority and its 'execucion' by the council and he did so willingly.[36]

Among the concepts which bolstered the power of the governing council was the expectation that the king would authorise its deeds when he came of age. The lords declared this in 1427, but found that the principle could be used against them.[37] Gloucester replied, as he apparently had before, that if he had 'doon eny thing that touched the king his soverain lordes estat, therof wolde he not answere unto no persone on lyve, save oonly unto the King whan he come to his eage'.[38] If the king was not physically competent to rule in person, then his authority could not be presumed. In effect, the duke was repudiating the council's authority by asserting the inseparability of the king's private and public *personae*.[39] The exchange reveals the precarious nature of the council's position. It depended on just such a separation, which in turn depended on a widespread acceptance that Henry possessed no character. This was easy to contrive while the king was an infant, but it would become less so as time went by, even if it were true. When the king was old enough to license the deeds of the council, he would also be able to license the deeds of others. In 1427, the lords were able to compel the duke to agree to be 'ruled and governed' by them because, with no authority to be had from the king's private will, they represented the greatest accumulation of power and their claims of 'execucion' stuck. But the king was getting older all the time and the council's argument of 1428 – that it could not allow Gloucester greater powers because the king would shortly be able to exercise them himself – undermined, rather than strengthened, its position.[40]

In the event, the council sealed its fate with the coronations of 1429 and 1431, the necessary sequel to Joan of Arc's triumphant crowning of Charles VII at Rheims.[41] In November 1429, the protectorate was ended on the grounds that Henry had now personally undertaken the protection and defence of realm and Church.[42] In this way the private and public *personae* of the king were moved a step closer together, yet the council still claimed the 'execucion' of the latter in practice. Gloucester's response to these changes shows that he understood their implications. Having changed the council ordinances to fit the circumstances of a ruling king, he removed the three great officers within weeks of Henry's return early in 1432.[43] A few days later, a new steward and chamberlain of the household were appointed, the king's secretary was dismissed and his signet deposited in the treasury with Gloucester's own.[44] These measures directly reflected the increased significance of the king's person. Gloucester took no action until Henry had returned, implicitly invoking the direct authority of the Crown against the assumed authority of the councillors.[45] The fact that he found it necessary to make changes in the household is highly illuminating. It had become important to have influence about the king's person: sure evidence that the 1422 council's monopoly of the 'execucion' of royal authority was weakening.[46]

The move failed because Beaufort, the great defender of the 1422 settlement and intended victim of Gloucester's *coup*, was saved.[47] Even so, the duke continued to use Henry to subvert the power of the council. It is surely this which lay at the heart of the protest of the earl of Warwick, the king's tutor, in November 1432.[48] The earl claimed that his powers about the king's person no longer sufficed, but what he really needed was an assurance that they still applied.[49] It was no longer clear whether the king was a child or a ruler, or even whether this distinction was valid. It was this uncertainty, more than any insight into the king's 'personality', which was betrayed by Warwick's fears regarding the king's growing resistance to punishment. Behind his request that Gloucester and the councillors should help chastise the king, that they should tell Henry that they had all agreed that he should be punished for bad behaviour, and that they should persuade him from any indignation against the earl, lay an evident fear that the king's personal wishes might become the recognised basis of royal will in the near future. In Warwick's absence, the king had been taken aside from his studies and told of matters 'not behovefull'. The earl's response was to try to restrict private access to the king – exactly what the conciliar regime demanded. Gloucester retaliated by invoking his closeness in blood, and so retained the right to see the king alone.

The duke had changed the basis of his campaign against the minority council and, in doing so, inaugurated a new politics. He, not Beaufort or Suffolk, was the first to exploit the dependence of the monarchical system upon the private person of the king. If formal councils were, in some sense, representative, there was a better form of representation inherent in access to the royal person. The king's power of equity, guided by his prudence, meant that the individual might obtain absolution from the law, even as the substance of law and its general validity were preserved by the king's sense of justice. This balance of predictability and grace was what made monarchy so persistently vulnerable to criticism, and yet so fundamentally irresistible. It offered, or appeared to offer, government without strings: a force which bound everyone, but released you when you needed it. In 1432 the duke of Gloucester revived the monarchy and so ended the minority. From this time onwards, politics were shaped by the not unfamiliar preoccupations of achieving the right mixture of law and grace, of balancing the public and the private. These issues could be swiftly resolved by the right sort of royal character, but this was something which the ten-year-old king did not possess when his private person first became the focus of politics.

The power concentrated in the hands of Bedford in late 1433–4 must be seen as a check to the uneasy drift of attention towards the king's private person: a corporate act of self-denial. On the advice of some of the lords in parliament, the king asked Bedford to stay in England and he agreed, subject to various articles making his 'advis' a precondition for changes in the council, offices of state, household and duchy, for calling parliament and for appointments to vacant sees.[50] The dominant group on the council was reasserting a conciliar monopoly of 'execucion' via the paradoxical expedient of increasing the powers of the king's elder uncle.[51] No longer was it necessary to assert the king's rule against a bid for autonomy from the royal dukes. What had instead become important was to preserve the separation between the king's *persona publica,* which was in public hands, and his *persona privata* which still could not look after itself. The lords openly revived the council – described in 1433 as '*prius existente*'[52] – and focused it on a proven arbiter and defender of the peace.[53] In other words, the events of November 1433 involved a deliberate repudiation of the king's personal exercise of his powers in the interests of political harmony at the centre, the essence of the common good.[54] It is significant that, as in the 1437 appointment of the council – in many ways a parallel development – this repudiation came ostensibly from the king in person: the defenders of public 'execucion' of the king's authority needed a mascot too.[55]

Once Bedford had returned to France, his brother again attempted to transfer power to the king's private person. The resultant confrontation at Cirencester inevitably focused on the king's capacity to execute his authority himself.[56] The same lords who had wheeled the king on to arbitrate between his uncles earlier that year were now in the difficult position of telling the king to his face that his attempt to assume the execution of his authority himself was not in his own interests.[57] They were able to achieve this because the king was not quite thirteen and could still pass for a child and because he was supported only by Gloucester. In later years, it would not be this simple.

Before turning to the events of 1435–6 which brought about the first general recognition of the exercise of power on the part of the king himself, let us look at the methods by which the executive power of the council was communicated. There were two main methods by which the council authenticated its issues: one was the formula, in the minutes,

'*Concordatus* . . .' or '*Concessus est per dominos de consilio*';[58] the other was the practice of councillors signing the document concerned – be it a petition, a draft letter or whatever.[59] In the years that followed, these methods of authentication were to change, often illuminating the difficult question of who actually disposed of the king's authority during the long and uncertain process of transition. Where before there had been doubts, now there was action, but the fact that the first successful transfer of power to the king in person came in the summer of 1436 does not mean that the question of who ruled was either closed or opened then. Undoubtedly the main reason for the king's personal accession to some of his powers was the threat to his overseas possessions which resulted from the defection of Burgundy in September 1435.[60] A new air was apparent in the endorsements of council issues in the early part of 1436. Alongside those denoting conciliar authority, just described, the form '*Rex de avisamento consilii* . . .' began to appear.[61] It was still always accompanied by the signatures of councillors present, which showed where practical authority still lay, but the new form must have reflected a new involvement in the process of government on the part of the king.[62] A letter written in March to Cardinal Orsini in Henry's name made explicit reference to his long minority and went on to look forward to the day, now close at hand, when the king would be able to reward those who aided him.[63] Two months later, his tutor, the earl of Warwick, was discharged.[64]

Perhaps the most important factor influencing this process was the decision to place the king at the head of an army destined for Calais.[65] If the king was to lead an army into Flanders, it was plainly desirable for him to emerge from behind the skirts of the councillors. More specifically, since it was undoubtedly to encourage participation – actual or financial – in this crucial campaign that it was decided to send the king, an important part of Henry's leadership would be the power to reward: the royal prerogative of grace. In the event, leadership of the royal expedition passed to Gloucester, perhaps because Burgundy's early success made an experienced general desirable, but the king remained very much at the centre of events.[66] He was at Canterbury by 21 July in order to attend to the passage of those going overseas with Gloucester.[67] His government was at his side. Five days later, Henry VI made his first known grant by his own personal authority: a release to the duke of Gloucester, hero of the hour, of 5,000 marks which he borrowed in 1425.[68] It was authenticated by his signature alone: 'henry'. Two days later, the king made another grant by sign-manual – this time to Beaufort – and on 5 August, at Merton, he signed a memorandum recording two more grants made on his sole authority.[69] It has been suggested by Dr Harriss that Beaufort led the king into making grants on his sole authority behind the council's back, but since Gloucester and others were able to obtain them as well, perhaps they were an obvious, though unofficial, development of the leadership increasingly accorded to Henry at this time.[70] It seems very likely that the great council which met in late October 1436 resolved that the king was now fully competent to make grants, at least during pleasure, on his sole authority: a stream of signs manual followed.[71]

There is no reason to suppose that this train of events was set in motion by anyone other than the lords of the council. A military crisis on two fronts – Flanders and the Ile de France – stretched resources to the limit. To raise support for a second major expedition a new ingredient was needed: royal leadership, with its promise of decision, direction and reward. The magnitude of the problem in the Low Countries made it inadvisable to send the king in person, but his presence at Canterbury was a spur to noble participation in the venture. The attribution of powers of patronage to the king was the natural consequence of the lordship thrust upon him; indeed these powers had never been formally withheld. The only impediment to the king's personal exercise of them had been the general perception that he was a child. This perception had been under threat since 1432. Four years later, circumstances required an adult king and, with the nobility temporarily united at Henry's side, there was no danger in allowing it to collapse. The king ruled in fact as well as theory. If approaches to the royal grace remained tentative until the autumn, this was surely because some sort of formal recognition of the validity of royal grants was necessary for the security of the recipients.[72] This recognition could only be secured by some form of great council and such a council would not be called until the autumn. Once the authenticity of royal grants was accepted and publicised in this way, the floodgates opened. That Henry was scarcely in control of the situation is demonstrated by the enormous preponderance of grants to those who had easy access to the royal person: the staff of the household and the nobility of the court.[73]

The councillors kept control of matters of state. This was another indication that the initiative to delegate powers to the king lay wholly with them. If the king had been behind the developments of 1436, it would have been a small step from granting minor offices to granting major ones and becoming actively embroiled in the decision-making process.[74] Instead, government remained in the hands of the council for a considerable length of time. Power over grace they had never really claimed nor had: the 'execucion' of the king's authority which they had demanded had been concerned with rule. Although the king's personal exercise of his grace was a new development, it did not immediately affect the rule of the land: the relationship between counsel and government did not change. The councillors continued to meet and, in fact, govern.[75] During the great councils of autumn 1436 and spring 1437, they met 'in presencia Regis',[76] but, in practical terms, the power of 'execucion' remained with them.

It was this state of affairs that was regularised by the reappointment of the council in November 1437.[77] On the 12th, 'thei that wer of consailx before beth appointed to be of counsailx now', with the addition of the earl of Salisbury, the bishop of St David's, Sir John Stourton and the keeper of the great wardrobe.[78] Then, or the next day, the councillors were granted powers based on those of the council established in 1406.[79] To the king were 'reserved' the powers which he had been exercising since 1436: grants of pardon, collations of benefices, offices and 'other thynges that stond in grace'.[80] However, considering the great labours involved in the government of his realms, and because 'he shal not mowe attende to hem in his owne persone as oft as he wold', the king needed to be 'supported' by councillors.[81] Those appointed were to have the power to discuss and determine all matters 'as shal happen for to be moved among hem'. In great matters, the king's 'advis' was to be had. He would also decide matters where there was a major division among the councillors.[82]

It is difficult to see where these provisions differed substantially from what had gone before. The king had been using his powers of grace since 1436.[83] Great matters had been intermittently referred to him for 'advis' since his first appearances at the council in the autumn of 1435. His position as final resort in the event of divisions among his leading subjects had been made public in 1434. The ordinance of 1437 breathed life into the concept that it was by royal appointment that the council executed the king's authority, but it made no real change to that execution. The monopoly of counsel, which was the key to conciliar rule, was preserved through the appointment of named councillors. Far from being 'the king's declaration', this was a formal restatement by the councillors of the *status quo ante,* made necessary by the increasing attention accorded to the king in person.[84] Just as in 1422, or at any time since, the overriding concern of the lords was that the king should be adequately counselled. Provision for this was as necessary now that the king was almost an adult as it had been when he was a baby: in fact, more so. Now that application could be made directly to the king for grace, the possibility of drawing the king away from his council became more real than before. In an absolute sense, adult kings chose their own counsellors. However, successful royal government depended on their doing so with sensitivity and discretion, taking counsel which was, at least in terms of power, representative. In 1437, the dominant lords at court decided that Henry VI was not yet capable of this. This decision required general recognition and endorsement, since otherwise political approaches to Henry – in ever-increasing numbers – were inevitable and the locus of government would shift, perhaps irretrievably, to a king who was unable to conduct it.

The 1437 settlement obtained for about a year and a half. From early 1438, the forms of royal authentication became settled: a simple 'RH'; the signet;[85] chamberlain's endorsements.[86] Meanwhile, issues of the council continued to bear simple notes of who was present, or formulae of the 'Concessus est . . .' variety, supplemented by 'in presencia Regis' when the king was there.[87] These forms help to convey the impression of two parallel agencies of government: matters of grace settled by the king's private person, matters of state dealt with by his public person – still in the grip of the minority council, led by Cardinal Beaufort.[88] However, the separation was not complete: the council made formal reference to the king in person on several occasions.[89] It also, more importantly, retained an interest in the areas which had been 'reserved' to him in 1437, attempting twice in February 1438 to persuade the king to be less open-handed.[90] A more striking intervention was the unprecedented rôle accorded to the clerk of the council, Adam Moleyns, a few months later.[91] On 28 May 1438, he recorded that the king had made a grant at Windsor, in the presence of Lord Bardolf, John Hampton and Robert Felton.[92] Two of these men were not councillors and it is plain that this was not a council meeting. Since endorsement by Moleyns, using the 'Rex apud . . . concessit, praesentibus . . .' formula, rapidly became the most common way of authenticating royal acts of grace, the inescapable conclusion to be drawn is that the council still had little faith in the independence of the king's will. If it remained important for the council to know who was present when the king made grants, this surely indicates that the king's private person was held to be as susceptible to the control of others as his public person.[93]

Now that the king was no longer a child, this problem could be confronted in two ways: either the separation of powers – and personae – characteristic of 1437 could be rigorously maintained, or the process of representation in the king's public person which the council had provided for since 1422 would have to be extended to the king's private person. The former policy was artificial and unnatural and depended on almost total unity amongst the leading men. The latter more closely resembled the normal situation, but depended on the virtuous character of the king for success. But to state the problem in these terms grants the lords a greater opportunity for objectivity and abstraction than they actually possessed. For them, the fundamental question was: could they resist the operation of the king's adult, private will, even if they suspected that will to be operated by other people? The answer is that they could no longer do so corporately, while to do so individually courted treason. Corporate action on the 1436–7 model was undermined in three ways. For one thing, many of the councillors of 1437 enjoyed ready access to the king in person.[94] For such men, there must have been little incentive or point in reserving their counsel for meetings of the king's public body. And could they have been so pressingly aware of the king's inadequacy when it was their policies he was pleased to endorse? For another, the act of 1437 had anticipated and so licensed the king's later acquisition of full power. Normal royal leadership, the desired end, was typically exercised informally, away from any form of corporation. Finally, there were major divisions over the best way to preserve the king's French realm. Had the king been an infant, these divisions would have had to be settled by corporate action, but there was now an alternative: appeal to the Crown in person. As a result, the lords began, in 1439, to drift towards what was ostensibly normal royal government, but was really something rather different.

The first major change came in the spring of that year when '*Rex de avisamento consilii . . .*' became the normal form of endorsement for council issues.[95] When this formula first appeared, early in 1436, its force had been to show that the king was personally involved in the decisions made. In 1439, it emphasised the activity of the council instead: the king may or may not have been involved and was frequently elsewhere when issues were made.[96] In various other ways, the council's independence diminished: it met more rarely in the latter part of 1439 and after; it was not always noted who was present; no regular minutes were apparently kept; and finally, and most importantly, matters of state began to be decided at the king's side.[97] These developments were by no means clear or consistent: this was not a steady decline, but it remains true to say that by early 1441 conciliar government had been more or less abandoned.[98]

Uncertainty was the principal result of this situation: it was perhaps the hallmark of the 1440s. The lords hovered between the false security of a formal council and the traditional security of informal counsel to the king in person. The acceptance of the latter form, which was soon unavoidable, made the former ridiculous. At the same time, however, a formal council was the only means of ensuring adequate representation of views, except that it could not do so, on account of the natural drift towards the king's private person. It was perhaps with a view to resolving this paradox that, in the autumn of 1441, an attempt was apparently made to revive formalised counsel. A series of draft minutes extends from then till at least July 1443. This may simply reflect the haphazard survival of evidence,[99] although the fact that they were written by a new clerk, Henry Benet, suggests more than this.[100] New men, with influence in the household, seem to have been appointed to the council.[101] Membership was fixed,[102] and notes of attendance were carefully kept. Contact with the king was fairly frequent, but perfunctory: in practical terms, the councillors seem to have regained possession of the 'execucion' of the king's authority.[103] Finally, there is some evidence to suggest that the initiative to establish conciliar control over matters of grace, usually dated to 1444, may have arisen at about this time.[104]

Not long after the addition of new councillors in the autumn of 1443,[105] the revived council began to wither. Benet was gradually replaced by a new clerk, Thomas Kent, and the series of minutes came to an end.[106] The records of royal activity become proportionately greater, as the councillors once again – just as in 1439–41 – made the king the focus of government. It is difficult to find any specific reason for the abandonment of the council, just as it is difficult to explain why it was revived in the first place. Underlying these developments was surely a delicate equilibrium between the limited commitment of the lords to a governing council and the fear that, without such a contrivance, the king could not be adequately advised. Under these circumstances, the interpolation of a clerk who kept minutes and took note of attendance may have been decisive in maintaining the momentum of a thoroughly artificial enterprise. Later, perhaps, as in 1441, political divisions over dealings with France persuaded the court group, who necessarily dominated the council, to retreat to their power base about the king's private person and hope for the best. So far as we can judge, nothing like the revived council of 1441 was attempted again until the king's private person was removed from politics by his mental collapse in 1453–4.

Looking back over the reign in the light of this analysis, we can see that Henry VI's lack of character was confronted in two basic ways. One approach was to disregard the king's private person altogether, dissociating it utterly from politics and basing government on an artificial royal will which derived its efficacy wholly from the willing recognition of a majority of leading men. The other was to believe the king to possess an independence of spirit and accordingly to focus politics on his private person, on the logical assumption that he would provide for the normal operation of government, which was the function of his public person. The former policy prevailed until 1432 and remained influential, though fatally weakened, thereafter. The latter policy was first attempted in 1432 and enjoyed a lengthy, but uneasy, hegemony from 1444. The artificial royal will devised in 1422 proved difficult to defend against claims, advanced by those about the king, that Henry himself was physically competent to wield it. A partial solution was advanced in 1436–7, when the leading men of the moment – Gloucester, Beaufort, Suffolk – thought they had equal access to the king's person. Henry took up the administration of grace, but not of affairs of state. The artificiality of the distinction is reflected by the council's continued intervention in matters of grace – on the grounds of their fiscal and political implications – and the later drawing of the king into matters of state. This last was ultimately irresistible: partly because it was closer to the natural model of rule; partly because the simple response to the action of an authority tacitly admitted is to seek to influence that authority, not to deny it, and this in turn makes every person an individual and frustrates corporate resistance. Doubts remained, fed by those who could not get access to the king's person and recognised by those who could and who knew that free counsel, which alone bound the realm and made government possible, would not be preserved with Henry at the helm. Only the irreducible, untraceable force of the king's private *persona* could hold him in place above his people and guarantee their universal participation in his government. Henry had no such force, or not enough. From 1432, vacillation over this insoluble problem was the basis of politics, until Richard of York's attempt, in 1460, to solve it by replacing the useless king altogether. Henry VI's minority ended when he was ten: the rest of the reign was a prolonged and weary struggle, initiated and conducted by the nobility, to manage his personal rule. The monarchical state was hung with fictions: modest indeed was the independent power of its head, but majesty required some grain of resistance at the nub. To take counsel was finally not enough. Perhaps I can end by returning to Oz, where, amid the broken glass of another shattered polity, another ruler faced the music:

"'I think you are a very bad man," said Dorothy.

"Oh no, my dear; [said Oz] I'm really a very good man; but I'm a very bad Wizard, I must admit".'[107]

Notes

1   I am most grateful to my supervisor, Dr Christine Carpenter, for her criticisms of earlier drafts of this paper.

2   L. Frank Baum, *The Wizard of Oz,* Fontana edn, (London, 1969), pp. 113–14.

3   Chastellain's famous comment on the king in his forty-ninth year, quoted by B.P. Wolffe, *Henry VI* (London, 1981), p. 344.

4   This tradition owes much to John Blacman's famous biography, which was first printed as early as 1510: M.R. James, ed., *Henry the Sixth. A Reprint of John Blacman's Memoir* (Cambridge, 1919), p. vii. Its value as a source has been confirmed by R. Lovatt, in his essays 'John Blacman, Biographer of Henry VI', R.H.C Davis and J.M. Wallace-Hadrill, eds, *The Writing of History in the Middle Ages: Essays Presented to R.W. Southern* (Oxford, 1981), pp. 415–44 and 'A Collector of Apocryphal Anecdotes: John Blacman Revisited', A.J. Pollard, ed., *Property and Politics* (Gloucester, 1984), pp. 172–97. More or less the same view appears in W. Stubbs, *The Constitutional History of England in its Origins and Development,* 3 vols (Oxford, 1890), III, pp. 132–4; J.H. Ramsay, *Lancaster and York,* 2 vols (Oxford, 1892), II, pp. 1, 25, 49; K.B. McFarlane, 'The Lancastrian Kings', *Cambridge Medieval History* (Cambridge, 1936), VIII, pp. 398–9.

5   J. Nichols, *A Collection of All the Wills . . . of the Kings and Queens of England* (London, 1780), p. 293.

6   A parallel treatment is perhaps to be found in N. Fryde, *The Tyranny and Fall of Edward II, 1321–6* (Cambridge, 1979).

7   B.P. Wolffe, 'The Personal Rule of Henry VI', S.B. Chrimes, C.D. Ross and R.A. Griffiths, *Fifteenth Century England* (Manchester, 1972), pp. 29–48; pp. 30, 44.

8   For the classic treatment of this distinction, see E.H. Kantorowicz, *The King's Two Bodies* (Princeton, 1957), especially chs I, II and VII.

9   The importance of counsel was widely stressed. For examples, see J.G. Nichols, ed., *The Boke of Noblesse,* Roxburghe Club (London, 1860), p. 57; R.R. Steele, ed., *Three Prose*

Versions of the Secreta Secretorum, EETS, extra series, 74 (1898), p. 209; F.J. Furnivall, ed., *Hoccleve's Works*, III, EETS, extra series, 72 (1897), pp. 175–81 (stanzas 695–717), which also contains an account of the counsel process which implies this model of royal public action (see especially lines 4873–5).

10   For a discussion of the unique authority of royal will, see J.L. Gillespie, 'Sir John Fortescue's Concept of Royal Will', *Nottingham Medieval Studies*, 23 (1979), pp. 47–65 and J.W. McKenna, 'The Myth of Parliamentary Sovereignty in Late Medieval England', *EHR*, 94 (1979), pp. 481–506.

11   It is in this sense that the Bractonian '*Addicio de Cartis*' finds the king's curia to be superior to the king himself, because '*qui socium habet, habet magistrum*': B. Tierney, 'Bracton on Government', *Speculum*, 38 (1963), pp. 295–317; p. 314 and *passim*.

12   The point being that if it were not, there would be no guarantee that the king would not simply go back on his word. Obviously, the king's private will might be expected to change under the influence of counsel.

13   C. Morris, *The Discovery of the Individual* (New York, 1972), pp. 76, 78.

14   J.G.A. Pocock, *The Machiavellian Moment* (Princeton, 1975), pp. 25–8. Prudence was frequently depicted as the virtue which most inclined the bearer to the common good: ibid., p. 24; J.P. Genet, ed., *Four English Political Tracts of the Late Middle Ages*, Camden Society, 4th series, 18 (1977), p. 119.

15   See my article, 'The Counsels of King Henry VI, *c.* 1435–1445', *EHR*, 106 (1991), pp. 279–98.

16   It may be considered what part this had to play in the use of fixed councils made by the Tudors.

17   *CCR, 1422–9*, p. 46. The king received the seal from Langley and then, by Gloucester's hands, presented it to Simon Gaunstede. By July 1424, the king, now two and a half, was able not only to receive the seal, but also to give it to Beaufort 'by advice and assent of the council' (ibid., p. 154).

18   *RP*, IV, p. 261; C.L. Kingsford, *Chronicles of London* (Oxford, 1905), p. 285.

19   *POPC*, III, p. 233.

20   *RP*, IV, p. 174.

21   Ibid., p. 326.

22   Ibid., p. 175. The question of who appointed the counsellors is neatly avoided in the roll by the use of the passive form ('*furent . . . nomez . . .*'). In this way, the gap between the theory (the king appointed them) and the reality (the lords, or some of them, chose them) was bridged.

23   The men are described as being named '*Conseillers assistentz*'. The charge they undertook was '*tiele assistence a la governance*' as was depicted in the articles which followed (*RP*, IV, p. 176). The fact that their brief extended beyond counsel was thus noted.

24   This was implicit in the publications of lists of councillors' names in the 1422 and 1423–4 parliaments, in the ordinances which accompanied them and in the practice of swearing in new members (*RP*, IV, pp. 175–6, 201; *POPC*, III, 22–3, 147). The ordinances read at Reading in 1426 and agreed in the parliament of 1429–30 made it quite explicit that no one 'of what degree or condition that he be of' was to be present when the council debated, apart from councillors and people specially invited by authority of the council (*RP*, IV, p. 343; V, pp. 407–9).

25   *RP*, IV, pp. 176 (1422), 201 (1423–4), 343 (1429–30).

26   See the ordinances of 1422, 1423–4 and 1429–30: *RP*, IV, pp. 176, 201, 343. Special arrangements were devised to take account of the higher status of Bedford and Gloucester.

27   In the 1422 ordinances, it was declared that names of those present should be taken 'to see what, howe and by whom, eny thyng passeth': *RP*, IV, p. 176. See also ibid., pp. 201 (1423–4) and 343 (1429–30).

28 *POPC*, III, p. 233. The lords' awareness that this was a usurpation is shown by their determination to justify it: 'that the said lordes may for default of the said rule . . . falle in ayenst the king . . . the whiche God ne reson ne wolde' (ibid., p. 234).

29 The regency claims of the duke of Gloucester, based on a rather strong interpretation of Henry V's will and the duke's hereditary right, could not be admitted on exactly these grounds. Not only did Bedford have a superior hereditary interest, which he soon asserted, but any kind of regency threatened to accroach the royal power in a potentially damaging way. For Gloucester's claim, see S.B. Chrimes, 'The Pretensions of the Duke of Gloucester in 1422', *EHR*, 45 (1930), pp. 101–3 and, more generally, J.S. Roskell, 'The Office and Dignity of Protector of England, with Special Reference to its Origins', *EHR*, 48 (1953), pp. 193–233, *passim*. Bedford's claim, in his letter of October 1422, appears in R.R. Sharpe, *London and the Kingdom*, 3 vols (London, 1894–5), III, pp. 367–8. A general disapproval of regency is shown by the statement made by the lords in January 1427 (*POPC*, III, pp. 232–4), specifically the comment that no one single person may 'ascribe unto himself the said rule and governaille' (p. 234).

30 Such an attribution was, in any case, habitual. The writs for the 1422 parliament were sent out in the new king's name by a fairly representative group of peers meeting in the king's presence (*CCR, 1422–9*, p. 43). As the lords were to point out in 1428, Gloucester's acceptance of his summons sealed the fate of his proposed regency (*RP*, IV, p. 326). Once the king's authority was recognised in this way, the organisation of means of counsel around it was inevitable.

31 In January 1426, for example, Gloucester was told that the king, at barely four years of age, charged him upon his love to come and discuss his ill-will towards Beaufort and offered him a just and reasonable consideration of his heaviness. If the duke protested against the presence of Beaufort at such a meeting, he was to be told that it was not fitting for the king 'to weyve the presence of any of his lige men nor to lymitte him who shal be or not be in his presence' (*POPC*, III, pp. 183–4).

32 According to the statement of January 1427: ibid., p. 233. Note the rôle of parliament in the settlement of some of the more important noble disputes: e.g. Talbot-Ormond, 1423 (*RP*, IV, pp. 198–9), Fitzhugh-Scrope, 1424 (ibid., pp. 212–13), Warwick-Marshal, 1425 (ibid., pp. 262–75), Gloucester-Burgundy (ibid., p. 277), Gloucester-Beaufort, 1426 (ibid., pp. 296–9), Norfolk-Arundel, 1433 (ibid., pp. 441–3). Consider also its part in licensing the council to issue, from the royal estate, securities for loans (ibid., pp. 210–11 and *passim*).

33 For example, *RP*, V, pp. 406–7 (1425), 408 (1426); IV, pp. 344 (1429–30), 421–2 (1433).

34 Note, for example, the terms of Bedford's commission as parliamentary lieutenant, which was made '*de avisamento consilii*', but which does not otherwise mention the council. Most striking is the absence of the '*de assensu*' rubric, which so enraged Gloucester in 1422 (*RP*, IV, p. 296; *POPC*, III, pp. 6–7). The power of licensing councillors to reveal what had been discussed on the matter of the Gloucester-Beaufort dispute belonged to the king and Bedford alone (ibid.). The instructions to the envoys to Gloucester in January 1426 were given by the king by Bedford's sole advice (*POPC*, III, p. 181: note that this could be explained by a gap in the document, however).

35 Bedford was not among the arbitrators in the 1426 parliament: rather, he presided over their award. He had come, as Chichele told the king, to work for a solution to the great dispute and, when Beaufort made his declaration, it was Bedford who announced that the king had understood him and was willing to declare him true (*RP*, IV, p. 298). Note that Bedford's superiority did not derive from his position as heir presumptive alone: it also rested upon his personal conduct of the French war, his political skills and, no doubt, his long absences from England which saved him from getting involved in the feud between Beaufort and Gloucester (see Wolffe, *Henry VI*, chs 2–4, for details).

36   S.B. Chrimes, in his unpublished M.A. thesis, 'John, First Duke of Bedford: his Work
     and Policy in England, 1389–1435' (London, 1929), p. 145, suggests that Bedford
     engineereed this himself in order to ensure that Gloucester was similarly bound in his
     absence. However, since the lords made an unfavourable reference to 'diverse wordes
     and rehersailles that have be seid afore aswel by you my lord as by my lord of Glouc
     your brother, the whiche we passe overe at this tyme', it seems that the initiative came
     from them (POPC, III, p. 239).
37   Ibid., pp. 232, 238.
38   Ibid., p. 241.
39   In a sense, this had always been implicit in Gloucester's position: if the king could not
     rule in his private person in 1422, then he could not rule in his public person either. A
     regency was therefore necessary.
40   RP, IV, p. 327.
41   G.L. Harriss, Cardinal Beaufort: a Study of Lancastrian Ascendancy and Decline (Oxford,
     1988), p. 191; R.A. Griffiths, The Reign of King Henry VI (London, 1981), p. 189.
42   RP, IV, pp. 336–7. Note that similar policies were followed by the council with regard
     to Bedford's authority in France. The duke was to be made to accept a royal
     commission to govern the subject kingdom, though he was ultimately able to assert his
     independence: POPC, IV, p. 37; Harris, Beaufort, pp. 202, 208; B.J.H. Rowe, 'The
     Grand Conseil', F.M. Powicke, ed., Oxford Essays in Medieval History Presented to H.E.
     Salter (Oxford, 1934), pp. 207–34; pp. 227 and passim.
43   These almost unnoticed changes to the council ordinances, dated Canterbury,
     28 January 1432, before the king's return, were the necessary precursor to what has
     been called 'Gloucester's coup'. The changes specifically provided for matters associated
     with the offices of chancellor and treasurer to be dealt with in the presence of at least
     one of them and by a simple majority of one of the king's uncles (RP, V, p. 433). This
     made it easier to get rid of the current officers, but it also anticipated the demise of
     conciliar government, since a 'council' (really a bureau) composed chiefly of the three
     officers would not be unlike normal royal government. Gloucester was in possession of
     the seals during the night of 25–26 February (CCR, 1429–35, p. 181). Note that it was
     on the 25th that writs were sent out for the parliament which was to be the scene of the
     duke's attack on Beaufort (ibid., pp. 178–9).
44   POPC, IV, p. 110. Some use of the king's signet had been made during the coronation
     expedition, presumably without consultation (e.g. PRO, Warrants for the Great Seal,
     C81/1367/1, dated 18 Jan. 1432). It does not seem that Gloucester made use of the
     signet himself: perhaps his seizure of it was purely precautionary.
45   A point made by Dr Harriss, Beaufort, p. 217. Had Gloucester changed the officers
     before the king returned, he would not only have breached the ordinances of April
     1430 (POPC, IV, pp. 37–8). but would also, as in the 1420s, have appeared to be acting
     against both king and council, rather than with the king against some of the councillors
     – a subtle, but important, political difference. Nonetheless, a point often overlooked is
     that it was, in practical terms, control of the council which enabled Gloucester to
     reappoint the officers.
46   The steward and chamberlain were, of course, the key men in the household,
     controlling the 'household proper' and 'chamber' respectively: A.R. Myers, The
     Household of Edward IV (Manchester, 1959), pp. 104, 142.
47   Harriss, Beaufort, pp. 220–2 and also pp. 118, 132, 144.
48   POPC, IV, pp. 132–7.
49   The individual articles demonstrate this. For example, Warwick already possessed the
     power to remove anyone whom he suspected of 'mysgovernance', pending reference to
     Gloucester and the council (POPC, III, p. 300; cf. Wolffe, Henry VI, p. 13). If he was
     having to ask for it again in 1432, it was surely because it had been challenged,

presumably on the grounds that it was for the king to decide the company he kept: see n. 31 for an early enunciation of this principle, ironically by Gloucester's opponents.

50 *RP*, IV, p. 424. Note that it was only Bedford's 'advis' and not his assent which was to be sought. In practice, the two may have been much the same, but the former avoided raising the constitutional issue.

51 Roger Hunt, who, as Speaker, presented the commons' request, had been Speaker under Bedford in 1420 and had led the commons' deputation to him in 1426 (Harriss, *Beaufort*, p. 151; *RP*, IV, p. 296), but was also associated with Beaufort (*CPR, 1436–41*, p. 219; Harriss, *Beaufort*, pp. 151, 194, 203) and his ally Tiptoft (J.S. Roskell, *The Commons and their Speakers in English Parliaments, 1376–1523* (Manchester, 1965), p. 208). It seems fair, therefore, to see the defenders of the council behind these events.

52 *RP*, IV, p. 446.

53 PRO, T.R. Council and Privy Seal, E28/55/8 Nov. 1434 shows how the attribution of power to the absent Bedford, addressed somewhat extravagantly as 'Right hiegh and myghti Prince oure right worthi and ful noble lord', protected the power of the council ('Your servantes the consaillers of the kyng . . .'). The letter deals with the council's advice on the promotion of Thomas Brouns to Rochester. There was no question of the king being a part of the process.

54 An example of this repudiation is given by the councillors' refusal to endorse Bedford's petition for lands in Guienne on the grounds that they dared not give away the king's inheritance in his nonage: *POPC*, IV, pp. 246–7. This stands in contrast to the large number of grants of lands in France made at Dieppe in 1432 as the newly-crowned king returned to England: Rowe, 'Grand Conseil', p. 225.

55 The request of the commons that Bedford should stay was delivered to the king, who was present to receive it, although the ensuing request to the duke was made by the mouth of the chancellor (*RP*, IV, p. 423). Other public appearances by the king at this time included the arrival of an embassy from Basle in October 1433 (Harriss, *Beaufort*, p. 231) and the great council of spring 1434, when Henry ended the quarrel of his uncles – significantly '*de ipsius consilii voluntate et assensu*' – (*POPC*, IV, p. 211). The king's personal announcement two days later that Beaufort should be repaid the £6,000 lent in 1432 must be considered in the same light (ibid., pp. 236–9).

56 *POPC*, IV, pp. 287–8. Gloucester was absent from the meeting, between the king and nearly all the other councillors, which took place in the heart of his 'contree'. The inference that he had taken the king away from Westminster and the council in order to commence personal rule seems inescapable (see Harriss, *Beaufort*, p. 242).

57 Their unease is reflected in the elaborate form of authentication for their declaration: '*de advisamento, consensu et mandato de consilio . . . et per eundem dominum Regem gratanter admissus et acceptatus*' (*POPC*, IV, p. 288). These events cannot be used as evidence for Henry's character (cf. Wolffe, *Henry VI*, p. 65; Griffiths, *Reign*, p. 231), since it was essential for both Gloucester and the council to emphasise the king's authority, which was necessarily associated with his person once he was more than an infant.

58 This form appeared on instruments as well, e.g. PRO E28/55/11, 19 June 1434 ('*concordatus et concessus fuit*'), 6, 8 Nov. 1434 ('*lecta et concordata fuit*') etc.

59 E.g. PRO E28/56/26 Oct., 29 Nov., 4 Dec. 1435, 18, 20 Feb. 1436. This practice had been ordained by the council in November 1426 (*RP*, V, p. 408), but seems to have begun to be common earlier in that year: e.g. PRO C81/1544/62, 65.

60 The parliament of October 1435 was dominated by fear of imminent war. Burgundy's defection was mentioned in the chancellor's address, which centred on a request for funds for a campaign to defend the king's title (*RP*, IV, p. 481). The king is first known to have attended a meeting of the continual council at Kennington on 1 October 1435: PRO C81/1545/55. In the ensuing parliament, he may have made a personal request to the lords then present to show their goodwill for the rescue of Calais and presumably

the other areas in jeopardy (according to the articles of the 1436 loan commissioners printed by Nicolas: *POPC*, IV, pp. 352b–e, p. 352c).

61   For example, 20 and 22 February, 9 March, 27 April–1 May 1436 (PRO E28/56, 57). Patent letters issued under the minority often used this formula, but the endorsements on drafts always reflected the real authenticating authority. A good example of this process is *POPC*, IV, p. 130, where the minute records '*xx⁰ die Novembris anno xi⁰ apud Westmonasterium lectus et concordatus fuit sequens actum per dominos de consilio*', while the 'actum' following begins '*Memorandum quod x die huius instantis mensis Novembris, dominus Rex, de gracia sua speciali, de avisamento et assensu consilii . . .*'. However, when the '*Rex de avisamento . . .*' formula appears in the *endorsement* as well, actual royal involvement would appear to be indicated.

62   Whether the usage indicates that the king was actually present at these meetings, or was informed afterwards of what had been decided, or whether it was a change in administrative philosophy slowly gaining ground in the privy seal office cannot be known, but the significance is the same in each case: the king was now really, and not only formally, a participant in the 'execucion' of his own powers.

63   PRO E28/56/20 Mar. 1436. I am most grateful to Dr G.L. Harriss for his kind interest and advice regarding the authorship of this letter and to Dr A. Sapir Abulafia for helping me with the tortuous Latin.

64   PRO E28/57/19 May 1436.

65   This is revealed by a letter to the abbot of Bury St Edmunds, dated 16 June: BL Add. MS 14,848 (Register of Abbot Curteys of St Edmunds, 1429–46), fo. 191v. I am indebted to Dr Michael K. Jones for this reference.

66   Another letter, dated 30 June 1436 (ibid., fos 191v–192r) announced that Burgundy, having taken Oye, proposed to assault Calais on 2 July and that, as a result, the duke of Gloucester 'hath desired of us to goo thedir in persone'.

67   R.R. Sharpe, ed., *Calendar of Letter Books of the City of London, Letter Book I* (London, 1909), p. 206.

68   BL Cotton MS Vespasian F XIII, fo. 79. The grant was made 'of [the king's] grace especiale and by thadvis of his counseil', but the principal source of authority is plainly the sign-manual. The grant by sign-manual to Beaufort, mentioned below, was not, therefore, the first (cf. Griffiths, *Reign*, pp. 231–2 and Harriss, *Beaufort*, p. 275), though it was the first appearance under Henry VI of the phrase '*de mero motu nostro*'.

69   PRO E28/58/as dated; *POPC*, IV, p. 345 (grants to Thomas Lisieux and the dean of Gloucester's chapel, Richard Wyot).

70   Harriss, *Beaufort*, p. 275. The development was a natural one. On 30 June, for example, the councillors obtained the king's advice before granting a petition relating to the duchy of Lancaster (PRO E28/56/as dated). Meanwhile, four other grants made on 26 July were endorsed as being granted by the king, which suggests a development from the '*Rex de avisamento consilii . . .*' formula, since the absence of an advice clause implies independent royal authority (E28/57/as dated, one, a petition from the earl of Salisbury, being wrongly assigned to 26 June). Even so, they were also signed by the councillors present. The explanation is perhaps that no one was sure how far the king's powers might be held to extend, but everyone knew that conciliar authentication was universally accepted. Interestingly, the last warrant signed by councillors which I have been able to find before the 1450s was endorsed as granted by the king's command (E28/57/17 Aug. 1436), which suggests that, by then, the royal command had become a crucial component.

71   The great council met from late October to early November (PRO E28/58). On 1 November, the first of a long series of letters patent was issued upon a warrant under the sign manual (ibid./as dated). The conclusion that the great council formally approved the king's power in this area is further implied by the fact that no letters patent

based on royal grants were issued between 1 September and 31 October 1436 (evidence from *CPR, 1436–41*). A similar conclusion is reached by Dr Harriss, *Beaufort*, p. 275.

72   A similar process may be noted in the types of grants made (which reflected, of course, the types of grants asked for). With the exceptions of Beaufort's life grant of Canford and Poole, the permanent release to Gloucester of his debt of 1425 and grants of ecclesiastical positions, all the grants made up to the end of January 1437 were during pleasure only. In the following two months, there was only one life grant: the appointment of a serjeant-at-arms (*CPR, 1436–41*, p. 47). From the beginning of April 1437, life grants began to be made in much larger numbers. A great council seems to have met from 7 April at the latest to 17 April and it is possible that it made some sort of ruling on the validity of royal grants for life (*POPC*, V, pp. 6–15). It was during this council that Beaufort claimed that the king was now of such an age 'that he [Beaufort] may the better absente him' (ibid., p. 9).

73   Of 173 grants recorded in the patent rolls for the fifteenth year of the king's reign, 146 were to people in the court and household (see *CPR, 1436–41*, pp. 20–91). The proportion in November and December 1436 – seventeen out of nineteen – is even more dramatic. Henry's lack of discretion is suggested by the council's note to warn him to give offices to men appropriate to them (*POPC*, V, p. 3).

74   Cf. Richard II's struggle for influence by means of the court, described by M. McKisack, *The Fourteenth Century* (Oxford, 1959), ch. xiv.

75   The endorsement '*concessus fuit per dominos de consilio*' and its relatives remained common throughout the year: PRO E28/58/*passim*. Although the councillors no longer signed their issues, it was still always noted who was present. In the minutes printed in *POPC*, V, this note of attendance seems to have been the only form of authentication necessary. This implied a tacit recognition that the living authority of the king underlay council activity, but also that the council enjoyed a continuing monopoly of 'execucion' of that authority in government.

76   E28/58/21 Oct.–6 Nov. 1436 (the formula used is 'the king in his great council granted . . .' with slight variations). For the great council of April 1437, see *POPC*, V, pp. 6–16, where the '*in presencia regis*' formula is used. Following this assembly, king and council met together on a number of occasions, culminating in the arrangements of November 1437: e.g. 11 May (*POPC*, V, p. 25), 16 June (ibid., pp. 33–4), 8–12 July (ibid., pp. 42–5).

77   Note that another – and rather fuller – version of my views on the arrangements for counsel made between 1437 and *c.* 1445 appears in my article, cited in n. 15, above.

78   *POPC*, V, p. 71 (full list: *POPC*, VI, p. 313). In fact, the earl of Warwick, who had been a councillor, does not appear in the list, perhaps because he was in France. Lord Scrope is another omission, though he may have been expelled from the council when he lost the treasurership, since he does not appear in the list of councillors in the 1433 parliament (*RP*, IV, p. 446). The new councillors had close connections with the king; Salisbury was Beaufort's nephew; Rudbourne was one of Henry's chaplains and Stourton held a post in the household (Griffiths, *Reign*, p. 278).

79   This appears under the minutes of 13 November (*POPC*, VI, pp. 312–15), identified as a translation of the less contentious parts of the 1406 appointment with appropriate additions by B.P. Wolffe, 'Personal Rule', p. 45.

80   *POPC*, VI, p. 313.

81   Ibid., pp. 312–13. The use of the word 'supported' evokes the terminology of 1422, in which the councillors were appointed not only to counsel, but to assist: see n. 23, above.

82   *POPC*, VI, pp. 313–14.

83   The power of pardon may well have been new in autumn 1437.

84   Cf. Griffiths, *Reign*, pp. 275–6, 277. Professor Griffiths argues that since Henry was unusually young to be 'bringing his minority formally to an end' it is unlikely to have

been the council which 'proposed such a major political and constitutional change' (p. 276).

85   The sign-manual was standardised from February (PRO E28/59/12, 20, 26 Feb.); the signet had been in use since the beginning of 1437 (PRO, Warrants for the Privy Seal, PSO1/5), but the first reference to a secretary since 1432 is a patent of 13 February 1438 (*CPR, 1436–41*, p. 134). It seems to me doubtful whether earlier letters issued 'By the king' among E28/56–8 are actually signet letters (cf. Harriss, *Beaufort*, p. 274). They do not bear the phrase 'given under the signet' and one, E28/56/27 Jan. 1436, actually concludes 'yeven undre oure prive seale.'

86   The first endorsement by the chamberlain was 10 February 1438 (E28/59/as dated), though I have found one example of its use as early as 1424: BL Cotton MS Vespasian F XIII, fo. 84.

87   E.g. 16–29 November 1437 (*POPC*, V, pp. 73–82, PRO C81/1545/64, 66), 7, 14, 16 February 1438 (PRO E28/59/as dated), 5–7 May 1438 (*POPC*, V, pp. 93–5), 9, 13–14 May 1438 (*POPC*, V, pp. 95, 98–9). There is no evidence for the council's activities between May 1438 and February 1439. Note that '*in presencia Regis*' hardly suggests that the king was much more than a bystander at these meetings.

88   Beaufort seems to have enjoyed the sort of presidency over the council which the king might have been expected to wield: signalling his assent without having to attend in person (*POPC*, V, p. 27); conducting diplomatic and domestic affairs apparently by himself (ibid., pp. 81–2); holding several meetings at his church of St Mary Overeys (PRO E28/59/14 Feb., 24 & 28 Mar. 1438; E28/61/6, 10 & 12 June 1439); receiving a higher wage from December 1437 for his services '*in assistendo consiliis nostris*' (PRO PSO1/5/280, *CPR, 1436–41*, p. 126). Dr Harriss comments on the hegemony of the Beaufort group on the council and the cardinal's rôle as referee: *Beaufort*, pp. 293–4.

89   The payment of the wages of the duke of York in February 1438 is perhaps the best example. The council offered the duke certain jewels as pledges if it should please the king. Thirteen days later, the king, at Windsor, in the presence of Suffolk and the chancellor, commanded that this should be done (PRO E28/59/10 Feb. 1438).

90   *POPC*, V, pp. 88–90.

91   Only McFarlane, 'The Lancastrian Kings', p. 399 and A.L. Brown, *The Early History of the Clerkship of the Council* (Glasgow, 1969), pp. 32–3, have really attached much significance to this strange development.

92   PRO E28/59/as dated.

93   Moleyns himself was not always present when these grants were made (e.g. on 20 May 1439 he wrote 'and this saide to me the Chaunceler and the Tresorer of England': E28/60/as dated), but his endorsement remained important, which suggests that he had some sort of recognised duty to record the king's actions, rather than simply being coincidentally at hand.

94   For example, between 15 November 1437 and 31 August 1441, Gloucester was present about the king on 15 recorded occasions (against 23 in council), Bishop Stafford on 58 occasions (against 89), Suffolk on 40 (against 29) and Cromwell on 29 (against 77). Since the records for presence about the king are weighted towards occasions of patronage rather than government and there is thus no need to expect major lords to be there, it is striking how often the leading councillors were at Henry's side.

95   First used (since 1437) on 14 March 1439: E28/59/as dated. It is possible that this was simply Moleyns's own way of representing conciliar authority, since this was almost the first council issue endorsed by him (though C81/1545/69, dated 23 February 1438 and signed by Moleyns, simply records which councillors were present). Even so, in the light of other changes, such as the absence of regular council minutes between May 1438 and the autumn of 1441, the change is unlikely to have been without meaning.

96   E.g. E28/59/14, 16 Mar., 28, 29 Apr., 8, 11, 15, 16, 18 May, 6, 10 June 1439. Note

that this formula was used throughout the king's madness of 1453–4, during which time all those in the government, at least, knew that he was totally incapacitated. Obviously, communication with the king could be conducted through messengers, but it is hard to imagine this being done on every occasion. Moreover, unless the king was actually present, he could take no part in the discussions preceding a decision. This means either that his assent was anticipated, uninformed and largely formal or that those who counselled him when he actually gave it were not necessarily councillors, and were certainly not the council in a corporate sense.

97   Instances of government recorded as emanating from the king include business concerning the lands of the alien priories (from November 1440: PRO E28/65/4, 28; 67/61–2), new appointments at Calais (February 1441: E28/66/68), a letter telling Lord Grey of Codnor to keep the peace (March 1441: E28/67/20) and instructions for ambassadors going to Calais (*POPC*, V, pp. 139–40).

98   Though council meetings continued to take place: e.g. 9, 10, 13 February 1441 (E28/66/30, 31, *POPC*, V, p. 134), 11, 23 May 1441 (E28/68/10, 30).

99   The files of Exchequer T.R. (Council and Privy Seal) documents, which tend to reflect extra-conciliar activity are very thin for late 1442 and 1443 (E28/70 and 71).

100 The minutes have a distinctive style and we can link them to Henry Benet by his reference to 'me Benet' on 29 August 1442 (*POPC*, V, pp. 207–9). On 5 July 1443, a warrant to pay Benet for the attendance 'that he hath had aboute oure counsail by ii yere last passed' was issued (PRO, Exchequer Warrants for Issue, E404/59/265). Benet was never actually appointed clerk, and it seems possible that he simply replaced Moleyns in practice. See no. 106, below.

101 On 14 October 1441, Bishop Ayscough, Viscount Beaumont and Lord Sudeley first attended a council meeting: *POPC*, V, p. 153; cf. R. Virgoe 'The Composition of the King's Council, 1437–61', *BIHR*, 43 (1970), pp. 134–60; p. 157, n. 2, where no distinction has been made between formal and informal counsel. Lord Fanhope, who attended once before (on 8 May 1440: E28/63/69), began a regular attendance on the same day.

102 The word 'counsaillers' appears beneath some of the names of those present at a great council meeting on 28 November 1441, for example: *POPC*, V, p. 173.

103 For example, on 18 October 1442, the council, meeting at Eltham, with Henry presumably on the premises, decided to send messengers to Cardinal Beaufort to ask him 'the Kynges entent' (*POPC*, V, pp. 220–1; Wolffe, *Henry VI*, p. 363). In March 1443, Stafford and Moleyns 'commanded for the K' that certain letters should not be made (*POPC*, V, p. 250) and in April, a petition for grace was passed in Suffolk's inn by the earl and the same two men (ibid., p. 259). There is plenty of other evidence to show that the king's part was often assumed, played by others or overridden.

104 A rather inconclusive discussion of the dating of this document appears in my article, cited in n. 15, above.

105 Lord Dudley is known to have been sworn to the council in November 1443: PRO E404/61/114. It is possible that Bishops Brouns and Lowe and the marquis of Dorset joined at about the same time. Dorset first attended on 14 November, Lowe on 13 January and Brouns on 31 January (E28/71/27, 29, 53); cf. Virgoe, 'King's Council', p. 157, n. 5.

106 Kent was appointed clerk on 22 November 1443 (E28/72/88: patents dated 15 March 1444 – *CPR*, *1441–6*, p. 235). By March 1444, he was signing the great majority of warrants, both conciliar and royal. Benet's last minutes (until 1446) were those of 4 March 1444 (*POPC*, VI, p. 28). Interestingly enough, Moleyns signed the minutes of 14 and 28 November 1443 (E28/71/27, 28), about the time that Kent became clerk. Two months later, Moleyns had ousted Beckington from the privy seal. It is intriguing to speculate whether Moleyns' fortunes had a decisive role in determining the rise and fall of formal counsel.

107 Baum, *Wizard of Oz*, p. 117.

8

Aliens, Agriculturalists and Entrepreneurs: Identifying the Market-Makers in a Norfolk Port from the Water-Bailiffs' Accounts, 1400–60

Terence R. Adams

In the study of medieval English towns, the county towns, market towns and villages are all placed firmly within a rural context, their economic activity being related to the agricultural or semi-industrial hinterland which they serviced and which justified their existence. With port towns, however, the emphasis has been traditionally placed on the nature of their international trade, and their rôle as local markets is often ignored. It is this approach that accentuates the apparent differences between ports and country towns, obscuring the fact that international trade had its roots in the economic life of the countryside and discounting the community of interest that linked the English rural producer and consumer to his alien customers and suppliers. In reality, a port – as with any other kind of town – succeeds by being the marketplace for its hinterland, and the only real differences between it and an inland town are that some of its frequenters come greater distances to market, that these men come by sea, and that some of them are aliens.

The water-bailiffs' accounts of Great Yarmouth provide some evidence for the operation of just such a market-town-on-sea.[1] As they list the place of origin of the rural producers and consumers and the English and alien importers and exporters who came to the town to trade, and the goods they exchanged, some of the market-makers can be identified and their use of the town as a market explained, and the international trade of the port can be placed in its rural and domestic context.

Great Yarmouth occupied a strategic position in the coasting trade of the North Sea (see Map I). It is situated at the mouth of the three river systems that drain the fertile arable and pastureland districts of its hinterland; a region of East Anglia where good waterborne communications kept transport costs, even of bulky products, low.[2] The water-bailiffs ('ballii aque') were responsible for collecting the tolls and charges levied on ships using the port. Their accounts cover not only the import and export of goods by sea but also the waterborne trade with the interior. As road travel in any direction was more difficult and slower than

Map I

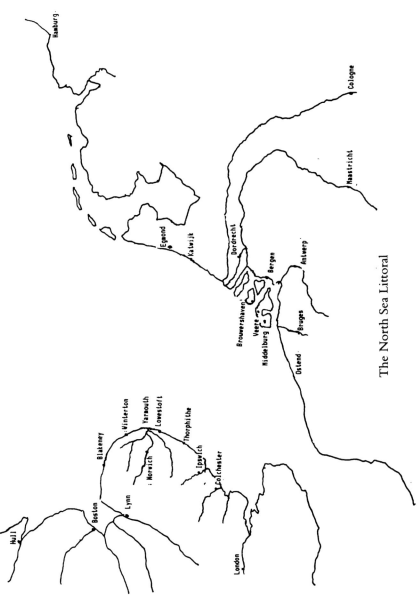

The North Sea Littoral

travel by water – Great Yarmouth was then almost entirely hemmed in by marshes[3] – these accounts record the majority of the trade on which tolls were charged. They do not accurately represent the real level of activity, though, as the burgesses of Yarmouth and Norwich, who did not pay toll, must have dominated the carrying trade and been heavily involved in import and export as well. Both they, and merchants from places such as London and Newcastle which had charters antedating Great Yarmouth's (1209) and gave full exemption from local tolls, only appear in the records when paying cranage and tronage or murage, or when being charged measurage on grain or on coal.[4] Some Norwich merchants operated their own ships, while others hired space in vessels from Great Yarmouth or from other English and alien ports. Great Yarmouth, however, was the place to which aliens came to trade – there is little evidence in these accounts of aliens penetrating upriver – and it was that town to which merchants and mongers of Norwich brought goods for sale to aliens, and from which they bought imported products.

When the places of origin of the goods brought into Great Yarmouth from the hinterland are plotted on a map of East Anglia (see Map II) it becomes obvious that both river and coastal craft were being used as a means of transporting the surplus agricultural produce of the region into the town for sale. The fact that some products and places of origin appear infrequently in the accounts is of less importance than that they appear at all, for the surplus production of most small landowners or tenant farmers would normally have been purchased direct from the producer by mongers and merchants of Norwich or Great Yarmouth, who would have transported it to the town in their own or in hired lighters. There are hundreds of entries in these accounts for petty entrepreneurs from Norwich or Great Yarmouth, often described as lighterman or waterman, who deal in 10–15 qtrs of grain at a time, paying customs dues because they were not citizens of either town and were not otherwise exempt: unfortunately, the records do not show where in the hinterland these cargoes had originated, only where the shipper was from.

Norwich merchants often dealt in very large quantities of grain and exported it both in English and in alien ships. For example, in 1404–5 they brought 568 qtrs of mixed grains through the town, including 120 qtrs described as 'ex' (exeunt) versus Colchestre' and 30 qtrs 'ex' le 12 die Novembris in navi Brix Outresson de Campver' (Holland), and in 1446–7, 810 qtrs of which 100 qtrs of barley was exported by Richard Aylfeld in a ship of Dordrecht owned by Will Elyson, who also paid toll on 50 qtrs on his own account. Men from Norwich also brought in thrums – an entry in the roll for 1431–2 records 2 hampers of thrums being exported in Henry Gronyng's ship (an alien) on behalf of Jacob Petrisson 'ducheman' of Norwich; and hides – three non-burgess merchants of Norwich, John

Map II

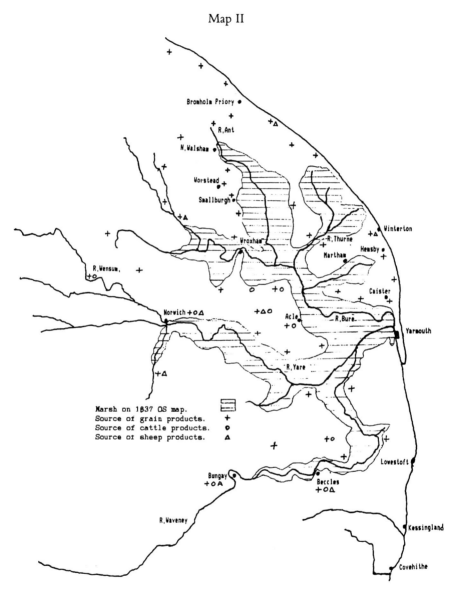

Sources of Agricultural Products 1399–1460

Reyner, Richard Vigerous and Will Lardyner paid customs dues on entering the town with 13 packs and 1 parcel of 'calvyskynnes' containing 300 skins and also 2 packs of woollen cloth 'pan en grayne'. In 1440–1 a merchant, Herman Haberdasser (described as 'alien' up to 1445 and 'of Norwich' thereafter), settled in Norwich, and as he was not a freeman we can see his activities in detail. He brought into Great Yarmouth and then exported 2 parcels of 'wombis', 100 'pell agnell' and 4 dakers of calfskins 'in navi Coppe Cole' (of Antwerp); later in the year he exported more woolfells and calfskins, 1 wey of cheese and 1 sack of thrums. In 1445–6 he paid on 1 fardel containing 30 calfskins and 200 lambskins, 3 pokes containing 13 'pac' of thrums, 2 dakers of calfskins, 1 wey of cheese, 2 barrels of tallow and 1 roll of frieze entering the town, and for anchorage; later in the year he exported 2 fardels of rabbitskins and 8cwt of tallow in the ship of Paul Gilison 'alien'.

To select a few examples from the villages on the rivers Yare and Wensum: Robert Colkirk of Hempnall paid dues on 40 qtrs of malt and 40 combs of barley in 1439–40, and on a further 24 qtrs of barley later in the year: he was active throughout the 1440s. John Kidman of Blofield paid custom in 1427–8 on 60 qtrs of barley, though he claimed that he was a tenant of the bishop of Norwich and should be free from toll. Men of Bawdeswell and Witchingham were charged on imports of malt (26 qtrs), wheat (20 qtrs) meat (14 barrels) and tallow (1 wey). From Ringland came hides (1445–6) and 'hayre' (1446–7). Villages on the Bure were the sources of up to 100 qtrs of grain at a time, and also contributed hides, wool-fells and malt. Some of these rural dealers also exported directly: Robert de Martham exported and paid the customs dues on 40 qtrs of barley in the ship of Martin Matheson of Brill (Holland) in 1404–5, and in 1440–1 John Skitting of Potter Heigham had 27 qtrs in a ship of Nicholas Crost of Dunwich, who paid the toll on his behalf.

What can be seen of the trade along the Waveney valley was almost entirely in the hands of the men of the two sizeable market towns of Beccles and Bungay, and the products of this area were mainly agricultural. For example: in 1427–8 Will Sadeler of Beccles brought in to Great Yarmouth 8 barrels of meat, 8 qtrs of oats, 1 wey of cheese, 200 shearlings and 6 dakers of calfskins, and on a second visit 60 qtrs of barley; John Rede, described as 'indigena et shipmaster de Becclys' imported and paid on 20 qtrs of oats, 1 wey of cheese, 1 hamper containing 80 stirrup leathers ('strrevelyng'), 2 barrels of thrums, 100 calfskins, [?1c pillettys] and 500 horns, all 'in navi suo' at a total cost in dues of £2. Other products of this area were malt, rabbitskins, tallow and butter. The victualling of Great Yarmouth would have absorbed much of the production of this region, but there is also some evidence for men of the Waveney valley exporting their surplus direct to the Low Countries or to elsewhere in England. For example, John Rede exported the items listed above within the week, paying a further £2 in export dues; Will Butt exported 50 qtrs of oats and 3 dakers of calfskins '*in navi Petri Best* (of Antwerp) *exeunt primo die June*' [*sic*], and also 5 qtrs of wheat and 5 qtrs of malt '*in navi Peto Wouterson, alien*'; and John Haldeyn exported 2 weys and 4 stones of tallow '*in navi J. Carvyng, alien, exeunt 21 Decembris*' (also in 1428).

The small ports to the north of the town and the villages near them were also suppliers of agricultural products. Winterton was heavily involved in the grain trade.[5] A typical year was 1440–1, when 236 qtrs of malt and barley were traded, including 180 qtrs by John Wasy who had been active in previous years but against whose name is the note '*quare burgensis est*' and who paid no toll.[6] In 1452–3 Thomas Iryng paid 25s. 0d. on 600 qtrs and in the following year he dealt in imports and exports of cloth, wood, 'ores' and grain in quantities that contributed over 35s. 0d. in income to the town. In 1454–5, in addition to bringing in four loads totalling 132 qtrs he had 50 qtrs of malt in J. Knyst of Colchester's ship and 80 qtrs of malt in John Rugge of Great Yarmouth's ship; presumably he was paying them to carry it southwards.[7] Other Winterton shippers, charged on smaller quantities of grain, usually paid anchorage at the lowest rate. It seems likely that coastal vessels were bringing in small quantities of grain which were made up into larger loads for export.

Even though the majority of the waterborne traffic into Great Yarmouth from the hinterland must have been in the hands of Norwich or Yarmouth burgesses and was therefore largely invisible, there are sufficient entries recording the input of products from small inland and coastal places to demonstrate the wide area from which the town drew its supplies. It is clear that its hinterland was a source of agricultural production for surplus and for export which was brought to the town for sale and then shipped out through the port. This implies that the agriculturalists in the rural areas looked beyond the town for their ultimate market, although few of the rural producers were dealing with alien shippers directly or were exporting their own produce from Great Yarmouth themselves.[8]

Having shown that Great Yarmouth was a market-place for the produce of the rural hinterland, it is necessary to show who purchased and transported it away. Shippers from the small ports of Suffolk and Essex carried grains southwards, usually taking 15–20 qtrs per trip, with some animal products. Merchants from places such as Colchester and Ipswich took larger quantities of malt and barley on a regular basis, both for brewing and for the victualling of London, whose merchants were also very active in the export of grain,[9] but for whom these accounts are rather unrevealing, their free status usually enabling them to avoid the attentions of the water-bailiffs. Grain also went north[11] to Newcastle and Scotland in exchange for coal and salt, but the bulk of the payments for customs dues were made by aliens, who had no exemption from tolls and were heavily involved in exporting in their own right, not just acting as carriers for English merchants. When aliens, many of whom have a territorial designation as well as a surname, and are often also described as 'alien' or 'Ducheman', were trading in the town as principals, and thus paying local customs dues on their purchases, their activities are shown in the accounts, and with the exception of re-exported coal and lead the items they bought are the products of the agricultural hinterland.

Most of these aliens came from the towns of the Low Countries, especially from Holland and Zeeland. A typical shipper and merchant from the estuary of the Scheldt was Herman Hermansson of Middelburg, active from 1447. In 1449–50 he exported 7 fardels and 4 packs of cloth, 10 qtrs of wheat, 300 sherling and mortkin [sic] and 6 weys of 'talwe'. He shipped out 170 qtrs of barley, a large quantity of calf- and rabbitskins, 3 weys of 'talwe' and some meat in 1451–2; and in 1453–4 he exported 10 dakers of leather, 'conyskynnes', candles and thrums; the next year 60 qtrs of oats, 60 qtrs of barley, 80 qtrs of wheat, 3 barrels of candles, 2 weys of tallow and 3 barrels of butter in at least two different ships. For part of the year he lived in Yarmouth, as in the account for 1451–2 there is a payment for 'firma domus'. In 1457–8 his exports were 320 qtrs of malt, 120 qtrs of barley and some cloth, and he had a share in a further 248 qtrs of malt and 24 qtrs of barley exported by two other Dutchmen in their own ships. In 1459–60 he exported tallow, 7 rolls of rabbitskins, 1 pack of coverlets and 280 qtrs of oats.

Men of Westenschouwen and the ports on the island of Walcheren took out meat (including live pigs!), cheese, tallow and candles; oats, peas, wheat, malt and barley; rabbit- and calfskins, thrums and woollen cloth. In 1427–8 a Petrus Jacobsen 'de Westonskowe' exported three separate loads of grain: on 4 October 1427 12 qtrs of wheat and 40 qtrs of oats in the ship of Cornelius Wale; on 5 December 1427 in his own ship 16 qtrs of wheat, 20 qtrs of oats and 1 wey of tallow; and on 1 June 1428, again in his own ship, 80 qtrs of barley and oats; he also carried 180 qtrs of wheat for Robert Wilby and 12 qtrs for Thomas Cadewyn of Thorphithe (Suffolk).[11] Coppe or Copyn Cole of Antwerp was a shipmaster who traded in cloth, meat and Newcastle coal in 1438–9 and 1439–40, and also worked as a carrier for Herman Haberdasser (q.v.): in 1445–6 he carried 50 qtrs of barley for Bone (Bowen) Janson and 260 qtrs of barley for a number of other aliens. In 1447–8 Petrus Williamson of Zerickseepaid dues on 50 qtrs of barley, 7 qtrs of oats, 2 fardels of shearling fells and 2 weys of tallow; all described as 'owtwarde'. Brouwershaven merchants exported cloth and grain with quantities of shearlings, candles, cheese, rabbit- and calfskins: in 1440–1 quantities of 'wombis', meat, peas, cheese and barley were handled and in 1446–7 the massive total of 1280 qtrs of barley and oats was bought at Great Yarmouth. In 1407–8 Heyne Martisson, 'magister navis vocat' le

Longlyse de Dordrac' (Dordrecht) imported wine and exported wheat, calfskins and a feather bed, paying toll of 16*s.* 4½*d.*, and during the 1440s and 1450s average quantities of grain totalling 200 qtrs a year were exported by men of Dordrecht.

Noord Holland had few big towns, and although the records are of the carriage of grain, skins and cloth, the quantities are usually small. From Zandvoort came both fishermen and merchants, who exported pike, pigs and meat (*'caro bovum'*) as well as grain. In 1437–8 Herman Blocke, who in 1434 paid 18*d.* for *'Magnum Theolonium'*[12] and therefore must then have been merely a fisherman, exported two loads of grain, one of 30 qtrs and one of 80 qtrs, and in 1446–7 he exported 40 qtrs of barley and 40 qtrs of oats (he had imported oil, fish and iron).

These examples show what aliens were buying and exporting, and one point is clear: alien merchants know that at Great Yarmouth supplies were available of agricultural commodities drawn from an area that was geared to the production of a surplus for sale. Grain was the most important element in the export trade, though cloth and woolfells occurred regularly enough to show that not all the business was in the hands of the burgesses. There is evidence for the purchase of grain as late as mid-summer, implying that it was stored in bulk in the town from one harvest to the next (100 qtrs of grain is equivalent to 1,000 cu ft and weighs approximately 20–25 tons), in addition to substantial quantities of cloth and skins, and barrels of meat, tallow, candles and butter. The Patent Rolls contain numerous entries for dealings by English merchants in enormous quantities of grain obtained at Great Yarmouth,[13] and the water-bailiffs' accounts prove the existence of an export trade to the Low Countries by aliens in addition to this, though not on quite the same scale. The consistency with which grain was exported shows that to some extent the towns of the Low Countries relied on the production of the hinterland of Great Yarmouth to make up any shortfalls in the output of their own countryside.[14]

The substantial quantities of calfskins, tallow, candles, meat and butter recorded in the accounts suggest that at various places in the hinterland there must have been a group of semi-industries based on the slaughtering of cattle to supply both local demand and the export trade. Curing hides, rendering tallow and making candles, packing meat in barrels with brine or salt – and the cooperage that this required – were clearly on a larger scale than the local market required, and this argues that some agriculturalists had an awareness of the existence of a market overseas and a determination to exploit it. It is a reasonable assumption that some country producers were increasing their herds in order to be able to supply this market of opportunity.

The evidence of these water-bailiffs' accounts is that the hinterland of Great Yarmouth was an area where agriculturalists were heavily involved in production for export to the towns of the Low Countries and elsewhere, and that Yarmouth was the point of exchange – the place where visiting merchants expected to obtain victuals and other materials of animal origin in quantity. However, the trade was not all one way: these accounts also show that the inhabitants of the agricultural districts could, and did, purchase the imported products that were essential to their own economic activities at Great Yarmouth or in places served by the river distribution system centred on Great Yarmouth; thus proving that the water-bailiffs' accounts show a true regional market in operation.

The commodities imported through Great Yarmouth fell into two main categories – the indigenous manufactures of the towns and villages of the Low Countries and their own agricultural hinterland, and the re-export or merchant trade. By origin most of the salt and wine came from the south via the operations of the Bay fleet; while the wax, pitch, tar, ashes, cinders, timber and bowstaves were from the Baltic. Relationships between England and the Hanse were strained throughout the first half of the fifteenth century[15] and although these accounts contain entries for shippers described as 'de Hanse', 'de Dansk' and 'de Almayne' they were never popular either in England or in Great Yarmouth itself. Instead, the ships of Dordrecht and Middelburg were visiting the town with a waterborne chapman's pack of goods, and the break-bulk operation must have already taken place in the Low Countries.

The imported goods were all for use – there are no 'apes, japes'[16] in these accounts! Much of the salt would be absorbed by the herring fishery[17] but the trade in rabbit- and calfskins, leather and woolfells would require supplies of salt to be redistributed inland to the producing and processing areas for curing the skins. The production of meat, cheese and butter stored in barrels also consumed large quantities of salt. The pitch and tar from the Baltic must have been mainly for shipbuilding and ship-repairing but the woolgrowers would also have used some of it for marking and doctoring their sheep after shearing. Ashes would have been used for making lye soap in quantity, less for domestic than for commercial use in the wool and cloth industries, although, as we have seen, much soap was also imported. The other Baltic products, the timber, bowstaves and wax, were of obvious utility, and there was even a trade in ships: aliens frequently sold their ships in Yarmouth and presumably the sailors returned home with one of their compatriots.

Certain products imported into Great Yarmouth were the output of manufacturing processes or semi-industrialised agriculture in and around the towns of the Low Countries. In the latter category were hops, dyes and teasels,[18] the last two of which are essential raw materials for the cloth industry, and there is evidence in these accounts for the redistribution of these items into the cloth-producing areas by small-scale dealers, although

Norwich merchants imported in bulk and dominated the wholesaling and retailing of dyes. Aliens brewed beer in the town under licence from at least as early as 1431–2[19] but although a large quantity of hops was imported in most years thereafter, there are only a few entries in the accounts for hops being distributed inland. Presumably this was because beer was originally introduced by and for alien fishermen visiting the Herring Fair; the townsmen may soon have acquired the taste for bitter beer from the visitors, but this fashion would be slow to spread into the rural districts. There were also substantial imports of wine, both by aliens and by Englishmen.

The manufactured products that appear in the accounts are soap, nails and iron, tiles, glass, millstones and quernstones. The soap was a component in a reciprocal trade: tallow was produced in the hinterland and brought to Yarmouth where aliens bought it and shipped it abroad. It was then made into soap and re-exported to Great Yarmouth for redistribution, and from the quantity imported and the regularity with which it appears it is likely to have been coarse soap for use in the wool and cloth industries; Spanish soap is specified as such. There are many entries for iron, iron nails and osmund. There are no records of the import of iron and iron products from English sources, and as with tiles and bricks, the Low Countries were the main supplier until well after this period.[20] Most of the millstones were 'cullens' from Cologne, although there were some from the Peak District and from Normandy, and some building stone was imported, both from Germany and from various sites in England, notably Corfe. Glass was also imported in some quantity – never less than a wey at a time. Water transport would minimise breakage, just as in the case of building stone, millstones and quernstones it made for cheap carriage relative to the weight involved.[21]

Sluys, Westenschouwen and Antwerp were sources of salt (marked '*intrante*') and madder, oil, osmund, 'waynescot', hops, nails, soap, wine and 'garlek'. In 1423–4 John Clayson of Sluys imported 2 pokes of madder, 4 weys of salt and 1 barrel of tar, and exported grain and animal products. In 1447–8 John Je of Middelburg imported a total of 20 weys of salt, 1 barrel of oil and 1 poke of madder '*intrando*', buying grain in exchange, and in the following year the entry in his name reads: '*custuma 2 pipe vini intrando et exeunto et eodem pro 2 bal madder, 1 barrel sope et 1 barrel oler*'. This was probably an occasion when an alien both imported and carried the goods inland himself. In the same year Jan Grenewold paid 10*d.* as dues on the import of 40 barrels of onions. Court de Middelburg paid cranage on '*unus petrus voc' marbill*' in 1454–5, and Littel Herman de Middelburg [*sic*] paid customs dues on 5 sacks of hops, 2 pokes of madder, 100 bowstaves, 1cwt of alum and 6 barrels of soap. A second trip brought in half a last of soap, 4 barrels of saltfish (cod), 100 bowstaves and 3 millstones, and a third trip 2 millstones, 200 'borde', and 1 last of tar. In 1455–6 Herman Hermanson (alias 'Littel Herman'?) imported 1 last of osmund, 9 millscots, 6 barrels of pitch, 150 wainscots, 4 barrels of soap and 160 'clapholdr', and used Shipper Engler de Burgh to carry 1 last of osmund, half a last of soap, 100 'borde', 1 last of tar and half a last of pitch; Shipper Cole to carry 20 '*sort frutus*', half a last of soap and 1 last of osmund; and Shipper Thomas to import 1 last of tar, half a last of soap, 1 last of osmund and 1 ton of vinegar. In 1459–60 Herman brought in 2 sacks of hops, 100 'borde', 400 pavingstones, 2 tuns of wine, 6 sacks of hops, 3 bales of madder, 1,000 'borde', and 1,000 wainscots. Herman was obviously a merchant with interests in the Baltic trade, re-exporting from the Hanse depot at Middelburg into Great Yarmouth. But he was also dealing in the products of the Low Countries – madder, hops and soap; and the building stone and millstones probably came from as far inland as Maastricht and Mayen-neidermendig, travelling by water from the quarries to Middelburg for export.

The minor ports in this region dealt in salt, madder, teasels (60 'sheve'), tar and pitch, 'scaffold' and 'borde', saltfish, onions, soap, alum, nails (*clavi*) and sulphur (16 '*pec fumitus*'). In 1453–4 Kempe de Zericksee – shown later in the roll as '*magister unae navis voc' Cogshippe*' – paid duty on 4 barrels of tar, 4 barrels of pitch, 2 barrels of soap, 1½cwt of salt '*et divers' mercandisorum*'; and Cornelius Ison of Brouwershaven paid custom on unspecified goods '*intrando*' of 6s. 2d. and the same sum '*exeundo*', and was also charged for tronage on 3,600 nails and 3 bales of madder, and for cranage on 15 tuns of wine '*intrando et exeundo*'.[22] The next winter seems to have been a stormy one, and unfortunate for the men of Brouwershaven. Wytte Clayson paid 13s. 4d. for '*grondage unae navis et custuma bonum salvat' in eodem navi*'; Coppe Martisson paid the same for his ship and goods; and Coppe Lovesson, who had already sold 6 weys of salt and exported herring and 60 qtrs of grain, made the best of a bad job by '*vendit unius battel perdu per wrecc' maritimum soluend' in festo Pasche proxime futur' pro obligat' 23s. 4d.*'

Men of Dordrecht imported wine, soap, tiles, teasels and millstones. In 1448–9 Will Dordrecht imported 22 'anic' of wine, '2ml pathyngtyle', 2 barrels of soap, 2 weys of glass and 2 lasts of quernstones – total customs dues were 9s. 4d.; and sold the ship. In another of his ships he carried 12 weys of salt, 2 barrels of soap, 2 barrels of osmund, '1ml tyle pathyng', 1 wey of glass and 2 pokes of hops, and exported 120 qtrs of oats and 2 fardels of shearling fells. He also paid tronage on 7cwt of iron and a further 3 pokes of hops of which there is no record in the customs rolls.[23] In the following year, described as '*Will Elyson alias de Dordrecht*', he imported 5 tuns of soap and 6 millstones '*intrando*' and 15 'anic Rhenysh wyne', 1 last of quernstones, half a last of tar, 4 barrels of osmund, 4 barrels of salmon, 1 ml of nails and 100 wainscots and also paid tronage on 3 sacks of hops, 15cwt of nails, 7 millstones and 3 vats of Rhenish not otherwise accounted for; a joint cranage account with Will Taverner of Norwich for 13*d*. indicates who his customer was.

The men of the northern group of towns imported madder, oil, salt and soap, but quantities were small. Germans, whether described as '*de Hanse*' or not, dealt in wine and Baltic products, especially woad and wax, and sometimes sold the ships they arrived in. In 1432–3 Henry Cologner imported '*22 doli vine de Ryne*', paying 13*s*. 4*d*.; paid 3*s*. 8*d*. for '*licenct tappandi vini [sic] infra villam*', and then took away what he did not manage to sell. Poule Rode de Colonia, '*mercator*', brought in '*28 doli wadde*' and took out cloth, tallow, fish, candles and calf-skins in 1440–1, and other men bought grain. Court de Colonia paid customs dues of 12*s*. 0*d*. on a consignment of millstones and a sack of hops in 1453–4. Hamburg, Stettin, Luneburg, '*Pruce*' and '*de Dansk*' are all represented in the accounts; and to the south, Dieppe, Normandy, Brittany, Gascony and Portugal. The latter all brought wine and bought grain. None of these places was very important in the trade of Yarmouth in terms of the numbers of shippers visiting the port, and it is obvious that the towns of the Low Countries were the main trading partners of Great Yarmouth and were the entrepôts which fed the town with goods from both the Baltic and the South.

The water-bailiffs' accounts suggest that aliens dominated the import trade, but the limitations of the records make it impossible to make any realistic assessment of the level of English participation. Most English merchants trading at Yarmouth must have been free of local tolls. With the exception of non-free citizens of Great Yarmouth and Norwich, only Londoners bringing in wine and salt and Newcastle merchants dealing in coal were significant amongst the English, and they only appear in the records because they paid cranage or measurage on these items, although there are sufficient entries for shippers from other places to show that Great Yarmouth's trading network stretched as far as Dartmouth and Brixham (imports of wine and exports of grain) and Scotland (imports of salt and exports of grain).

These accounts are more revealing as to the distribution of imported goods by water into the hinterland (see Map III) although while a definite pattern of trade can be seen, it must be recognised that much of the trade must have been in the hands of the burgesses of Yarmouth and Norwich and thus will not appear in the accounts. A wide range of products went upstream to Beccles; it was doubtless a centre for distribution in its own right. In 1427–8 Robertus Cuppe, described as 'alien', paid custom on salt and 1 tun of wine '*ex*' *versus Beccles*' – presumably he was sailing upstream to deliver it to a merchant there. Frequent entries record the re-export upstream of oil, wine and millstones; the accounts for 1439–40 list a total for Beccles men of 5½ weys of salt, 4 barrels of onions, 3 millstones, 1 barrel of oil, 7 barrels of soap, 1,100 teasels, 3 barrels of osmund, 1,500 nails and 2 tuns of wine. In 1445–6 John Smith of Beccles bought 4 bells in Yarmouth.

Map III

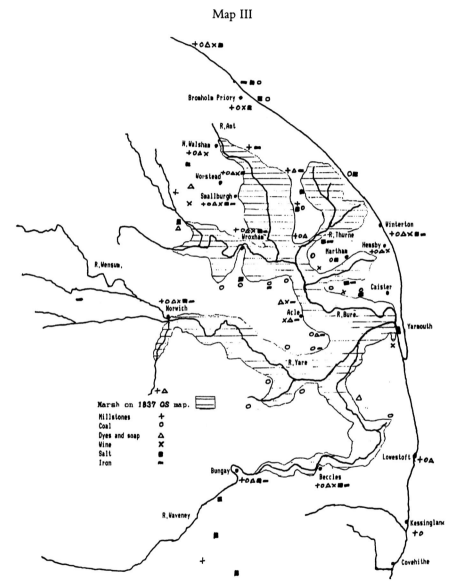

The Destinations of Goods Re-exported from Yarmouth 1399–1460

John Oldryng paid on 9 weys of salt and 20 wainscots in 1447–8 and on 1 bale of madder in 1449–50. In 1452–3 Will Grene (who sold grain, cheese, meat, butter and woolfells in Yarmouth) bought 10 weys of salt, 2 lasts of quernstones and 2 barrels of oil, and in 1454–5 he purchased 2 tons of building stone, 1 pipe of wine, 16 'sheve' of teasels, 50 'borde' and 8 weys of salt. A man from Frethingfield bought '12 quernstonys and 4 houndstonys' and 1 barrel of tar in 1438–9, and Will Skitting of Stradbroke bought a gravestone in 1447–8 and paid 2*d.* in toll on taking it away.

Norwich was a major consumer of imported items, and provided a market and distribution function for its own hinterland, but only those products which had to be weighed or measured are normally shown in these accounts. In 1428–9 John Marwe had 20 tons of building stone carried inland by Engleberd de Dansk, and John Reyner had 18 barrels of tar in his own ship. In 1434–5 a total of 50 weys of salt was taken inland, and in 1436–7 osmund, woad, 3 millstones, and 1 pipe and 1 hogshead of wine. The cranage roll for 1445–6 reveals purchases of 5 pipes of oil, 3 pipes of vinegar, 3 fardels of flax and 18 millstones; and in the following year 9 tuns and 8 pipes of wine, 10 fardels of flax, 19 tons of woad, 2 tons of oil, 3 barrels of beer, 11 'stran' of wax and 5 barrels of copper – for none of which is there a corresponding entry in the customs account. Some of these merchants operated their own river craft: John Rook, variously described as '*forinsecus*' and '*de Norwich*', paid cranage in 1454–5 on 6 tuns of wine 'in Rokyslyghter' and on 30 tons of building stone 'freeston' in the same vessel later in the year.

It is hardly surprising that there are few entries for the villages along the Yare and none for the Wensum above Norwich as the Norwich men must have virtually monopolised the trade. The large village and route centre of Acle only took 2 barrels of osmund and 1 pipe and 1 hogshead of wine in the sixty years under investigation, and the entries are 25 years apart – clearly the needs of the village and the surrounding area being met by carriers and merchants of Norwich or Yarmouth. There was more discernible activity on the river Bure. John Cooper of Tunstall bought 1 barrel of tar, 1,000 tiles and 1,000 nails in 1445–6 (to build a house?), and 1 barrel of oil and 1 barrel of soap in 1448–9. Will Colinson of Scottow bought 23 weys of salt, 6 barrels of tar and 1 tun of wine and paid anchorage. At Ranworth Roger Iryng purchased an average of 3 weys a year between 1445 and 1455, and also some pitch. The dual village of Wroxham/Hoveton must have been a local distribution centre as it imported wine, almonds(1424–5), wax ('*custuma pro Xc cere exeunt versus Wroxham*' in 1434–5), millstones, nails, salt, osmund, oil and fuller's earth (in 1451–2 and 1455–6).

On the rivers Ant and Thurne, Thurne village took woad and a gravestone; Hickling, salt; Worstead, wine, vinegar, canvas and teasels; Brumstead, millstones and soap; Walsham, wine, 'stokfysh' oil and osmund; Stalham and Ingham, teasels. Smallburgh was the base of a middleman named Thomas Spicer who bought wax, oil, salt, tin (27 *cuppel stanni*) soap, alum and wine in 1439–40. In the next year he paid 6*s.* 8*d.* '*pro divers' mercandisorum*', and also paid directly for oil, soap, salt and vinegar. He dealt with alien shippers, taking responsibility for paying the customs dues on goods entering the port as well as on their departure inland. Successive entries in the accounts for 1445–6 show '*custuma 1 pipe oler, 1 pipe vinagre, ½ pipe oler intrante*' and '*custuma 1 pipe oler, 1 pipe vinagre, ½ pipe oler, 3 barrel sope exeunte*'; in confirmation, the cranage roll has matching entries marked '*intrante*' and '*exeunte*'. In 1449–50 and 1450–1 he paid '*fine pro custuma aque toto anno 13s. 4d.*', but also paid duty on purchases of millstones and coal, and on sales of grain, and in 1454–5 he paid 13*s.* 4*d.* '*custuma vini mercimon' usque St. Michaelis Archangelis proxime futur'*.

Some of the small ports to the north of the town and the inland villages they served do appear in the accounts as consumers of salt and coal, with frequent cargoes of nails, osmund, millstones and wine. The most important merchant here was Thomas Iryng of Winterton. In 1453–4 he paid a total of 19*s.* 0*d.* on his purchases during the year which were then itemised, though not completely: 100 'borde' 4*d.*, 1 last of white herrings 2*s.*, 1c. [*sic*] of 'ores' and 1 tun of nails 2*d.*, 100 combs of malt 4*s.* 2*d.*, 140 qtrs of malt 6*s.* 8*d.*, 30 qtrs of malt 3*s.* 4*d.*.. He also paid separately for other purchases of iron (4 tuns), salt (4 weys) and 3 'Norwych Whytes' and on sales of barley and malt. In the following year he bought fish and teasels, and in 1455–6 wax, madder, oil and salt. The small ports to the south of Yarmouth were mainly concerned with the coastal trade in grain, buying in Yarmouth and shipping southward to Colchester, Ipswich and London, but these shippers did undertake some redistribution of imported goods. Men of Lowestoft took oil, coal, millstones, hops and freestone; Kessingland the same plus iron, wine, salt and pitch; Southwold and Walberswick took osmund, wine, salt, madder and pitch.

The evidence for the redistribution of imported goods into the hinterland of Great Yarmouth is not comprehensive, but it is sufficiently detailed and geographically spread to allow inferences to be drawn. Great Yarmouth and Norwich merchants would have attempted to act as an interface between the importers and the rural consumer, and they would also tend to control the means of distribution – the fleets of river and coastal vessels. Few rural consumers would have thought it worthwhile to maintain their own vessels and the necessary crew when the shippers from the big towns would be already providing this service. The scale of their purchases would hardly have justified it. Even those people who can be identified as rural middlemen do not appear in the accounts consistently year after year – so it is all the more surprising that there are as many entries for rural consumers buying and shipping goods out of Great Yarmouth as there are. In view of the bulky nature of the commodities – barrels, tuns, bales and millstones – this demonstrates the facility with which trade could be conducted by water in this area. While less numerous than the records for the entry into the town of grain and other agricultural produce, the details available for the distribution of imported products into the hinterland indicate where the market for these products lay – with the agriculturalists who supplied Great Yarmouth with the materials for its export trade.

By excluding much of the operations of the burgesses of Norwich and Great Yarmouth, these accounts throw into sharper relief the activities of aliens and smaller local traders and shippers – the dealers not in bulk loads but in smaller quantities. They show that the rural hinterland of the port was an area where production of grain and animal products for surplus and export was widespread, and that despite the demands of London and other English towns, a substantial proportion of the grain was exported in alien vessels for the victualling of the Low Countries, as were most of the animal products. In return, aliens supplied Great Yarmouth's hinterland not only with their own indigenous products but also with items from the Baltic and from southern Europe, competing with merchants from elsewhere in England to satisfy the needs of the agriculturalists whose surplus production they bought in the town.

The water-bailiffs' accounts of Great Yarmouth provide a valuable insight into the economic life of the town and of this region of East Anglia in the first half of the fifteenth century. This once-rich port was slowly recovering from the disasters of the latter half of the fourteenth century, but its harbour was prone to silting up and was costly to maintain, and it had lost much of its former significance as an exporter of wool. The only real justification for its continued survival as a major centre of population was its rôle as the market-place for the produce of its region, a place where the surplus of that production could be exchanged for goods imported by alien and English merchants and in demand in the rural areas; an inland trading operation that was facilitated by a waterborne collection and distribution network that shrank the time and cost of transporting goods between the hinterland and the port. These accounts reveal a functioning economic system in which the port of Great Yarmouth was acting successfully in the rôle of market town for its hinterland and was also serving the needs of buyers and sellers from a significant part of the littoral of the North Sea.

Notes

1   I am indebted to the staff of the Norfolk Record Office, Norwich, for the opportunity to make use of these records. The format of the rolls varies from clerk to clerk, but in good years the name of the shipper (the person responsible for paying the toll); the shipmaster (if different); the place of origin of either or both; the individual products carried, with the quantity and the amount of toll paid on each product; the amount of

anchorage paid (which depended on the size of the ship); whether the goods were being imported or exported; and even the day of the month on which the ship entered and left the port are shown. The rates of local customs duty appear to be almost identical to those of Southampton, see H.S. Cobb, ed., *The Local Port Book of Southampton for 1439–40*, Southampton Records Series, 5 (1961), pp. xi–xlvi.

2   L.J. Redstone, ed., *The Cellarer's Roll Account for Bromholm Priory, Norfolk, 1415–16*, Norfolk Record Society, 17 (1944), pp. 45–91, records the purchase of 1 wey of salt at Great Yarmouth in 1415; the cost of ferryage to Horning and cartage from there to the priory was 15*d.* as opposed to the 20*s.* 0*d.* cost of the salt itself (transport costs approx. 6%). A boat which sank at Cantley in 1343 on the journey upstream to Norwich contained 40 people, 3 barrels of osmund, sea coal worth 10*s.* 0*d.* and a quartern of Riga boards, plus quantities of herrings, salt, onions and other items; W. Hudson and J.C. Tingey, *The Records of the City of Norwich*, 2 vols (Norwich & London, 1906), I, no. lxxxviii.

3   J. Boyes and R. Russell, *The Canals of Eastern England* (Newton Abbot, 1977), pp. 118–32. See also *Ordnance Survey of Norfolk 1837* – it is unlikely that any of the marsh shown in this survey had ever previously been drained.

4   Cranage was the charge for using the town crane, e.g. millstones 4*d.* each, pack of cloth 4*d.*, sack of hops 4*d.*, hogshead of wine 1*d.* Tronage was the charge for using the town weighbeam, e.g. 1 sack of hops 4*d.* Measurage was charged on cargoes of grain or coal landed in the port by merchants exempt from customs dues. Murage was a royal grant of the right to charge a tax for the maintenance of the town walls; the duty actually to spend the money on the fortifications was more honoured in the breach than in the observance.

5   *Antient Deeds*, V, p. 265. Elizabeth Clere instructed that 181 qtrs and 4 bushels of barley to be received in rent from manors in Ormesby should be sent to Winterton and Yarmouth for sale (1457). See *The Cellarer's Account for Bromholm Priory* . The priory both farmed on demesne and received rents in grain: barley and malt were sold to mongers from Winterton.

6   He was admitted to the Freedom in this year: see *Calendar of Freeman of Great Yarmouth, 1429–1800*, Norfolk and Norwich Archaeological Society, Norwich, [?1910].

7   These particular entries do not specify whether the grain was coming into the port or leaving it.

8   The Pastons occasionally sold grain and other produce southwards down the coast and also overseas, see N. Davis, ed., *Paston Letters and Papers of the Fifteenth Century* (Oxford, 1971, 1976), pp. 533–4, no 236 (17 Feb. 1467). From John Paston III to John Paston II: '. . . we have the most part of your barley safe [at London] from Wynterton'. Also see *Paston Letters*, I, nos 71, ll.8–11, 72, ll.125–30, II, 650, ll. 24–31. Sir John Fastolf did likewise; see *Paston Letters*, II, no. 572, l. 25 and K.B. McFarlane, 'The Investment of Sir John Fastolf's Profits of War, *TRHS*, 5th series, 7 (1957), pp. 115–16.

9   *CPR, 1436–41*, pp. 344, 351, 355, 358, 361, 362 and 366 record the issuing of licences for the purchase in Yarmouth and dispatch to London, Colchester and Ipswich of 2,700 qtrs of mixed grains: *CCR, 1435–41*, pp. 199–200. In a letter dated 22 Dec. 1438 the customers of Great Yarmouth were told to allow Londoners to ship grain without interference, as they had done in the past.

10   *CPR, 1429–36*, pp. 313, 326–7; licences issued to the abbot of St. Mary's, York, Richard, earl of Salisbury and Thomas Louthe to buy 1,300 qtrs of barley, 300 qtrs of wheat and 800 qtrs of malt for the victualling of the North parts (York, Carlisle etc.)

11   Both of these men, who never gained the freedom of the town, were active in the coastal trade in grain and malt to the south.

12   *Magnum Theolonium* gave fishermen visiting the town for the Herring Fair, held between Michaelmas and Martinmas, the right to enter and leave the harbour as many times as they wished within the forty days of the Fair. R.H. Teasdel, *Great Yarmouth, the Cinque Ports and the Free Fair in Herring* (London, 1928); J.W. deCaux, *The Herring and the Herring Fishery* (London & Norwich, 1881).

13 *CPR, 1401–5*, p. 483, 26 Jan. 1405; Hugh and Robert Fenne (burgesses of Yarmouth) were given licences to ship 1,000 qtrs of barley and oats from Yarmouth to Holland and Zeeland. *CPR, 1436–41*, pp. 375–6, 12 Feb. 1440; Robert Clere (he was later to be a trustee of William Paston I's will) was given a licence to ship 60 qtrs of wheat, 500 qtrs of barley and 1,000 qtrs of malt from Great Yarmouth to London, Boston, Ipswich, Colchester, Winchester or Sandwich.

14 Sir George Warner, ed., *The Libelle of Englyshe Polycye* (Oxford 1926), ll. 114–18. This market overseas was so attractive to rural producers that trade had to be restrained in the interests of English consumers, e.g.: *CCR, 1429–35*, p. 199, 13 Oct. 1432; prohibitions on the export of grain: see also *CCR, 1441–7*, p. 115, 14 Nov. 1442. *CCR, 1402–5*, p. 199, 22 Dec. 1403: list of the ships arrested on royal order for fear that they were about to take grain and fish abroad for sale – five ships out of seven were from Yarmouth.

15 E.E. Power and M.M. Postan, eds, *Studies in English Trade in the Fifteenth Century* (London, 1933); Chapter III.

16 Warner, ed., *The Libelle*, ll. 348–9 .

17 N.J.M. Kerling, *The Commercial Relations of Holland and Zeeland with England from the Late 13th Century to the Close of the Middle Ages* (Leiden,1954), pp. 89–90, 99.

18 Ibid., pp. 123–5.

19 Beer was imported in barrels much earlier. The brewery was operated by aliens, outside the walls and over the river in Southtown. Jacob Brewer '*de Southton*' paid 13*s*. 4*d*. for '*custuma beer*' in 1431–2, and in succeeding years '*Petrus Beerbrewer de Southton, alias Symondesson*', and his sons paid similar sums. In 1445–6 Arnaldo Orgonmaker, Arnaldo Couper, Lutekin Ducheman, Clays Beerbruer and others paid various sums '*custuma bere*' between the feasts of St Michael and St Luke.

20 Sir John Fastolf imported tiles; see H.D. Barnes and W.D. Simpson, 'The Building Accounts of Caister Castle A.D. 1432–1435, *Norfolk Archaeology*, 30 (1947–52) pp. 186–8. So did the Pastons; see *Paston Letters*, I, no. 329, ll. 117–18 to John Paston II, in March 1469: 'John Pampyng hath had home to Caster as good as Xml tyle fro the plase at Yarmouthe'. Hollanders often ballasted their ships with bricks which they sold on arrival; see J.A. van Houtte, *An Economic History of the Low Countries 800–1800* (New York, 1977), p. 87, and Kerling, *Commercial Relations*, p. 128.

21 Carriage of 18 tons of stone brought from the Isle of Wight to Great Yarmouth cost £2 10*s*. 0*d*. in 1411–12; see E.C. Fernie and A.B. Whittingham, eds., *The Communar Rolls of Norwich Cathedral Priory, No.1068*, Norfolk Record Society, 1974. For trade in the opposite direction, see *Paston Letters*, II, no. 669, ll. 11–15, 5 July 1462, Richard Calle to John Paston I: '. . . wherefore it were wele done to selle some nough at London . . . one quater carrying from Yarmouthe to London will cost you 6*d*. a quater'. At this time the price at Yarmouth was 26*d*. per quarter.

22 The basis on which tronage and cranage were charged is often ambiguous. This entry suggests either that tronage and cranage were merely taxes, having no objective reality, or that he had sold the nails and madder in the town but failed to sell the wine and was forced to load it into his ship again.

23 But (cf. 22 above) these aliens may have been bringing in goods ordered and paid for by a denizen, and therefore not liable for customs dues, but were being forced to use the weighbeam to confirm that the goods were as specified.

N.B. For a fuller discussion of the issues raised in this paper, see my M.Litt. thesis of the same title (Birmingham University, 1993).

9

The Aims and Interests of the London Chroniclers of the Fifteenth Century

Mary-Rose McLaren

At some time between 1755 and 1811 the London chronicles ceased to be regularly updated as records of current events and became documents of antiquarian interest. To the best of my knowledge the last London chronicle to be printed with a contemporary continuation appeared in 1755.[1] In 1811 *The New Chronicles of England and France* was edited by Henry Ellis, and was followed by *A Chronicle of London*, edited by Nicolas and Tyrrel in 1827.[2] These were published not because they contained new continuations, but because of the light they shed upon the fifteenth century. Clearly a change in the ways that the London chronicles were perceived had taken place.

Since Nicolas and Tyrrel's edition of MS Harley 565 as *A Chronicle of London*, many other manuscripts have also been edited, most of these by Gairdner in the Camden Series, by C.L. Kingsford in his *Chronicles of London* (1905) and *English Historical Literature in the Fifteenth Century* (1913) and by R. Flenley in *Six Town Chronicles* (1911).[3] Although a further eleven manuscripts have been found since Kingsford wrote in 1913, the only subsequent edition of a full London chronicle (as opposed to fragments being published in journals like the *English Historical Review*) has been the publication of MS Guildhall 3313 as *The Great Chronicle of London* by Thomas and Thornley in 1938.[4]

Despite a continuous interest in the London chronicles for the last 170 years, and a veritable flurry of interest at the beginning of this century, no-one has yet asked why the London chronicles were written. Modern scholarship has tended to consider the chronicles either as useful in simply providing a more or less accurate narrative of events, or as propaganda tools and therefore, generally speaking, worthless. I want to direct my attention here to the chroniclers' aims, first by providing an outline of the nature of the London chronicles and by examining what their contents tell us of the chroniclers' interests, and then, by drawing on the accounts of three processions, to highlight what the chroniclers' aims actually were. It will then be evident that the London chronicles cannot be understood and fully utilized by modern historians unless many of our assumptions about their purpose and the skills of their writers are changed.

The earliest document that might be considered a London chronicle is the *Liber de Antiquis Legibus*, written in Latin around 1274, probably by Andrew Horn.[5] Like the *Annales Londoniensis* (1329)[6] and the French chronicle of London (1345),[7] it is related in form, but not in content, to the later London chronicles.[8] Another early text of a London chronicle appears in Letter Book F (initial text concluding 1354, but continued in various hands to 1548).[9] Although slender, a relationship between this and some later London chronicles can be observed.

My own work focuses on the forty-one extant manuscripts of London chronicles from the fifteenth and early sixteenth centuries. The sources of all later printed chronicles can be found in these manuscripts. The fifteenth-century London chronicles are grouped together primarily because they share a common form. It is usual for the manuscripts to begin at 1189[10] and to date by mayoral years, giving accounts of events under the names of the mayors and sheriffs in any given year. The chronicles appear in commonplace books, as continuations to Bruts, or occasionally in Corporation records, or they are bound on their own. Some of these manuscripts have clearly been copied by their owners for personal use; others appear to have been professionally copied and then continued by their owners.[11] A third group may have been kept by guilds or the Guildhall as semi-official records.[12] Although some authors or types of authors can be guessed at, the manuscripts are, without exception, anonymous.[13]

Although grouped together as the London chronicles, the extant manuscripts represent more than one original text. In general terms, Kingsford's idea of a Main City Chronicle (the extant manuscripts all allegedly representing versions of one text) is misleading.[14] At least three, and possibly four different source chronicles can be found embedded in the fifteenth-century texts, although they have been copied with a large number of variants and additional materials. Furthermore, there are ten texts which bear only very slight relationships, or no relationship, to any other extant text.

The extant manuscripts of the London chronicles therefore constitute a puzzling group. Although they share a common form, they differ widely in the material they record (particularly on contemporary events), the amount of detail included, and their apparent use (either personal or semi-official). Furthermore, they are anonymous. We can therefore rely only on internal evidence in attempting to determine why they were written.

Although often different in style and content, the London chronicles are surprisingly similar in the type of material they record. Accounts focused on London and on royal activity are the most commonly recorded, providing about 35% of all entries. A further 10–15% of entries consist of religious references and accounts of rebellion and treason. Weather, prices, heresy, plague, supernatural occurrences, taxes, laws, incidental events and events outside England are also recorded, although these usually account for a relatively small percentage of entries.

The contents of the London chronicles support the idea that the authors had an interest in London and access to London sources. However, they were not exclusively interested in London: events in York, Leicester, Northampton, Pleshy, Bristol, Oxford, Sandwich, Tewkesbury, Coventry, Lincoln, Reading, Bromholm, Salisbury, Bedford and Norwich are mentioned, as are a limited number of events beyond England. Thus there is a high proportion of London information, with selected material from beyond London also considered to be of interest.

Such interests reflect, to a degree, the sources available to the chonicler. These fall under several headings.

1. *Letter Books*. There are no explicit references in the London chronicles to the use of Letter Books as sources. However, the appearance of a very early London chronicle in a Letter Book, Letter Book F, suggests that a close relationship probably existed between the two types of records. This is supported by the appearance in MS Gough London 10 of indices to ordinances in several Letter Books.[15] It should be noted that Gough London 10 is particularly beautiful, and is clearly the work of a professional scribe. Its inclusion of material like oaths of guilds and letter book indices along with the chronicle suggests that it may have been a book kept for some official purpose. As the chronicler appears to have had enough access to the Letter Books to have an index of them, it seems reasonable to suggest that some of his material may have come from them. A comparison of the later sections of Gough London 10 and the corresponding passages in Letter Book K supports this view.

2. *Other City records*. Again, there is little explicit evidence of these as sources. However, there is some similarity in content and style between certain chronicle accounts and the records of some crafts and guilds. Margaret of Anjou's entry into London in 1445, for example, is found in the Goldsmiths' records. Henry IV's death and burial in the Brewers' Book is similar to the account in MSS Cotton Julius B II and Longleat 53.[16] If these chronicle accounts were not drawn from company records, they were almost certainly drawn from similar sources. Records of prices and weather also occur both in company records (weather being recorded where it has a direct bearing on prices) and the chronicles, and the charters granted to the city and to particular guilds are found in Letter Books, company records and chronicles. However, actual guild matters are recorded in the chronicles only if they affected the city as a whole. Guildhall 3313 (*The Great Chronicle*), for example, records the bakers' attempt to bribe sheriffs in 1271, and their fraudulence in 1476; and the fraudulence of the goldsmiths in 1278. In 1372 we are told only that John Norwold, mercer, was killed, which caused a great dissension. The drapers' and taylors'

dispute is mentioned in passing in MS Trinity College Dublin 509 (*Bale's Chronicle*) in 1448. Although the chronicles and company records have different emphases and serve different purposes, it is possible that in some cases they were written by the same people. Certainly, any city official who wrote a chronicle, like the author of Egerton 1995 who was a mayor, would also have access to the records of his, and perhaps other, guilds.[17] In this context it is interesting to note that one manuscript, MS Rawlinson B 359, appears to have been kept and updated by the Grocers' company.

3. *Official documents.* There are many examples of official documents providing sources in the London chronicles: the deposition of Richard II (probably from parliamentary records);[18] the debate between the duke of Gloucester and the bishop of Winchester;[19] and letters (not only those which were directed to the city – these may have come from city records – but also those to others such as sovereigns or the duke of Burgundy).[20] Also included amongst official documents are the numerous treaties from the French wars.[21]

4. *Pamphlets in circulation.* That pamphlets were circulated as propaganda tools in the fifteenth century is evident in the existence of several pamphlets such as the ceremonial account of the marriage of Margaret, Edward IV's sister, to the duke of Burgundy and the extended pamphlet on Edward IV's arrival, and in the seditious rhyme mentioned in Guildhall 3313 as being nailed to the cross in Cheap in 1484.[22] It is possible that pamphlets were mainly a Yorkist tool, but C.A.J. Armstrong's article on the use of pamphlets following the first battle of St Albans suggests that Edward exploited a form already in existence.[23] In the chronicles, those accounts which may have been taken from pamphlets occur only from the end of Henry IV's reign – quite possibly from within the lifetime of the first London chroniclers who wrote contemporaneously with the events they recorded. Such accounts include the battle of Agincourt and the response to it in London;[24] Henry V's marriage feast, including the menu;[25] and Henry VI's coronation and his entry into Paris.[26] Some aspects of these accounts point to their being copied verbatim from a pamphlet source. For example, manuscripts which are otherwise diverse may agree on the account, as in the case of Henry V's wedding where the texts in the Egerton and the St John's families of manuscripts differ before and after this account. Some accounts of heresy and treason are also possibly taken from pamphlets like the account of Prince Henry's attempt to save a heretic in the St John's manuscripts under the year 1409. This is formulaic and moralising. It also appears in the Harley 565 family and the Egerton 1995 family. In each appearance it concludes with a verse, suggesting that each account was copied verbatim from a document. Also included in this

category are ballads. An excellent example occurs in MS Cotton Cleopatra C IV where the chronicler tires of translating the ballad into prose and records the second half of it in verse.

5. *Eye-witness and hearsay.* There are several examples of eye-witness and hearsay material being used. In the account of 1425, for example, MS Egerton 1995 records:

> And that yere there were many worthy men of London apechyde of treson by A false Peloure by excytacyon of the Byschoppe of Wynchester as many men noysyde and sayde yf were trewe or no I remytte me to gode.

Similarly, in 1461, the same author writes:

> as hyt ys sayde . . . and sum men sayde that . . . God knowythe the trought.

There are further examples of eye-witness and hearsay accounts in many other chronicles. Those manuscripts with detailed accounts of the French wars appear to have relied upon eye-witness reports. MS Cotton Cleopatra C IV, for example, is more detailed than similar chronicles, and the details may have been added from eye-witness records. Similarly, the accounts of Cade's Rebellion in MSS Egerton 1995 and Trinity College Dublin 509 are almost certainly eye-witness, as are the descriptions of the second battle of St Albans in Egerton 1995 and the punishment of Dame Eleanor Cobham in MS Trinity College Cambridge 0.9.1.

6. *Other chronicles.* The single most common source for the chronicles is other chronicles. It is possible that very few of the extant manuscripts ever drew on city or official records as their sources, but that they have copied these from other chronicles. Most chronicles show signs of having drawn, at least in part, on other chronicles. It is therefore misleading to suggest that every chronicler had access to the sources he seems to have used.

Determining the interests of, and sources for, the London chroniclers may indicate some of their general aims. Their interest in civic affairs may suggest an aim to record the events of the city for posterity. Their access to letters and documents, and the frequent copying of these, also points to an attempt at a documentary or perhaps official history, rather than the cyclic and in part fabulous history of the Bruts.[27] The probability that they were both commercially and privately copied indicates a broad-based interest, suggesting that these aims were not exclusive to the official civic leaders. To determine why they were written it is necessary to examine not simply the contents of the chronicles, but the ways in which the material is recorded. The aims of the London chronicles surviving from the thirteenth, fifteenth and seventeenth centuries are, I think, quite different. Of the three groups, the aims of the chroniclers of the fifteenth century are the most difficult to identify. The difficulty stems essentially from the diversity of the texts and the differing emphases they place on the material they record.

Royal processions feature prominently in the fifteenth-century chronicles. Almost every text which is more than simply a list of city officials refers to or describes at least one procession. Furthermore, because they are highly ceremonial, rôles and *mores* are clearly defined, both within the procession, and in the chroniclers' recording of it. The chroniclers' presentation of processions therefore provides an appropriate case study through which we can attempt to identify the chroniclers' aims in recording. This is all the more so as the frequent recording of pageants and processions ranks highly on the list of criticisms directed at these texts.[28]

Royal processions recorded in the chronicles were clearly orchestrated. It is almost impossible to determine, however, whether they were orchestrated primarily by the protagonist, or by the chronicler in his process of recording. Certainly they were not orchestrated by the people of London. An examination of the way in which processions are recorded by the chroniclers indicates that the latter were concerned with the projection of images and could produce very sophisticated pieces of writing. Particular elements of importance can be discerned: the appearance of the processor on horseback; his clothes; his retinue; and the road he takes. In ideal combination these elements project an image of order and firm monarchical rule. However, an inversion of the ideal is also possible. In the following discussion it will be evident that through recording processions the chronicler indicates the quality of the kingship, and draws on a shared vocabulary to comment on the state of the world and the nature of leadership. A comparison of three processions highlights the central issue of how far the chronicler consciously manipulates his material to present certain images.

The first processional account to be considered is the duke of York's arrival from Ireland in 1460 in MS Egerton 1995. The account begins with Richard's landing at Redcliff in Lancashire. To this point the chronicler's prevailing attitude has been Yorkist. The chronicler records in detail the physical appearance of York's retinue. Clearly, it is perceived as being of primary importance in describing his arrival and consequent movements. The initial sentence includes a striking visual image, 'hys lyvery was whyte and brewe in hyr clothyng and i-brawderyd a-bove with fetyrlockys'. As the account continues the visual image is built upon. Richard comes towards London and 'hys lady the duchyes met with hym in a chare i-coveryd with blewe felewette'. He arrives in Abingdon, and there he sende for trompeters and claryners to bryng hym to London and there he gave them baners with the hole armys of Inglonde with owte any dyversyte and commaundyd his swerde to ben borne uppe ryghte be-fore hym and soo he rode forthe unto Lundon tylle he come to Westemynster to Kyng Harrys palys and there he claymyd the crowne of Inglonde.

It appears that the chronicler, as well as the duke himself, is concerned with the visual impact which Richard makes. Of greater interest, however, is what these images implicitly denote. The contrast between the style and devices of the London chronicles and monastic chronicles is clearly seen by a comparison here with Whethamstede.[29] For the same year, Whethamstede records much detail which is not apparent in the Egerton account. He notes that some believed York's arrival was peaceful while others suspected his intentions, and describes York's interruptions of parliament and the Lords' refusal to support him. By contrast, the Egerton account places a heavy emphasis on the procession towards London (rather than the events on York's arrival) and the clothing and accoutrement of Richard, his duchess and his retinue.

The colour and fabric associated with the duchess are traditional signs of nobility and were set as such by statute.[30] The perceived importance of clothing is evidenced by the bequeathing of clothes in wills.[31] Perkin Warbeck, according to his confession, modelled clothes for his employer, and was taken to be a prince by the people.[32] Further, the mayor, aldermen and men of the guilds were expected to wear specific colours in certain processions, particularly for Henry IV's burial (russet) and triumphant processions (red).[33] Royalty are almost always recorded as wearing blue in public. Richard's presentation of himself and his wife, therefore, firmly places them in the high orders of nobility on an occasion of public ceremony. The use of banners is usually associated with triumphal procession. In this account the implicitly triumphal statement is reinforced by the organisation of the musicians to signify unity. The chronicler explicitly states that their banners were 'with owte any dyversyte'.[34] The effect is to produce an image, not of a motley group making their way to London, but of a unified group processing with purpose. This is particularly relevant in the context of the past month's events. The chronicler's reference to the banners as 'the hole armys of Inglonde' establishes an implicit contrast between the unity and purpose of Richard's men in claiming the throne and the disunity and disorder in the realm which had been manifest a month earlier in the battle of Northampton (at which Richard was not present). The purpose of such imagery, whether orchestrated by Richard, or constructed by the chronicler, is to present Richard as projecting himself as leader of England, processing triumphantly towards London. That Richard bears his sword upright before him further reinforces this image. The sword is used as a sign of power and just leadership by the king in coronation and by nobles in procession. Here, in the context of the events that follow, it is suggestive also of the king bearing his sceptre in coronation procession, symbolising control over the land. Through this accumulation of images, the chronicler presents Richard as offering a restoration of the peace. He is perceived as a powerful and unifying leader. Add to this the aural image of fanfare, and the chronicler's recording of Richard's procession to London may be interpreted as a worthy prologue to coronation.[35]

Throughout this description, the chronicler has selected that material which emphasises and builds the imagery. Richard's gradual movement towards London, and the corresponding increase in the ceremony with which he is attended, reflects the chronicler's perception of Richard's development as a *de facto* leader. On the journey Richard is depicted as becoming more and more a physical manifestation of the perception of kingship. This process mirrors the procession recorded earlier in the chronicle when the child Henry, on his return from his Paris coronation, is taken through the streets of London to view pageants which show him the stages of kingly development.

It is impossible to determine the impact this series of images had on the people of London. It is evident from other accounts that some sort of procession into London took place. However, it is impossible to determine how far the chronicler has retrospectively constructed these images of Richard to present him as a kingly figure, and how far Richard himself orchestrated this self-projection. It is clear from parliament's response to Richard that gaining the throne was not a natural progression from his processional presentation or his ceremonial claim to the throne (through action, and not initially through words). It is quite possible, therefore, that the chronicler, writing in retrospect, presented Richard in a manner appropriate to the later parliamentary compromise, and the subsequent rule of Edward IV. The chronicler has employed a series of well-known images echoing those found in pageantry, to record, not what he saw or knew, but what he considered most appropriate. The fact that the account is not written as an eye-witness report may provide further evidence for the view that the chronicler is here writing a literary account of the events. Thus although the account of Richard's arrival may reflect what actually happened, it may be primarily a fitting literary way for the chronicler to describe Richard's journey and to suggest his status and power.

The processions associated with the restoration and second deposition of Henry VI recorded in MS Guildhall 3313 provide a telling contrast. The first processional account, leading to Henry's restoration, is as follows:

> The said duke accompanyed wyth the Erlys of warwyk & of derby
> [*sic*] & of Shroysbury and the lord Stanley wyth many othir noble
> men Rode unto the Towyr and ffett thens kyng Henry and conveyed
> hym soo thorwth the hye stretys of the Cyte Rydyng In a long
> Gowne of blew velvet unto pawlys and when he hadd there offird at
> the Rode of the North dore he was then conveyed thorwth the
> Chyrch Into the Bysshoppys palays & there lodgyd.

Although we are not told the precise route of the procession, the fact that
it went 'thorwth the hye stretys of the Cyte' and ended at St Paul's and the
bishop's palace suggests that it was the usual processional route through
London. The clothing, 'a long Gowne of blew velvet', is appropriate to the
king, as is the retinue of noble men, mirroring the acclaimed support of
the nobles necessary to the king at his coronation. Like Richard duke of
York, Henry and his supporters are on horseback. This is consistent with
the normal triumphal procession through the city.

In striking contrast to the procession of Richard, however, is the fact
that this procession is not presented as being orchestrated by the
protagonist. Although within the procession Henry is presented as the
king, the chronicler perceives him as passive. He is 'ffett' and 'conveyed' by
the duke, the earls and Stanley, who are clearly intended to be seen as the
initiators of the action. The word 'conveyed' is ambiguous. Although
elsewhere in the chronicles it is used to mean 'convoy', the association of it
here with 'ffett' seems to compromise its meaning, suggesting rather the
alternative nuance of the word, to control or direct.

The picture of Henry as passive is reinforced later in this account when
the chronicler describes him as 'this Goostly & vertuous prince'. The
chronicler further states that Henry held 'noo thyng [with] the pomp or
vanytees of this world'. The recording of pageants and processions, however,
suggests that such 'pomp or vanytees' were important in reflecting a hierarchy
of rule and a sense of order. The contemplative image of Henry, projected in
his passivity in procession and his saintly attributes, establishes, therefore, a
sharp dichotomy between the rôle of a king and the rôle of a saint.[36] Such a
dichotomy is encapsulated within the procession itself. Henry's passivity,
implicit within the chronicler's account, is directly opposed to his supporters'
attempts to present him as king. When the chronicler consequently compares
Henry to Christ, claiming that Henry might repeat the words '*Regnum meum
non est de hoc mundo*' ('my kingdom is not of this world') he is highlighting the
failure of Henry as a king. His rôle as king requires that he rule on earth. It is,
therefore, an abdication of his responsibility, and also implicitly of the
monarchy, for Henry to adopt the contemplative life. In presenting Henry as
passive in his claim to the throne, and as a mystic saint in private life, the
chronicler strips him of those qualities most essential for kingship.

Henry's passivity and his failure as a king are highlighted in the chronicler's account of the procession immediately prior to his second deposition. Edward, earl of March, with 'hys strength myghtyly encreasid', advances on London. Sir Thomas Cook '& ffewe othir' try to arrange for Edward to be denied entry to the city. The passage continues:

And ffor to cawse the Cytyzyns to bere theyr more ffavour unto kyng henry, The said kyng henry was conveyed ffrom the paleys off pawleys thorwth Chepe & Cornhyll and soo abowth to his said lodgyng agayn by Candylwyk strete & wattlyngstrete, Beyng accompanyed wyth the archbysshop of york whych held hym alle that way by the hand and the lord Sowch [*sic*] an old & Inpotent man which þt day beyng Shere thursdaye abowth IX of the clok, bare/ the kyngys sword, and soo wyth a small company of Gentyllmen goyng on ffoot beffore, and oon beyng on horsbak & beryng a pool or long Shafft wyth ii ffoxe Taylys ffastenyd upon the said Shafftes eennde, held wyth a small Company of servyng men ffoluyng, the progresse beffore shewid/ The which was more lyker a play then the shewyng of a prynce to wynne mennys hertys, ffor by this mean he lost many & wan noon or Rygth ffew, and evyr he was shewid In a long blew goune of velvet as thowth he had noo moo to chaunge wᵗ.

In many ways this procession is the inverse of the ceremonial procession. The route itself is the reverse of the usual route. Although this might be explained by Henry residing in St Paul's Palace at the time, such inversion still marks, in literary terms, a movement away from the seat of royal power, rather than to it. The conditions under which the procession takes place reflect this. It is orchestrated in response to an explicit threat with the primary aim that the king should display royal qualities 'to wynne mennys hertys'. Here, the procession is not essentially assertive, but defensive. Thus, in conjunction with this inversion of purpose, the procession away from the palace appears as a strikingly inappropriate choice for a king wishing to retain power.

The sense of ill-applied images is reinforced by the presentation of individuals within the procession. The king is not accompanied by 'many othir noble men' as previously, but by 'a small company of Gentyllmen' and 'a small Company of servyng men'. Further, it is implied that many were on foot – perhaps even the king himself – as we are expressly told that 'oon' of the gentlemen was on horseback.

As in the previous procession the king is presented as passive. We are told he 'was conveyed' and 'was shewid'. Moreover, he is incapable of independent action. The archbishop of York leads him 'alle that way by the hand'. There is a marked contrast to the child Henry's participation in his coronation pageant, recorded in this manuscript in Lydgate's poem, and the presentation of Richard of York in MS Egerton 1995. Such an image strongly suggests that the king was either child-like or frail. That Henry may have been popularly perceived as child-like is suggested by the accusations of treason by words brought to court. An example is provided by John Merfeld of Brightling and William Merfeld of Brightling who allegedly called Henry 'a natural fool'.[38] Even if such cases were created simply to get a defendant to court to argue a different issue, they do indicate that such opinions of the king were considered believable and were threatening enough to be taken to court.[39] The image of Henry as frail is reinforced in the description of 'the Lord Sowch', 'an old & Impotent man', bearing the sword of might and victory presented to Henry as a child. Such an accumulation of images serves to comment on the nature of Henry's rule and question the legitimacy of his kingship. Whether or not this is exactly how the procession appeared, the chronicler has manipulated the images to suggest that the power and order of good rule is inverted. Thus the procession is defensive not triumphant, the king follows rather than leads, and the sword is associated with impotence and weakness. These implicit criticisms of the king are more overtly stated in the second half of the description. The chronicler considers the shaft bearer to be more a jester, and the whole procession to be like a play. The comment indicates the chronicler's acknowledgement that the two forms of public show are dependent on the projection of images. However, there is a clear distinction to be made in the chronicler's mind between the purpose and impact of plays and processions as public performances. There is a suggestion in this distinction that in 'reality' the outer form should reflect the inner state. This is consistent with the notion of clothing as an appropriate means of distinguishing between various classes of people. In a play a disunity between presentation and reality is acceptable. Meg Twycross's article, 'Beyond the Picture Theory: Image and Activity in Medieval Drama' suggests an extra dimension to the perceived distinction between the play and the procession.[40] She claims that the visual representation of events authenticates the real event and, in miracle plays, asserts a desire to make evidence visible. The same may be said of processions. They are perceived as presenting a visual image of a spiritual reality – that the king is King. Similarly, where the instruments of the Passion in a miracle play might be 'a common visual mnemonic for the entire process of the torture and death of Christ', the instruments of coronation may act as a mnemonic for the nature of kingship and good rule. However, whereas medieval theatre is concerned with representation and insists on the disjuncture between reality and illusion, the procession, while drawing on mnemonic images, is concerned with presentation, with showing what is real. In the serious 'shewyng' of a prince, therefore, the chronicler is unprepared to accept an incompatibility between state and presentation. The terms in which he expresses this incongruity are telling: that this was more like a play than the showing of a prince. This is a direct allusion to the understood rôle of theatre. A German/Latin dictionary of the fifteenth century defines the word '*ludus*' as an occasion when a beggar dresses up as a prince. Through a complex series of inversions, and comparisons of the procession to the performance of a play, the chronicler implicitly questions the reality of Henry's nature as a prince. In so doing, he suggests his acceptance of the Yorkist perception, supported by parliament, that Henry VI held only a secondary right to the throne after the duke of York and his descendants. In this case, Henry's procession is indeed 'more lyker play' because his actual state cannot be reflected in the images projected by procession.

These interpretations are supported by the two following comments: that as a result of the procession Henry lost many followers; and that his 'blew goune of velvet' was inappropriate. The loss of followers is a logical response to a loss of faith in the king's nature as monarch, which is suggested in his failure to present himself in that rôle. The blue gown, usually a sign of nobility, is incongruous among the other images in the procession and also, therefore, becomes inverted, suggesting Henry's poverty ('as thowth he hadd noo moo to chaunge w^t') rather than his regality.[41] Finally, in considering the description of Henry's person, it is noteworthy that he is not wearing a crown. This may be due to the chronicler's selection of material. If Henry wore a crown, it would be the one indisputably regal symbol. As such, it would be inconsistent with the general unkingly image of Henry in the account.

In this account, Henry is not presented as a king, but as a poor humbled man. His advisers are weak old men, and his sword of justice is almost too heavy to bear. This is the inverse of the image of the ideal king which is otherwise seen in processions and pageants. In processions and pageants, the perfect king becomes momentarily real, as he is described, clothed, and given the gifts of wisdom, mercy, justice and courage. Here, those images are inverted primarily because, as such, they can suggest levels of disorder and misrule.

The literary use of inversion to suggest ideas of disorder is also evident in poems and ballads of the period. 'On the Times' expresses through contradiction and juxtaposition the social manifestations of the 'world turned upside down':

> Many knyghtes, and lytyl of myght;
> Many lawys, and lytylle ryght.[42]

Similarly, 'On the Corruptions of the Times' uses inversion to comment on the confusion of Henry's reign:

Wyght ys blak, as many men seye,
And blak ys wyght, but summe men say nay.[43]

Clothing and rôle reversal are intricate parts of this 'world turned upside down'. Peter Burke's analysis indicates that such images could symbolise chaos, disorder and misrule.[44] Clearly, in describing this procession the chronicler has drawn upon a formulaic vocabulary and inverted it. Thus, the chronicler not only marks Henry out as an incompetent king, but also strongly suggests the social disorder resulting from Henry's lack of kingly attributes. The description of Henry as the inverse of the triumphant monarch therefore not only implies his lack of kingliness, but also the state of inversion, of social chaos, which his rule spreads through the land.

The processions of Richard duke of York and Henry VI in the chronicles, and the ways in which they are presented, suggest that a number of symbols and formulae could be used to create a demonstrative image of kingship which might be a substitute for, if not superior to, a prescriptive right. Implicit in the chroniclers' accounts is the idea that the king must project an image of himself as king, and must be perceived by the people to be doing so. A pageant or procession, therefore, may be used to create images of an ideal which are momentarily real to the observer, and perhaps to the reader. A successful pageant or procession is one where these images are convincingly projected and so, briefly, create an ideal king. Conversely, the chronicler may manipulate his material to present an inverted procession as a sign of the disorder and misrule naturally resulting from a failed king. It is therefore clear why processions are recorded at such length in the chronicles. They, along with pageants which often, but not always, accompany processions, are used by the chroniclers as a device to create a context within which the qualities and rule of a king may be examined. We cannot, from the chronicle accounts, determine what a procession looked like. The use of symbols and formulae by the chronicler must open the possibility that the chronicler is not writing a description of what he saw, but is using images to write an account of what he believed it to mean. Clearly, the early London chroniclers had a problem. They represented a group (probably lay merchants and clerks) who had not previously had much reason to record in English, but who were attempting to write detailed accounts of events they witnessed or heard about. It appears that they perceived their task, at least in part, as translating the potent visual images of a predominantly oral culture into a written form.[45] They undertook this task with few models for style and construction. The process which the London chroniclers therefore adopted and developed was one uniquely suited to their work. It was not to describe and comment, but to construct accounts in such a way as to present patterns of visual meaning in words. If we consider this simply as propaganda, I believe we are missing the complexity of what the chroniclers were doing. The chroniclers sought ways to communicate what they believed to be happening, not simply what they wanted others to believe was happening. In other words, their aim was not to convince, but to record in writing what, so far as they were concerned, was obvious to all who saw it.

It is evident that the chroniclers sought both to record and understand the events they considered to be important. Underlying the selection of material is a subtlety concerned with the ownership of the past and the control of the present. By recording events under particular mayors' names, the chronicler implicitly suggests two things: his secular view of London, and perhaps of the events, and his desire (conscious or unconscious) to order and control his world. The first of these is important in defining the chronicler's personal rôle. He clearly identifies with the organisational structure of the city. By presenting his material in this context, he claims it as his own by virtue of his citizenship of London. This interpretation of the material corresponds neatly with the anonymity of the chronicles because both aspects, the anonymity and the structural use of the mayoral list, imply a common ownership of the history of London rather than a personal or personalised ownership.[46] The emphasis on recording and the appearance of documents in many London chronicles reinforce this understanding. The chronicler aims to write down things because the action of writing them will contain them and preserve them. In writing a London chronicle, therefore, he is recording, but not personalising, his own history as common with that of the city in a formal structure.

The process of recording also necessitates the process of ordering. It is important to remember that this was the first generation of lay people to make a practice of recording the events of their time. This movement into recording must also indicate an awareness of the need to order and organise material into some usable form, to take control of that material. By juxtaposition, contrast and allusion, the chronicler provides a literary meaning which he perceives as mirroring the visual meaning of the events he records.

The London chroniclers' aims in the fifteenth century can therefore be seen as fourfold. They aimed to record events for future generations; for reference; and to control and understand these events in a new, literary, form. The underlying suggestion here is that awe for the written word remained, and lent authority to the presentation of these accounts in the London chronicles. At the same time, a different group of people had control of this 'authority'. Finally, they sought to assert pride in, and ownership of, the history and affairs of the city of London. As many of the citizens were immigrants to the city, this last aim must not be overlooked. To write a London chronicle might well have asserted a claim to an alien history made personal by virtue of citizenship. Such a suggestion is consistent with what we know of the types of people who wrote and kept London chronicles.[47]

What, however, does all this suggest for us as we read a London chronicle or use one as a source? First and foremost it is essential that we appreciate that what we are reading does not only aim to be a record of what happened. It is an attempt to present the meaning of what happened. Of course the paradox underlying the chronicler's work is that he drew upon a variety of sources which were meant to be simply records of events, such as parliamentary records and letter books. Much of what he wrote, therefore, and particularly where these sources are copied verbatim, does provide us with the sources for an historical narrative. In this way, and in the chronological outline which they provide, the London chronicles are useful as strictly historical sources in the traditional sense. However, by examining the way in which this historical material is recorded, we also find in the London chronicles an attempt to transfer one system of communication (through visual images) into another (writing). As such, the London chronicles represent lay, vernacular, and self-conscious recordings of how the world was perceived to work; of the orchestration and understanding of images; of the perceived structure of power; of what was believed to matter. Perhaps most important for us, an examination of the aims and interests of the London chroniclers provides a picture of how fifteenth-century lay urban people saw themselves, and attempted to express an image of themselves, in relation to their past and their present.

Notes

1   This chronicle is included in J. Stow, *A Survey of the Cities of London and Westminster and the Borough of Southwark . . . Enlarged in the Year 1720 by John Strype . . . Brought down to the Present Time by Careful Hands*, 6th edn, 2 vols (London, 1775).

2   R. Fabyan, *The New Chronicles of England and France, in Two Parts*, ed. H. Ellis (London, 1811). *A Chronicle of London*, ed. N.H. Nicolas and E. Tyrrel (London, 1827).

3   *The Historical Collections of a London Citizen*, ed. J. Gairdner, Camden Society, new series, 17 (1878); *Three Fifteenth-Century Chronicles, with Historical Memoranda by John Stowe*, ed. J. Gairdner, Camden Society, new series, 28 (1880); C.L. Kingsford, *English Historical Literature in the Fifteenth Century* (Oxford, 1913); Kingsford, *Chronicles of London* (Oxford, 1905); 'Two Chronicles of London' in *Camden Miscellany 12*, ed. Kingsford (1910); R. Flenley, *Six Town Chronicles* (Oxford, 1911). Several fragments and extracts of London chronicles were also published by F.W.D. Brie as continuations to the Brut in *The Brut*, EETS, orig. series, 136 (1908).

4   *The Great Chronicle of London*, ed. A.H. Thomas and I.D. Thornley (London, 1938), repr. Alan Sutton (Gloucester, 1983). An extract of the chronicle in MS 2M6 (College of Arms) appears in 'The Historical Notes of a London Citizen, 1483–1488', ed. R.F. Green, *EHR*, 96 (1981), pp. 585–90. A new edition of the French chronicle of London

(ends 1343) forms part of D.C. Cox's London Ph.D. thesis, 'A Study of the French Chronicle of London', 1971.

5   *Liber de Antiquis Legibus*, published as *De Antiquis Legibus Liber: Cronica Maiorum et Vicecomitum Londoniarum*, ed. T. Stapleton, Camden Society, 34 (1846). The question of Horn's authorship of the *Liber* and the other texts attributed to him is thoroughly discussed by J. Catto, 'Andrew Horn: Law and History in Fourteenth Century England', in R.H.C. Davis and J.M. Wallace-Hadrill, eds., *The Writing of History in the Middle Ages. Essays Presented to Richard William Southern*, (Oxford, 1981), pp. 367–91.

6   *Annales Londonienses*, printed in *The Chronicles of the Reigns of Edward I and Edward II*, I, ed. W. Stubbs, RS (London, 1882), from a transcription of MS Cotton Otho B3, now preserved in BL Add. MS 5444.

7   The French Chronicle is found in MS Cotton Cleopatra A VI, fo. 54ff, and is published as *Chroniques de London depuis l'an 44 Hen. III jusqu'à l'an 17 Edw. III*, ed. G.J. Aungier, Camden Society, 28 (1844).

8   D.C. Cox, in appendix B of his article, 'The French Chronicle of London', *Medium Aevum*, 45.2 (1976), pp. 201–8, notes the few exceptional points of correspondence between the *Chroniques* and later London chronicles.

9   The chronicle in Letter Book F is printed almost entirely in the *Calendar of Letter Books of the City of London: Letter Book F c.1337–1352*, ed. R.R. Sharpe (London, 1904), pp. 276–303.

10 A few manuscripts do not begin at 1189. Many of these are imperfect, e.g. MSS Cotton Cleopatra C IV and West Yorkshire Archives, Bradford 3286D/42, and may initially have begun recording at 1189, but have now lost their first pages. A small group of London chronicles (MSS Trinity College Cambridge 0.9.1, University Library Cambridge H.h.6.9, Rawlinson B 173, Egerton 650 and perhaps Harley 540) are written as continuations of Bruts. These usually begin in 1421. Some sixteenth-century texts do not begin at 1189: MSS Balliol 354, Harley 2252, Harley 540. In these cases the changed beginning-dates may reflect a perceived change of purpose, as these texts begin around 1400, and may be concerned primarily to chronicle the period of the Wars of the Roses, rather than to provide an early documentary history of London.

11 Manuscripts which have been clearly copied or continued by their owners/keepers include Trinity College Dublin 509/604, Bodley 596, Cotton Vitellius A XVI, Cotton Julius B II.

12 For example, MSS Guildhall 3313, Rawlinson B 359 and Gough London 10.

13 The contents of the manuscripts and the chroniclers' evident access to records suggest that they were written by citizens of London, often aldermen or people of high status in guilds. However, it also appears that less influential people kept chronicles, e.g. MS Trinity College Dublin 509 was probably kept by a scribe, and we can associate the Bradford manuscript with a common clerk of the Guildhall. With two exceptions (MSS Guildhall 3313 and Egerton 1995) there is no evidence as to the sex of the chroniclers. They are therefore referred to here as 'he' for convenience.

14 For C.L. Kingsford's postulation of a Main City Chronicle, see *English Historical Literature in the Fifteenth Century* (Oxford, 1913), pp. 99–100. Evidence for the existence of more than one main strand of London chronicle is discussed in my article, 'The Textual Transmission and Authorship of the London Chronicles', in P. Beal and J. Griffiths, eds, *English Manuscript Studies 1100–1700*, III (Oxford, 1992), pp. 38–72.

15 MS Gough London 10 is published in part in R. Flenley, ed., *Six Town Chronicles* (Oxford, 1913), pp. 153–66, and is described by him, pp. 74–81.

16 Extracts from *The Brewers' First Book* appear in R.W. Chambers and M. Daunt, eds, *A Book of London English* (Oxford, 1931), pp. 140–91.

17 The evidence that the author of the text in MS Egerton 1995 was a mayor of London is overwhelming. However, it is extremely unlikely that he was William Gregory, as is

commonly suggested. See W.E. Lunt, *Financial Relations of the Papacy with England 1327–1534*, Medieval Academy of America, 74 (Cambridge, Mass., 1962), pp. 574–5. See also my article, 'The Textual Transmission and Authorship of the London Chronicles'.

18 The deposition documents for Richard II are recorded in MSS Guildhall 3313, Cotton Julius B II and Longleat 53. They also appear as an appendix to the chronicle in MS Bodley 596.

19 This appears in MSS Guildhall 3313, St John's College Oxford 57, Cotton Julius B I, Cotton Vitellius F IX, Egerton 1995, Longleat 53, Cotton Julius B II.

20 Letters appear in MSS St John's College Oxford 57, Guildhall 3313, Cotton Julius B I, Cotton Vitellius F IX, Cotton Vitellius A XVI and Trinity College Dublin 509.

21 Treaties are recorded in MSS Arundel 19, Egerton 1995, Cotton Julius B II, Cotton Julius B I, Cotton Cleopatra C IV, Guildhall 3313, St John's College Oxford 57, Cotton Vitellius F XII.

22 'Account of the Ceremonial of the Marriage of Princess Margaret', ed. T. Phillipps, is printed in *Archaeologia*, 31 (1846), pp. 326–38. Edward IV's arrival survives in a Stow transcript in MS Harley 543. It is published as *Historie of the Arrivall of Edward IV in England and the Finall Recoverye of His Kingdomes*, ed. J. Bruce, Camden Society, 1 (1838). A French version of the *Arrivall* exists in MSS University of Ghent 236 and BN 3887 and 11590, and is published in translation by E. Jerningham, *Archaeologia*, 21 (1826), pp. 11–23. A short English version also exists in BL Add. MS 46354 and College of Arms 2M16, published by R.F. Green as 'The Short Version of the Arrival of Edward IV', *Speculum*, 56 (1981) pp. 324–36. Green's accompanying article examines the chronological order of these texts.

23 C.A.J. Armstrong, 'Some Examples of the Distribution and Speed of News in England at the Time of the Wars of the Roses', *Studies in Medieval History presented to Frederick Maurice Powicke*, ed. R.W. Hunt, W.A. Pantin and R.W. Southern (Oxford, 1948), pp. 429–54.

24 In MSS Harley 3775, Guildhall 3313, St John's 57, Harley 565, Digby Rolls 2, Cotton Julius B I, Cotton Julius B II, Cotton Vitellius F IX, Egerton 1995.

25 Recorded in MSS Guildhall 3313, St John's 57, Cotton Vitellius F IX, Cotton Julius B I, Egerton 1995, Arundel 19, Longleat 53.

26 In MSS Trinity College Cambridge 0.9.1, University Library Cambridge H.h.6.9, Harley 540, Guildhall 3313, St John's 57, Cotton Julius B I, Cotton Julius B II, Cotton Vitellius F IX, Egerton 1995.

27 That Brut chronicles are clearly based on cycles is indicated by their regnal dating, their chronological accounting in eras, and their repetition of ideals in the characters of various kings. In contrast the method of dating in the London chronicles identifies them as strictly linear. For a study of the Brut chronicles, see J. Taylor, *English Historical Literature in the Fourteenth Century* (Oxford, 1988).

28 While some historians, like A. Goodman, *The Wars of the Roses* (London, 1981), accept the London chronicles for what they are, without deeply questioning their sources or ideas (pp. 10–11), others are highly critical of them because they do not fit their expectations of what historical narratives should be. G.R. Elton, *England 1200–1600: the Sources of History: Studies in the Uses of Historical Evidence* (London, 1969) considers the fifteenth-century chroniclers 'scrappy and often primitive' (p. 14). J.J. Bagley, *Historical Interpretation: Sources of English Medieval History, 1066–1540* (Harmondsworth, 1965) states that the lay chroniclers of the fifteenth century 'did not try to present a theme or assess the importance of events' (p. 215). J.R. Lander, *Conflict and Stability in Fifteenth Century England*, 2nd edn (London, 1974), states that the London chronicles suffer from 'poverty stricken vocabulary, limited vision, credulous reproduction of rumour and slander, long and immensely detailed descriptions of ceremonies and

pageants' (p. 14). A. Gransden, *Historical Writing in England, II, c. 1307 to the Early Sixteenth Century* (London, 1982) looks at several different aspects of the London chronicles, but does not comment on their emphasis on ceremony. In general, she notes simply that they 'do not compare in quality to the best chronicles of the previous century' (p. 241). S. Anglo, *Spectacle, Pageantry, and Early Tudor Policy* (Oxford, 1969) analyses the use of pageantry in Tudor England, but does not assess its appearance in the earlier London chronicles. To the best of my knowledge, C.P. Maddern, 'The Chronicling of Fifteenth-century England' (unpublished M.A. thesis, University of Melbourne, 1978), is the only modern scholar to comment on the importance of the recording of processions in some fifteenth-century chronicles. I am grateful to her for suggesting they may be useful as sources for understanding the chroniclers' techniques.

29   *Registrum Abbatiae Johannis Whethamstede*, I, ed. H.T. Riley, RS (London, 1872), pp. 376–8.

30   Statutes of the Realm, I, 380 (1363), and Statutes of the Realm, II, 468–70 (1483), printed as Documents 681 and 692 respectively in *English Historical Documents, IV, 1327–1485*, ed. A.R. Myers (London, 1969). A further act against the wearing of costly apparel, defining class and income by clothing, appeared in 1510. See Statutes of the Realm, III, 8, printed as Doc. 16 in *English Historical Documents, V, 1485–1558*, ed. C.H. Williams (London, 1967).

31   For the bequeathing of clothes in wills, see for example the wills of John Plot, Robert Averay, John Solas of Southwark and John Rogerysson in Chambers and Daunt, eds., *A Book of London English*, pp. 212–20. An emphasis on clothing and position can also be seen in the 'Lament of the Duchess of Gloucester' in MS Balliol 354 (a commonplace book also containing a London chronicle), printed in *Political Poems and Songs Relating to English History Composed during the Period from the Accession of Edward III to that of Richard III*, II, ed. T. Wright, RS (London, 1861).

32   Perkin Warbeck's confession in the London chronicle of MS Guildhall 3313 under the year 1499, printed as *The Great Chronicle of London*, eds Thomas and Thornley, pp. 284–6.

33   'The Brewers' First Book', fo. 71, extracts printed in Chambers and Daunt, eds, *A Book of London English*, pp. 142–6. Examples of the wearing of particular colours in triumphal and regal processions occur in the *Gesta Henrici Quinti: the Deeds of Henry the Fifth*, ed. and trans. F. Taylor and J.S. Roskell (Oxford, 1975), ch. 15, recording Henry V's reception into London after the battle of Agincourt; and the greeting of Henry VII in London after the battle of Bosworth, in MS Guildhall 3313 (*The Great Chronicle*, pp. 238–9). Stow also lists and explains colours and fabrics worn by various parties on different occasions, *Survey of London*, II, pp. 246ff.

34   This is almost certainly an indication that York sought the throne. What is of interest in this account is the context in which it appears, and the implications it has for the audience within this account. As this is not an eyewitness record, we must consider why the chronicler has chosen to include it here and in this way.

35   P. Maddern, 'The Chronicling of Fifteenth Century England', analyses the record of this procession as it is recorded in *The New Chronicles of England and France*. Although examined in different terms, she also reaches this conclusion.

36   Such a conclusion is also reached by reading John Blacman's contemporary biography of Henry VI, published as *Henry the Sixth, a Reprint of J. Blacman's Memoir*, with translation and notes by M.R. James (Cambridge, 1919). For an examination of the ways in which Blacman expresses this dichotomy, see R. Lovatt, 'John Blacman: Biographer of Henry VI', in R.H.C. Davis and J.M. Wallace-Hadrill, eds, *The Writing of History in the Middle Ages*.

37   The qualities essential for good kingship can be found in many sources: implicit in Romance (e.g. the Arthurian cycles and King Horn); in the first chapters of the Brut

chronicles (founders, warriors, charitable men, just, loved); in Fortescue's *The Governance of England*, ed. C. Plummer (Oxford, 1885) and *De Laudibus Legum Angliae*, ed. and trans. S.B. Chrimes (Cambridge, 1942) (prosperity, leadership, order). See also L.K. Born, 'The Perfect Prince: A Study in Thirteenth- and Fourteenth-Century Ideals', *Speculum*, 3 (1928), pp. 470–504. The comparison of Henry VI and Henry V in Hardyng's *Chronicle*, ed. H. Ellis (London, 1812), also implies a number of ideal qualities.

38 PRO King's Bench Ancient Indictments (K.B.9) file 122, m.28, printed as Document 145 in *English Historical Documents, IV, 1327–1485*.

39 R.L. Storey, *The End of the House of Lancaster* (London, 1966), suggests this as a reason for the number of cases, and notes the attitude reflected even by false cases (pp. 34–5).

40 M. Twycross, 'Beyond the Picture Theory: Image and Activity in Medieval Drama', *Word and Image*, 4 (1988), pp. 589–617.

41 The English continuation of the *Polychronicon* provides an interesting comparison here. It notes that in 1399 Henry duke of Lancaster and Richard II left so quickly for London on the eve of Richard's deposition that Richard 'was not suffrede to chaunge his clothes, but rode in symple apparayle thro the cuntre', despite the fact that he had garments of gold and pearls. We may suggest that the chronicler believed Henry did not wish Richard to be seen to appear as a king. (*The English Continuation of the Polychronicon*, ed. Rev. J.R. Lumby, in *Polychronicon Ranulphi Higden Monachi Cestrensis*, VIII, RS (London, 1882), pp. 508–9).

42 'On the Times' from MS 237, fo. 236v (Corpus Christi College, Oxford), published in *Political Poems and Songs*, II, ed. T. Wright, pp. 252–3.

43 'On the Corruptions of the Times', from MS F.f.1.6, fo. 134v (University Library, Cambridge), published in *Political Poems and Songs*, II, pp. 238–42. Wright identifies the hand as contemporary with the reign of Henry VI.

44 P. Burke, *Popular Culture in Early Modern Europe* (London, 1978), ch. 7.

45 There is some evidence of oral residue in the texts, particularly in the style of dating events, and the formulaic presentation of some accounts.

46 The appearance of several of the chronicles in commonplace books suggests that they may be considered as complementary to other shared material: recipes, puzzles, tax rates etc. When placed in this context the idea of personal ownership of the material is decreased.

47 As stated above, the London chronicles often appear to have been written by senior members of guilds, or by clerks. The degree of variation in the social status of the chroniclers is evidenced by the possible author of MS Trinity College Dublin 509/604 being a scrivener; an owner or writer of MS West Yorkshire Archives, Bradford 3286D/42 being a common clerk; and the author of MS Egerton 1995 (Gregory's Chronicle) being a mayor. On the immigration and classes in London see G. Williams, *Medieval London from Commune to Capital*, University of London Historical Studies, 11 (London, 1963).

10

The Churchwardens' Accounts of Thame, Oxfordshire, c. 1443–1524

Julia Carnwath

The boundary of the counties of Oxfordshire and Buckinghamshire follows the course of the River Thame for some eight miles as it flows from its source near Tring (Hertfordshire) to its junction with the Thames a little north of Wallingford (Berkshire).[1] Lying on the Oxfordshire bank, the town of Thame took its name from the river. It was its position that gave the town its growing importance in the medieval period, for it lay at the centre of a network of roads. The way from Aylesbury to Wallingford lay through Thame, and at Tetsworth (three miles to the south of Thame and in the same medieval parish) it met the Oxford–High Wycombe–London road. The fairs and markets of Thame were well established by the mid-thirteenth century, and the Oxford–Aylesbury road had been diverted to run through it.[2] Oxford lay fourteen miles to the west of Thame and London forty-six miles to the south-east. The significance of Thame in this web of communication is shown by the marking of the town on the Gough map.

The medieval town lay at the north of the parish. Before the parochial reorganisation of 1841 the parish consisted of the town (comprising New Thame, parts of Old Thame and Priestend) and the other liberties and hamlets of Old Thame and Priestend, together with those of North Weston, Moreton and Thame Park where there was a Cistercian abbey. The parish also included Towersey, then in the county of Buckinghamshire, Tetsworth and Sydenham. There was also Attingdon, the population of which was already declining in the period and which was soon to disappear completely.[3]

The landscape is pleasant and undulating, mostly between 200 and 250 feet above sea level. It rises gently from the river towards the Chilterns in the south. It was then a well-watered, lush country characterised by low hills and many streams. The rich soil and excellent communications ensured its relative prosperity throughout the later medieval period. In the second half of the fifteenth century enclosure began in the fields of Moreton and Attingdon, much of it initiated by Geoffrey Dormer, 'wolman of Thame'.[4] He was the richest resident in the parish after the death of Richard Quatremains in 1477.[5]

Besides giving its name to both town and parish, the river also gave its name to the hundred. All the parish of Thame lay in the hundred of Thame except for Sydenham (Lewknor hundred) and Towersey (Ashendon hundred, Buckinghamshire). The town was only in a limited way the nucleus of both parish and hundred. In the oldest part of the original township of Old Thame stood the parish church of St Mary the Virgin. Sydenham, Towersey and Tetsworth had their own chapels. Tetsworth also had the chapel attached to the hermitage founded by Richard Quatremains in 1447.[6] There was another chapel to the south-east of the town just outside the abbey gates, and also a private chapel of the Quatremains family at North Weston. There was a chapel attached to the prebendal house at Thame, and in the parish church itself was a chantry chapel to St Christopher founded in 1447, again by Richard Quatremains, and served by a single priest.[7]

The sporadic nature of the surviving evidence presents the usual problems in estimating late medieval population. In 1377 791 adults were declared liable for the poll tax in the whole parish excluding Towersey and Sydenham.[8] No 1522 muster returns survive for Thame, but adopting Julian Cornwall's method of calculation the total population then being served by the parish church, (that is, excluding Tetsworth, Towersey and Sydenham) in 1524–5 appears to have been in the region of 550.[9] Around 1550 the communicating population of Thame 'which is a great town' was said to be 800 when the retaining of the chantry priest to assist the parish priest was requested.[10] The chantry certificate itself puts the figure at 1200.[11] There are clearly problems with all these figures, but on such evidence as they provide we might hazard a conservative estimate for Thame and its hamlets of between 500 and 600 in the period of the churchwardens' accounts, rising quite quickly in Thame as elsewhere in the ensuing decades.[12] It is clear nevertheless that the market town of Thame attracted people from the surrounding villages of Oxfordshire and Buckinghamshire and from as far away as London.[13] In the later fifteenth and early sixteenth centuries we can see Thame, although it was never incorporated, as a flourishing, moderate-sized town.

The earliest surviving churchwardens' accounts cover the period approximately 1442 to 1524.[14] They constitute an invaluable indication of the lay contribution to parish affairs. The first leaf is of an earlier date. From the 1440s until 1496 the accounts are for New Thame only. From 1496 until 1524 the volume contains the accounts of the churchwardens of both New Thame and Old Thame. These two facts are of the greatest significance in the appreciation and interpretation of the contents of the accounts. The distinction between Old and New Thame needs now to be defined.

The old town appears to have grown up around the church in the late Anglo-Saxon period.[15] The new town was a planned seigneurial borough of the twelfth century which developed within the manor of Old Thame at the desire of the bishops of Lincoln who held the manor, and indeed held jurisdiction over the entire hundred of Thame. The bishops' officials conducted the three-weekly hundred court in Old Thame. Twice yearly the view of frankpledge was held on Milton Common, also a part of the hundred but in another parish. New Thame, however, had its own portmoot every fortnight and held its own view of frankpledge.[16] By the mid-thirteenth century there were seventy-six burgage tenements held by sixty-three burgesses.[17] From the fourteenth century tax returns it is also clear that the new town had outstripped the old in population, and was by then the most populous part of the parish.[18] This is also reflected in the surviving court rolls of both hundred and portmoot for the fifteenth century.

To the west of Old Thame lies the liberty of Priestend incorporating the earlier settlement of Shillingdon.[19] The name Priestend probably derives from the presence there of the prebendal house and its attached lands. In the twelfth century the parish of Thame was made into a prebend of the chapter of Lincoln cathedral.[20] Priestend had its own field system and court administered by the rector's bailiff. It was exempt from the jurisdiction of the bishop in his hundred court, and the entire parish was of course exempt from the jurisdiction of his archdeacon's court. The prebend was one of the richest in the diocese of Lincoln: in 1535 it was valued at £82 12s. 2½d. and the vicarage at £18.[21]

In the period covered by the accounts there were eight prebendaries. The earlier ones were generally men of national standing.[22] Only the last two, Adrian de Bardis (1480–1519) and Richard Maudeley (1520–31) appear to have been frequently resident.[23] The vicars whom they appointed in the period of the accounts perhaps numbered seven.[24] Chaplains were appointed by the vicars to the daughter chapels of Tetsworth, Towersey and Sydenham. The small population of Attingdon probably attended at Tetsworth.[25] Although this paper is not directly concerned with the parish clergy, but rather with the degree and nature of lay involvement in the administration of church and parish affairs, one essential point concerning them needs to be made. From the almost complete absence in the accounts of any reference to a parishioner of Tetsworth, Towersey or Sydenham being buried at Thame or even bequeathing to the parish church, it is apparent that the chapels had acquired burial rights.[26] It is also clear that the chapels had their own churchwardens keeping their own accounts.[27] Only in connection with the ecclesiastical jurisdiction are they mentioned. The fortunes of Tetsworth, especially, and Towersey may have remained quite strongly linked socially and economically with Thame (Sydenham looked more towards Chinnor to the east) but there was no single parish community, liturgically speaking.[28] *De facto* the parish church at Thame served the old and new towns, Priestend, North Weston and Moreton.

Churchwardens' accounts are primarily ecclesiastical documents kept by laymen and for the use of laymen. The first churchwardens' account book, or *Computus*, for Thame is a slim volume of eighty leaves. The accounts are handwritten on paper in English and Latin. 'The original binding of stout leather is affixed outside the new one.'[29] This refers to a modern binding probably of the late nineteenth century. The original spine is lost. Some leaves are missing, some misplaced, and others have been cut out. At some point the book was evidently in pieces and major restoration undertaken, almost certainly at the time of the rebinding. It is not known how it came to leave Thame, but it was in the hands of a member of the Wykeham family of Tythrop in the mid-nineteenth century.[30] In 1902 it became the subject of a bitter dispute between the honorary secretaries of the Buckinghamshire Architectural and Archaeological Society and Bodley's Librarian, E.W. Nicholson, amid allegations of theft, libel and defamation of character.[31] It is now quietly and safely in the Oxfordshire County Record Office. Two partial transcriptions have been published. The Rev. F.G. Lee,the grandson of a former vicar of Thame, produced some extracts in his *History* of the church published in 1883.[32] Between 1902 and 1914 W. Patterson Ellis began a serialised transcription and translation in the *Berkshire, Buckinghamshire and Oxfordshire Archaeological Journal*.[33]

There has been a renewal of interest in early churchwardens' accounts in recent years.[34] Unique in being ecclesiastical documents kept by laymen, they have come to be seen rightly as a valuable source which may shed light on parish organisation and lay commitment to the Church in the generations preceding the religious turmoil of the mid-sixteenth century. Studies of such local accounts as survive are important in the building up of a national picture.[35] Many sets were transcribed or extracted in a flurry of interest towards the end of the nineteenth century and at the beginning of the twentieth. These were listed and analysed in the classic study by J.C. Cox (1913), but his list, as he anticipated, can now be shown to be incomplete.[36] Since then few transcriptions have appeared. The most recent to be published have been those for Ashburton (Devon) in 1970 and Chagford (Devon) in 1979.[37] None have supplemented the text with a full introduction, making use of other accounts where relevant, or of other sources for the same parish, where they survive. Thus it seems that their potential value has remained under-explored. Sixteenth-century religious historians have dipped into them for anecdotal references, for example, to rood-screen construction or demolition, and for evidence of late Catholic or early Protestant practice.[38] This is a valid use of them in the broad-sweep approach. It does seem, however, that there might be equally great value in the long run in attempting to investigate at a more than superficial level the local context in which such events occurred. This can only be done if all other sources for the same parish are integrated into the study.

In that way we may approach the question of whether the parish was ever a community in more than a purely administrative sense, and to what extent it coincided with the contemporary social and economic community on which it had come to be imposed.[39] Further, by this we may come closer to the elusive matter of motivation. Churchwardens' accounts require more than transcription, translation or summary if we are to interpret and use them properly as an important witness to lay attitudes.

It is accepted that the appointment of churchwardens and the practice of account-keeping by them developed from the thirteenth century when the laity received responsibility for the material upkeep, internal and external, of the naves of the parish churches.[40] Few accounts survive for the fourteenth century.[41] Between 1400 and 1600 there are at present more than 200 sets known to be extant, of which perhaps only about seventy cover any part of the fifteenth century; the majority of these begin in the second half.

Many of these are fragmentary. Much loss and damage, either wilful or from neglect, has occurred over time. Some accounts, such as those of St Michael's, Bath (1349–1575), St Laurence, Reading (beginning 1410) and the complete century of Ashburton (1479–1580) are exceptionally detailed.[42] Some include precious highlights, such as the wealth of information concerning plays given in the Bassingbourn accounts of the early sixteenth century.[43] Some contain inventories (Thame, Bassingbourn, St Edmund in Salisbury) which give illuminating details of vestments, books and ornaments, often naming benefactors.[44] In others there are frequent gaps, and years where mere totals for receipts and expenditure have been recorded.

In terms of fullness the Thame accounts fall somewhere between the two. They appear to rank about seventeenth chronologically with respect to the first year of entry. It is clear from the opening leaves that accounts had been kept previously. It is possible to ascertain this by 'dating' individuals named in the accounts from information found in the court rolls of the hundred, and from the chance survival of an early case in Chancery involving one of the churchwardens named at fo. 1 who was clearly dead by the time the true accounts open in fo. 2.[45] Here the loss was probably due to neglect, for the first leaf is heavily encapsulated by repair material and was clearly loose at one time. For some years either the receipts or expenses are missing. Sometimes whole years are missing: 1483–7, 1492–3, 1499–1500, 1505–8, 1513–14, 1515–19 and 1520–1, a total of fifteen years out of eighty-one. The removal of leaves from the volume may have occurred because of the evidence they contained, or it could have happened at a later date at the hands of misguided antiquarian enthusiasts. As with other sets of accounts for the period, those of Thame vary also even where the accounts appear to be fully extant. Some years (e.g. 1443–9, 1462–4 and 1488–98), provide a great deal of information, and many individuals who also occur in other sources are named. In other years (e.g. 1503–4 and 1509–10), the entries are sparse. Sometimes, frustratingly, the scribe adopts the practice of naming a payment, but omitting both recipient and purpose.

The method of account-keeping therefore varied between sets, and within individual sets, between scribes and over time. In Thame receipts were listed first (a common practice) but no further attempt was made to subdivide them under headings, for instance those from rents or bequests. Sometimes a chronological order seems to have been observed, and the same is done in the case of the expenses which, perhaps naturally, are often much more extensive. There is a good deal of internal evidence to suggest that much of what survives in the account book is a fair copy of accounts previously kept. Reference occurs to bills and receipts '*prout patet in billa*', or '*ut patet per scedulam*'.[46] Two such receipts were sewn into the book. On one occasion (1453) the accounts were drawn up first in English and then reproduced in Latin.[47] In 1481 two accounts were produced, the one an elaboration of the other.[48] One gains the impression that Latin in the earlier period was the preferred language, at least for the rubric, perhaps because it conveyed a greater sense of being official. In late 1449 the scribe attempted a Latin rubric, but then appears to have given up.[49] Except for the accounts of John Manyturn (churchwarden 1441–9), the rubrics are always in Latin down to 1521 where Latin is finally abandoned in favour of the vernacular.

Most parishes in the period had two churchwardens, although there are occasional instances noted of just one. Thame had four, perhaps because of the size of the parish and perhaps also to reflect adequately the retained separate jurisdictional identities of Old and New Thame. The two New Thame churchwardens were responsible for the north side of the church, and the two Old Thame churchwardens (comprehending Priestend and possibly also North Weston and Moreton) for the south side. Expenses for lighting, maintenance of the bells, clock and organ, the payments to the summoner and chapter expenses were shared. At this time the prebendary and vicar had no hand in their appointment. The term '*electi sunt*' is used, and they were chosen by the more prominent parishioners at or after the audit of the accounts which was generally, but not invariably, held in the church once a year.[50] In most parishes in the fifteenth century the time of audit and election remained variable. In Thame, typically, there was no rule until late in the accounts. For example, new churchwardens took office at Christmas Eve (1441), 13 March (1446), Easter Saturday (1449), All Souls' Day (1446) and Epiphany (1478). There is a break in the accounts at 1483, and when they resume in 1487 the term of office commences consistently thereafter at Ascensiontide.

It seems that at Thame the formal audit (as opposed to informal 'reckonings' between times, for which there is much evidence) was presented to a body of parishioners for inspection; perhaps the election took place at the same time, and the new wardens took office at once or at the next important feast. Particularly in the earlier period of the accounts there is a strong tendency for the same people to be re-elected. Thomas Bunce, for example, held office for eleven years consecutively from 1441 to 1453, the first eight of these with John Manyturn. John Daunce and John Benet were elected for two years in 1462. Benet was back again with John King in Easter 1446 for another two-and-a-half years until All Souls' 1468. His son John Benet junior held office with John Garthorpe for three years from Good Friday 1474. In the last three decades of the accounts, where Old and New Thame are combined, a pattern had established itself for each man to hold office for two years, so that there was, as it were, a senior and a junior churchwarden each year for both Old and New Thame. The account-book alone can give no indication of how willingly or reluctantly these men assumed office. Information gleaned from other sources about their economic status and social position strongly suggests that in Thame, if not elsewhere, the office was willingly accepted and even sought.

In pondering the incentives for laymen to assume parochial office three principal questions may be asked of the source material. What kind of men became churchwardens? To what extent were other laity involved in parochial and liturgical organisation? What were the actual functions fulfilled and tasks performed by these lay officers of the church?

What kind of men became churchwardens at Thame in the period of the accounts? The first point to be made is that they were likely to have been literate.[51] In the eighty years spanned by the accounts perhaps twenty scribes contributed. They were of varying degrees of efficiency and calligraphic skill. Only three of the scribes can be identified with any certainty. John Manyturn (churchwarden 1441-9) appears to have written his own accounts.[52] He wrote in English, as did John Chapman junior in 1482 and 1483.[53] His father, John Chapman senior, was a churchwarden of many years experience, having first been elected in 1449. He was again churchwarden at the time of his son's keeping of the accounts, and indeed the son is also named in the accounts as a warden of the Sepulchre light. The third and last scribe who can be positively identified is Christopher Bridgeman, who for more than a quarter of a century until his death in 1503 was sexton and keeper of the clock.[54] He appears to have started to keep the accounts in 1488 and continued to do so for the remaining fifteen years of his life. That his skill as a scribe was valued is evident from entries in the accounts recording payments to him for writing the service for the Visitation in the great portiforium (1487). In 1495 he was paid 2*d*. '*pro scriptura copie citacionis pro parte nostra*'. In 1500 he received 6*d*. for copying three deeds 'of the rent of Thomas Bocher's howse'. Finally, he was again mentioned in his capacity as scribe in the roll of the court of the guild of St Christopher in 1492, for which he had written the bill of the chaplain's distraint of the goods of one John Pede.[55] Bridgeman wrote in both Latin and English, and his accounts are among the fullest in the set. Of the other scribes nothing has been discovered. There was, however, at least one other churchwarden who would have been capable of writing the accounts. John Cockys (churchwarden 1494–6) was paid 6d. during his term of office '*pro scriptura iij cartarum pro annuali redditu tenementi Nicholai Hagurston*'.[56] The scribe for New Thame was paid 4d. down to 1496, a small sum for the effort and time required.

It may therefore come as no surprise that the wardens appear to have been drawn from the higher ranks of townsmen. They were more than labourers or small craftsmen. In the earlier period, before 1483, for which the evidence of hundred courts, views of frankpledge, and hallmoot and portmoot rolls can be used, they can be seen to be combining the management of shops and tenements or inns in New Thame with farming in the fields of Old Thame, Priestend and Moreton. They appear as bailiffs, tithingmen, and holders of office such as constable, meat-inspector, or taster of victuals. They are pledges, jurors and affeerors, and commissioners to collect the lay subsidy.

John Chapman senior, for example, was churchwarden between 1449 and 1482 for at least eleven years. In this period he was listed as a burgess in views of frankpledge for New Thame, a free tenant of the bishop of Lincoln in his manor of Old Thame and a juror at the courts. He was both chandler and fishmonger and was amerced at the assize of ale.[57] John Benet junior, who held office for a total of thirteen years and whose father was bailiff to the bishop of Lincoln, was also a burgess of New Thame and a tenant of Old Thame.[58] His father was a commissioner to collect the lay subsidy of 1449 and was described as a yeoman in a case of debt when he was temporarily outlawed in the hustings court of London for failure to satisfy a London grocer's widow of £6 5s. 4d.[59] Both father and son were innkeepers with interests in fishmongery, butchery and candlemaking.[60] Both the Chapman and Benet families feature throughout the accounts.

John Daunce, who held office for two-and-a-half years (1464–6), was also burgess and tenant, tithingman and constable. He was employed on important business riding 'to Oxfford ffor owyr proktor'. He served the church as summoner to the chapter from 1457 to 1459, and in 1468 he was a commissioner to collect the lay subsidy.[61] His grandson, also called John, was knighted, became a benefactor of Thame Church, and in 1524 was appointed steward to the bishop of Lincoln in succession to the Stonors.[62] No trade is given for the Daunces. They held land in Old Thame, but it seems likely that they were salaried.

John Garthorp, holding office for a total of ten years, appears as chandler and fishmonger, juror and tithingman.[63] By the 1480s we are within reach of the first of the surviving court rolls for the guild of St Christopher. Garthorp appears in the homage, as do many of the churchwardens from the 1480s onwards.[64] Again the Garthorp family is prominent in Thame to the end of the period covered by the *Computus*.

Between 1442 and 1483, when the gap of five years appears, there are a total of eighty churchwarden-years, allowing that two men held office together. Thirteen men held office twice during this time. The average number of years of holding office, not necessarily consecutively, was just over six years. The turnover was not high. Thomas Bunce held office for eleven consecutive years, Chapman for a total of eleven years, John Benet for thirteen years and John King and John Garthorp for ten years each. Of the thirteen men named six occur in the rolls as chandlers, five were also fishmongers and eight were jurors.

The period 1487–96 seems to have been one of transition. New names appear and the average period for holding office drops to two-and-a-half years (i.e. eighteen churchwarden-years, and seven men holding office). At this point there is less court roll evidence, but the guild roll of 1492 is useful.[65] On this, four of the churchwardens' names appear. No occupations for this group are given, but three of the eight occur in the draft portmoot roll of 1481 as tithingmen, two are named in the list of burgesses and one is clearly a chandler.

From 1496 to 1524, when the *Computus* ends, the accounts for New Thame and Old Thame were combined. Thirty-seven men held office in 112 churchwarden-years (four wardens holding office annually). The average length of office, again not consecutively, was three years. In fact most men held office once only, and for a two-year period. It is clear that two men were chosen specifically for New Thame and two for Old Thame and Priestend, and eligibility seems to have had something to do with residence, although as already indicated many of these men had both commercial interests in New Thame and farming interests in Old Thame and beyond.

Walter Pratt, churchwarden from the Sunday after the Ascension (15 May) 1496 for one year only, and appointed again for 1507–9, appears from the accounts to have been, amongst other occupations, a chandler, for he supplied candles and wax in abundance from 1496 until his death, in office, in 1508. His brass remains in Thame church in the nave. In his will he bequeathed 3*s.* 4*d.* to the high altar at Thame, 6lb. of wax to the Holy Sepulchre light, 1lb. of wax to every other light, a cow to the church, twenty ewes to the masses of the Name of Jesus and a ewe to every godchild. He bequeathed land in Henley-on-Thames and in both New and Old Thame to his wife Elizabeth until his heir should be of full age.[66]

From a case in Chancery, dated approximately 1515, we know that he also had an acre of wood in Radnage, Buckinghamshire, and that the Thame property included a messuage of close and garden in New Thame, plus other unnamed property in both New and Old Thame. These were claimed by his sister Joanna on the deaths of both widow and heir. He is described as a husbandman.[67]

A second example in this period is William Goodchild, whose story shows that it was not necessary to be of an old-established family in order to achieve the position of churchwarden. It may even have been a position which one sought on the way up and then moved beyond, as the history of the Daunce family might indicate. Goodchild was elected churchwarden in 1496 (with Walter Pratt), but he died a year later while still in office. He bequeathed 3s. 4d. to the church and 6d. to the rood. A memorandum in the account book informs us that his executors, his wife Alice and his son Christopher, gave to the church in honour of the Blessed Mary and all the saints, 'a seute of vestymentes with a cope the coler rede velvet the orfrarys of clothe of golde powdred with . . . angelys and flowrys of golde braunches in the seid chirche to remayne for ever'.[68]

Only eighteen years earlier the patent rolls record a mandate to all bailiffs, etc. to permit 'William Pentland, alias Godechild, born in Scotland, dwelling in New Thame, county Oxfordshire, who has taken an oath of fealty to inhabit the realm peaceably and enjoy his goods'.[69] He was soon afterwards a tithingman of Eastquarter in New Thame and a constable; he was named in the 1481 view of frankpledge for New Thame as an innkeeper and fishmonger.[70]

Whereas the few surviving court rolls have helped to shed light on the social and economic status of earlier churchwardens, the last years have the benefit of the lay subsidy returns. In the 1524 anticipation just two names are given for New Thame; Richard Elys and John Goodwyn, both of whom paid £3.[71] The only name given for Old Thame is Geoffrey Dormer, who paid £3 6s. 8d. He was a 'gentleman' and was never churchwarden, nor were any of his family. But both Elys and Goodwyn had served for New Thame. Richard Elys had served the usual (by now) two years, 1510–12; John Goodwyn had served twice, 1501–2 and 1505–8. Court rolls for the guild of St Christopher survive for 1514 and 1520.[72] On each occasion both Elys and Goodwyn were guildwardens presiding over the court. In 1514 Richard Elys had been elected warden of the light of the Holy Sepulchre. Both men supplied wax and candles to the church. In the return of the 1524–5 subsidy, the year that the accounts end, there are seventy-eight names listed for New Thame.[73] Richard Elys and John Goodwyn head the list, both assessed on goods worth £60 and each paying £3. Elys is named as a chandler and Goodwyn is marginated as sub-commissioner to John Benet for the collection of the subsidy. Of the nine next most wealthy males named in the return, seven (the exceptions being the bailiff and one designated 'of Thame Abbey') had also been churchwardens in the past twenty years. Elys and Goodwyn were clearly at the top of their local hierarchy in economic terms.

Such evidence as can be adduced indicates that throughout the period the men who dominated the office of churchwarden were generally those who held other offices within the economic community of Thame. They emerge as men with diverse financial interests, who could be assumed to be capable administrators, able *and willing* from whatever motive to lead the body of men who served the church, and to handle the considerable amounts of property and wealth which were associated with parish government.

If this can be said of the churchwardens themselves, what of the subsidiary officers of the church and the laymen who occupied the positions such as sexton and summoner? Again, other sources, meagre as they may appear, are sufficient to show that they were drawn from largely the same class as provided churchwardens, and often from the same families.

In the church at Thame, apart from the high altar, there were several other altars in the period of the accounts. In the early fifteenth century there were those of St John the Baptist (in the south transept), Holy Trinity (in the north transept) and Our Lady in le Jesan. There was also the Holy Rood, of particular importance as is clear from numerous bequests. All these altars and the Rood had their own wardens. From time to time they are mentioned in the *Computus*, together with sums of money which they held or quantities of wax. The 1447–8 inventory compiled by the churchwardens John Manyturn and Thomas Bunce lists separately the vestments and ornaments pertaining to Trinity aisle and St John the Baptist's aisle (as they are called) and the altar of Our Lady.[74] In 1528 John Adam of Moreton died leaving in his will 100s. to the five altars of Thame besides the usual 3s. 4d. to the high altar.[75] In addition, from 1478 other lights are mentioned; the Sepulchre, All Souls', St Michael's, St Katherine's. Images of SS. Clement, Christopher, Erasmus, George and Thomas the Apostle also occur.

The number of subsidiary wardens or keepers ('*custodes*' as distinct from the '*procuratores*' or '*iconomi*' of the church) must have been at least six throughout the period and very probably more. The 1513 entry includes an incomplete list of lightwardens: nine are recorded.[76] The same names occur amongst them as in the list of churchwardens. John Chapman junior, whose father was churchwarden and who wrote the 1482–3 accounts, was keeper of the Sepulchre light in 1478–80 and was re-elected. John Garthorp, son of a previous churchwarden, was keeper of the Sepulchre light in 1496. William Young junior and William Young senior, both of whom served as churchwardens, were together keepers of All Souls' light in 1513. William Shadlock (churchwarden 1513–15) was also keeper of St Katherine's light and all the other lights in St John's aisle. John Ely, churchwarden in 1518–20 and again in 1524, was keeper in that same year of Our Lady pew. There are other examples. There is insufficient evidence in the Thame accounts to indicate exactly in what way and how often these lightwardens were chosen. It seems as though there might have been a general review of these offices at the same time as the new churchwardens were chosen and that some kind of election took place for them also.

Money was periodically handed over by the lightkeepers to the churchwardens, sometimes quite large sums. In 1519 the lightman of Our Lady in le Jesan handed over 13s. 4d. and a gold ring priced at 6s. 8d. The same year the lightkeepers of All Souls' handed over 10s.; and £3 was received from the keeper of the Sepulchre light. It is likely that these men kept their own accounts and only occasionally were surpluses handed over to the central fund. In 1513 Richard Elys and Peter Powlyn, both former churchwardens, were able to show 'magistro Johanni Parker ibidem vicario Galfrido Dormer generoso et aliis venerabilibus parochianis' at the audit that they had in hand for the light of the Holy Sepulchre £3 19s. 5d. and 120½lb. in wax.[77] In addition to the lightkeepers it seems that in the earliest period of the accounts two men were appointed to collect for the tolling of the great bell, and, from the prebendary or his representative, for the strawing of the church. The money collected seems to have been used to finance the clock. These entries exist only for the 1440s.[78] John Manyturn, churchwarden for the period, and one Richard Lavender were the two responsible. There is no indication as to whether this practice continued after Manyturn had retired from office.

The churchwardens and lightkeepers at Thame, as elsewhere, were unsalaried. The other lay officers of the church all received regular recompense. These were the sexton and the summoner throughout the Computus; the organ-keeper from 1488; and the clerk, distinguished from the office of sexton, only in the closing years.

The sexton or sacristan seems to have played an especially important rôle, though perhaps it was the man who made the job rather than the other way round. Six men held the position in the period and there is no suggestion that they were elected. In Thame the office was associated with the keeping of the clock and a payment of 20d. (from New and Old Thame) was made quarterly. That it was no sinecure is evident from the 1467 entry where John Sexton was paid by the New Thame churchwardens 10d. at Easter, Midsummer and Michaelmas quarters but 'for Christmas was non alowyd hym, for the clocke stode stille'.[79] By 1475 Christopher Bridgeman was sexton, remaining in the post until 1503 and writing the accounts for the latter part of this time. His brass survives at the entrance to the choir where he is shown in a long gown, lined and cuffed with fur. He wears a belt at his waist to which is attached a purse. His wife Matilda is shown beside him in a long, close-fitting dress, girdled and embroidered. John Bridgeman, who succeeded as sexton until 1515, was probably his son. They were succeeded by William Baret, who also received regular payments for the Jesus Mass.

Payments to the summoner or *apparitor* are recorded regularly throughout the accounts; in the accounts of New Thame to 1496 he was paid a fee of 4*d.* which became 8*d.* when the accounts of New and Old Thame were combined. There were six named in the period, John Daunce (churchwarden 1462–4) being one. The period of tenure seems again to have been long: John Hewlett, for example, was summoner continuously from 1462–82. Nothing is known of the others except for Jerome Holt of Priestend who is named as a tithingman in the view of frankpledge in June 1503 and appears in the 1517 assessment.[80] Perhaps they were Tetsworth men, for the chapter throughout the period seems often to have been held there. There are only three references to it convening at Thame, one called a general chapter in 1490.[81] In 1495–6 a chapter was held at the house of John Daunce, son of the churchwarden, and father of the knight who became steward to the bishop of Lincoln. The same year another chapter was held in Thame at the house of Christopher Holland, who was a servant of Sir William Stonor.[82] He was probably father of Robert Holland (churchwarden 1510–12).

An organ-keeper is mentioned from 1488, new organs and an organ loft having been installed in the late 1470s.[83] Like the sexton, he was paid quarterly, 10*d.* by both the New Thame and Old Thame churchwardens until 1502 when his payment was doubled to 13*s.* 4*d.* yearly. Only two are mentioned before 1510, when the references to an organ-player begin. Of the two organ-keepers, one was William Lewknor, a guild member from a long-established Thame family well involved in the upkeep of the church though never apparently holding the office of churchwarden. He accompanied the churchwardens to London at the expense of the parish when, in 1494–5, they attended the Court of Arches.[84] John Cockys (churchwarden 1494–6) held office as organ-keeper between 1489–98. In this decade he dominated the accounts, providing large quantities of wax, holding the office of keeper of the Sepulchre light and arranging for the mending of vestments, besides his duties as organ-keeper. In the closing years of the accounts the payment of substantial sums made to an organ-player occur. New organs appear to have been installed again in the period of the missing accounts 1515–19, and special collections were made by the churchwardens to pay the player.[85] In 1523–4 William Heyward, clerk, was paid £5 by the churchwardens in five unequal portions. It appears that the church music was being 'professionalised' at this time.

Finally, late in the accounts appear clear references to a parish clerk. By 1519 he was receiving 5s. every quarter, and was named as William Sentmond. In 1522 Richard Morgan was named as clerk, being paid 10s. a quarter. There is no indication of their duties, but at such a salary it was clearly a substantial contribution to the running of parish affairs, very likely including the accountancy. The office of clerk had now become dissociated from responsibility for the clock. Christopher Bridgeman (d. 1503), it may be remembered, had combined both functions.

Overall, the picture which emerges is that the churchwardens and the lightkeepers, the sexton (at least in the Bridgeman period), the summoner and organ-keeper were all drawn from a similar class of men. Clear references to a clerk appear too late for general conclusions. A reading of the accounts, supplemented by other material, conveys a firm impression of a dynamic parish life with offices held by laymen becoming increasingly defined during the period.

Finally, the office of churchwarden had arisen in the thirteenth and fourteenth centuries from the responsibility given to parishioners for the maintenance of the fabric of the church, excluding the chancel, and the ornaments and utensils. Sources of finance for these purposes varied quite widely but invariably involved these representatives of the laity in the handling of substantial sums of money and many precious objects. In Thame four principal sources of finance may be identified.

There was always a regular income derived from church lands (in Shillingdon) and tenements and houses in New Thame. In this the church was fortunate. Property was acquired either by purchase, as in 1443 when the churchwardens bought two acres of land for 6s. 6d. from Thomas Welles on which they grew barley, or by bequest. Butwell Leys (on one occasion suggestively designated 'the lampe londe') first occurs in 1469.[86] The account-keeping of rents, alas, leaves much to be desired. Rents were paid quarterly, twice-yearly or annually, but there are so many omissions and memoranda of debts that it is not possible to know even how many tenements, shops or houses the church was renting out at any one time. Even where house rents are recorded, the details are too sparse for continuous identification, a major problem being that church properties appear to have changed hands quite frequently. An exception is William Tebard's church land in Shillingdon, which he rented for 3d. (probably 6d. divided between the wardens of Old and New Thame) throughout the earlier period of the accounts and which in 1487 was sold by the churchwardens 'per consilium et avisiamentum [sic] xij^m hominum in die capituli generalis' to Geoffrey Dormer for 10s. 'ad opus ecclesie'. In 1469 Butwell Leys was producing an annual rent of 4s. 11d. and was still being rented out in the last year of the accounts. In 1466, a relatively detailed year, there appear to have been six church tenants paying rents. In 1497 there seem to have been three tenants paying a total annual sum of 12s. 8d. However, in 1510 the churchwardens calculated that they were owed £8 10s. 8d. in arrears of rent.[87] Their debtors included the abbot of Notley, who was seventeen years behind with his rent for 'a howse callyd Gilbardis'. (Richard Gilbert had been renting a house from the church in the 1460s and 1470s at 4s. a year.)

As elsewhere, bequests and gifts provided further income throughout the period. Sometimes this was in cash: 2d. to the roodlight from a poorer parishioner, 3s. 4d. from much more substantial ones. Occasionally houses were bequeathed: the sale of Genet Carpenter's in 1444 realised 16s. 8d., and in 1458 John a Bridge of Weston's house realised 23s. 4d. The generous bequests of Walter Pratt have already been mentioned: his flock of twenty sheep produced an income of 6s. 8d. a year until they were sold in 1513 for 20s. The cow also bequeathed in 1508 was rented out at 2s. a year, its demise being indicated in the 1513 receipt of 23d. for a cow's hide. A veil 'y made be þe maydenys' realised 23s. in 1443. Pots, pans and candlesticks, towels and coffers, and bushels of barley are recorded amongst gifts and bequests. In 1458 Beatrice Bates left 4lb. of flaxen yarn which was sold for 20d. The 1447–8 inventory records the bequest of many books and ornaments. William Goodchild, churchwarden, left a whole suit of vestments. In 1523 a whole suit of vestments with three copes was brought from London as the gift of Mr Michael Dormer (later knighted, and Lord Mayor of London, 1541).[88] Thomas Tomlinson in 1494 was holding 3s. 4d. which had come 'to the be hes of the church at the comyng to the towne of the bonys of the lady the kyngis Gramoder'.[89] Nor was it always parishioners who remembered the parish church in their testaments. In 1481 the wardens received 20d. '*ex legatu cuiusdam hominis de Lawnton*'. Thomas Pomeroy esquire, an outsider, taken ill apparently in Thame in the summer of 1508 and dying there in August (three of the six witnesses to his will were churchwardens and one was the summoner) left his chain of ten-score gold links to Our Lady in le Jesan in Thame church.[90] It remained in the care of Robert Pereson, churchwarden, until he sold it in 1511 for £4.[91] It is clear, however, that many bequests and gifts, for some reason or another, were not recorded. The most significant case is that of John Grene, who died in 1465 and left a messuage of land to provide an annual income of 5s. at Michaelmas and the Annunciation for the use of the churchwardens to find a lamp in St John's aisle and ornaments for the church, for repairs, and for the keeping of an obit for himself, his wife and friends on the morrow of the feast of SS.Peter & Paul (29 June). There is no mention of this important bequest in the churchwardens' accounts, although Grene is named as a benefactor in the benefactors' mass of 1492. Its existence only came to light because Thomas Tebard and William Cosyn of Thame both later claimed to be enfeoffed of the land with responsibility for the obit.[92] Sometimes payments are recorded in the accounts with insufficient detail to identify them as gifts or bequests; sometimes perhaps the Old Thame churchwardens were in receipt of them and the balance was sorted out in cash at the reckonings. Often, one suspects, bequests and gifts went directly to the lightwardens and were lost to the main accounts altogether.

The regular, dependable income in Thame came from the two annual collections at Easter and Christmas. Throughout the entire period the Easter gathering remained remarkably steady at around 20s., although it rose in the last decade. This might suggest some sort of rating system and also a fairly steady population of contributors. However, the sums from the Christmas gathering would run counter to this theory, for they show far greater fluctuation: 14s. was being collected in the 1440s, but it is by no means clear which population of the parish was contributing. If the 14s. was from New Thame alone it makes the explicitly combined collections of the early sixteenth century of between 14s. and 18s. look rather like a decline. Most of the income from the gatherings was intended for the purchase of wax and candles throughout the year as indicated by the yearly entries: 'on Ester day to the paschall and to the font tapyr and to the trendyll' and 'at Crystynmesse to the rode lyght'.[93]

Further income was derived from entertainments – plays and ales. Plays were evidently sometimes performed in the church and sometimes outside. By the end of the accounts Christopher Mixbury (of a churchwarden family) was in charge of the wigs and costumes and received an annual payment of 16d.[94] Sometimes, in the earlier years at least, there was a play organiser, or a play collector: in 1455 Edmund Toursey had 'in hys honde' the play money of 3s. 4d. and in 1462 the churchwardens received from him for play money 20s. 'pro nostra parte', which means that a further 20s. was almost certainly given to the churchwardens of Old Thame, quite a handsome sum in all. In 1467 the churchwardens received from John Benet and John Garthorp 'of the last play money, 29s. 6d.'. No names are given for these earlier plays, but in 1482 a St George play took place, and possibly one of Jacob and his Twelve Sons. The play of Fabine and Sabine was performed in 1488.[95] In 1495 there was a Corpus Christi play, and in 1496 and 1501 Robin Hood was associated with either a play or an ale. From 1514 there was an annual Resurrection play; in 1522, in addition, the play of the Three Kings and Herod was performed on Corpus Christi day. Ales were held regularly throughout the period but no clue is given as to location. From 1480 they appear to have been held annually in May. Interestingly, Old Thame and New Thame each held their own and both seem to have increased in popularity. The New Town ale was producing about 20s. between 1488 and 1512, but thereafter the profits began to soar. In the last year of the accounts £3 6s. 8d. was received from the ale of New Thame and 46s. 8d. from that of Old Thame.

These four principal sources of regular income – rents, bequests and gifts, entertainments and the two great annual gatherings – covered the year-by-year running expenses in general. They were supplemented by occasional fees for burial in the church, but these were too infrequent to make a big impact on the general finances.[96] However, if special and large projects were undertaken, extraordinary collections were made. Contributions to these seem to have been voluntary although, as in the case of the making of seats, a general standard rate sometimes seems to have been agreed. In 1444 John Manyturn and Thomas Bunce collected £9 1s. 0d. from 110 parishioners to rebuild the entire north transept. The total cost was £28 15s. 3d.[97] In 1449 Bunce and John Chapman raised 12s. 10½d. from sixty-two parishioners for the building of seats in the north side of the church.[98] In 1478 new organs and an organ loft were installed at a total cost of 91s. 8½d. for the organ and 24s. 2½d. for the loft.[99] The churchwardens made a special collection which produced 36s. 7d. The greater part of the money passing through the hands of the churchwardens always went on lighting, the bells, the clock and organ, salaries for the keepers, the maintenance of vestments, and books and ornaments. Occasional expenses covered all kinds of vicissitudes: the clearing of the snow from the gutters, the ringing of bells for visiting dignitaries, the repairing of the churchyard gates, and entertaining and negotiating with the dean of Lincoln in the churchwardens' important capacity as presenters.[100] An additional source of expenditure was also the maintenance of the church houses and tenements which often required minor repairs. Major surgery was carried out in 1457, 1459, 1461, 1464–6, 1488, 1491 and 1500. There does seem to have been a church-house in the more specific sense in Thame, but a clear list of references is hampered by the many references to people who lived in *a* church house – that is, paid rent for one to the wardens.

To conclude, a close study of the account book, supplemented by other sources surviving for the parish, indicates that the area served liturgically by the parish church centred upon the townships of New and Old Thame. The men who represented the laity in their collective responsibilities to the parish church can be seen to be taking the same leading rôle in the lay institutions of town and hundred.[101] The tasks which they fulfilled, unsalaried, were often onerous and time-consuming. It has often been suggested that their motives in holding these ecclesiastical offices were predominantly pious.[102] Yet there was also advantage to be had in terms of connection, prestige, and even financial gain. The accounts show clearly that money, land and riches could remain in their hands for some time before being appropriately disposed of. This is not to accept the view of Samuel Butler in the early seventeenth century, who observed that 'a churchwarden is a public officer entrusted to rob the church by virtue of his place as long as he is in it.'[103] By his day the office had undergone considerable development. But, in Thame at least, that later association of parish office with civic duties was already foreshadowed in the fifteenth century.

Notes

1 *VCH Oxon.*, VII, p. 162.
2 *Calendar of Charter Rolls, 1226–57*, pp. 33, 105, *1257–1300*, p.461; *Rotuli Litterarum Clausarum*, RC, I, p. 402.
3 See for example: PRO, Exchequer lay subsidy returns, E179/161/41 and 198.
4 Oxford, Bodleian Library MSS D.D. Bertie c16/37; *CCR, 1485–1500*, p. 61 (no. 226).
5 *VCH Oxon.*, VII, p.181. See PRO, Court of Common Pleas, CP 25(1) 31/37 for the extent of Geoffrey Dormer's estates in the parish of Thame in 1498.
6 *CPR, 1446–52*, p. 181.
7 Ibid.
8 PRO E179/161/41.
9 J. Cornwall, 'English Towns in the Fifteen Twenties', *EcHR*, 15 (1962), pp. 54–67; PRO E179/161/200 and 198.
10 Particulars of grants by Edward VI to Sir John Williams, quoted in F.G. Lee, *(The History, Description and Antiquities of the Prebendal Church of the Blessed Virgin Mary of) Thame* (London, 1883), p. 424.
11 R. Graham, ed., *Chantry Certificates and Inventories of Church Goods* (for Oxfordshire), Oxon. Record Society, 1 (1919), p.115 (hereafter Graham, *Chantry Cert.*).
12 Compare PRO E179/161/200 with 102/225.
13 P.D.A. Harvey, ed., *The Manorial Court Records of Cuxham, Oxfordshire circa 1200–1359* (HMSO, 1976), pp. 379, 417, 474, 564; idem, *A Medieval Oxfordshire Village 1200–1400* (Oxford, 1965), pp. 102, 110, 111; *CPR, 1429–36, p.159*; 1441–6, pp. 119, 214.
14 Oxfordshire CRO, MS D.D. Par. Thame c.5. The churchwardens' accounts resume in a separate volume at 1528 and are more or less continuous to 1617: Oxon. CRO, MS D.D. Par. Thame b.2.
15 *VCH Oxon.*, VII, p. 199.
16 A few court rolls survive for Thame: Bodleian MSS D.D. Bertie c16/1–34. These are: hundred court 1423–4, 1441–2, 1443–4, 1444–5, 1445, 1454, 1502–3; hallmoot 1426, 1429, 1445, 1451, 1502–3; portmoot 1431–2, 1433–4, 1436–7, 1442–3, 1444–5, 1449, 1461–2, 1472–3, 1502–3; guild of St Christopher 1492, 1512, 1514, 1520, 1525, 1527, 1528, 1529, 1530, 1534–5, 1535, 1538, 1541. The draft court rolls for the manor of Old Thame and the guild of St Christopher 1481–2 are ibid., c16/37.
17 Oxford, Queen's College MS 366, fos 23b, 25.
18 PRO E179/161/10, 9, 17, 41.
19 PRO E179/161/198 ; Oxon. CRO, Par. Thame c.5, *passim*.
20 *VCH Oxon.*, VII, p. 163.
21 *Valor Ecclesiasticus*, RC, II, p.168.
22 J. Le Neve, ed., *Fasti Ecclesiae Anglicanae 1300–1541, 1:Lincoln Diocese*, rev. edn by H.P.F. King (London, 1962), pp. 134–8.
23 *VCH Oxon.*, VII, p. 202.
24 The list in Lee, *Thame*, pp. 142–4, can be shown from the manuscript to contain at least two errors.

25 Tetsworth was closer than Thame (one mile, as opposed to three). No reference occurs in the manuscript to a parishioner who can be identified as from Attingdon. See Bodleian Library, Oxfordshire Archdeanery Papers c.141, pp. 125–6 for a copy of a thirteenth-century ordinance relating to the appointment of chaplains to the chapels by the vicars of Thame.

26 The only example is Nicholas Turnpenne of Tetsworth in 1452; Par.Thame c.5, fo.16.

27 The evidence is inferential. Only one reference occurs in the manuscript to the *iconomi* of a chapel: Par.Thame c.5, fo.45v. For sixteenth-century evidence of churchwardens in the chapels see Graham, *Chantry Cert.*, pp. 16, 49.

28 See D.M. Palliser, 'Introduction: the Parish in Perspective', in S. Wright, ed., *Parish, Church and People* (London, 1988) (hereafter, Palliser, 'Perspective,'), pp. 15–23.

29 *Bodleian Summary Catalogue of Western MSS,* VI, p.27.

30 I am grateful to Mrs L. Head, honorary librarian to the Buckinghamshire Archaeological Society, for this information.

31 Bodleian Library Records, d.1170.

32 *Ut supra.*

33 W. Patterson Ellis in *Berkshire, Buckinghamshire and Oxfordshire Archaeological Journal,* 7–14, 16, 19–20 (1902–14).

34 R. Hutton, 'The Local Impact of the Tudor Reformations', in C. Haigh, ed., *The English Reformation Revised* (Cambridge, 1987) (hereafter Hutton, 'Impact'), pp.114–38.

35 Ibid.

36 J.C. Cox, *Churchwardens' Accounts from the Fourteenth Century to the Close of the Seventeenth Century* (London, 1913).

37 A. Hanham, ed., *The Churchwardens' Accounts of Ashburton, 1479–1580,* Devon and Cornwall Record Society, new series, 15 (1970); F.M. Osborne, ed., *The Churchwardens' Accounts of St Michael's Church, Chagford, 1480–1600* (privately published, Chagford, 1979). A copy is held at the Devon County Record Office, Exeter.

38 Hutton, 'Impact', pp. 114–38; J.J. Scarisbrick, *The Reformation and the English People* (Oxford, 1985), pp. 27, 32, 89, 90, 101, 165–6.

39 See Palliser, 'Perspective,' pp. 5–15.

40 C. Drew, *Early Parochial Organisation in England: the Origins of the Office of Churchwarden,* Borthwick Institute of Hist. Research, Pamphlet 7 (York, 1954); E. Mason, 'The Rôle of the English Parishioner 1100–1500', *Journal of Ecclesiastical History,* 27 (1976), pp. 17–29.

41 St Mary's, Bridgwater, in T.B. Dilks, ed., *Bridgwater Borough Archives,* Somerset Record Society, 48 (1933), 53 (1938), 58 (1945), 60 (1948); St Michael's, Bath, in Bishop Hobhouse, ed., *The Churchwardens' Accounts of Croscombe, Pilton, Yatton, Tintinhull, Morebath and St Michael's Bath,* Somerset Record Society (1890); St Augustine's, Hedon, Yorkshire, in J.R. Boyle, *The Early History of the Town and Port of Hedon, Hull etc.* (1895); St James and St Nicholas, Hedon, Yorkshire (unpublished) which are now in the Humberside County Record Office, Beverley; Tavistock, Devon, in R.N. Worth, ed., *Calendar of the Parish Records of Tavistock* (Plymouth, 1887); St John's, Glastonbury, which are kept in the Somerset County Record Office and extracts from which have been published in *Somerset and Dorset Notes and Queries,* 4 and 5. Lists of surviving accounts are given in Cox, *Accounts,* pp. 15–43 for the fourteenth and fifteenth centuries, and pp. 44–52 for the sixteenth and seventeenth centuries. Publications are listed in E.L.C. Mullins, *Texts and Calendars: an Analytical Guide* (London, 1956), pp. 270–4, and in E.B. Graves, *A Bibliography of English History to 1485* (Oxford, 1975), pp. 894–5.

42 St Michael's, Bath, *ut supra;* St Laurence, Reading, in Rev. Charles Kerry, *A History of the Municipal Church of St Laurence, Reading* (1883); St Edmund, Salisbury, in H.F.J. Swayne, ed., *The Churchwardens' Accounts of St Edmund and St Thomas, Sarum, 1443–1702, with other Documents,* Wiltshire Record Society (Salisbury, 1896).

43 Printed in Cox, *Accounts*, pp. 270–4.
44 Par. Thame c.5, fos 28–31v; Bassingbourn, Cambs., partially printed in Cox, *Accounts*, pp. 108–9, 130–1; St Edmund, Salisbury, *ut supra*.
45 The churchwarden is Richard Higecok': Par. Thame c.5, fo.1–1v; PRO C1/11/462. His widow occurs in D.D. Bertie c16/12.
46 Par. Thame c.5, fos 25, 37, 38, 38v.
47 Par. Thame c.5, fos 38, 74; fos 16v–19.
48 Par. Thame c.5, fos 40–41v.
49 Par. Thame c.5, fo. 14.
50 See Par. Thame c.5, fos 25, 27, 28 for examples of rubrics indicating tenure in excess of one year. There is no indication in the manuscript as to whether the churchwardens were chosen for these longer periods or whether they were re-chosen annually.
51 Literate is used here in the modern sense of being able to read and write in English. In the period of the early Thame accounts *literatus* was used to denote a knowledge of Latin. There is no evidence in the accounts that any of the Thame churchwardens were literate in this sense.
52 See Par. Thame c.5, fos 4, 7(a)v, 8v for 'y Yhon Manytorn'. Fos 2–11 appear to be in the same hand.
53 Par. Thame c.5, fo. 42.
54 Par.Thame c.5, fos 43v, 45, 55.
55 D.D. Bertie c16/21.
56 Par. Thame c.5, fo. 52.
57 D.D. Bertie c16/16, /17, /19, /37.
58 D.D. Bertie c16/19, /37.
59 *CPR, 1452–61*, pp. 84, 327; *CFR, 1445–52*, p. 124.
60 D.D. Bertie c16/17, /19, /37.
61 D.D. Bertie c16/17, /19, /21, /37; *CFR, 1461–71*, p. 230; 'Chapter' is the term used throughout the manuscript for the local ecclesiastical court. Exempt from archidiaconal jurisdiction, Thame parish was subject to the jurisdiction of the dean of Lincoln cathedral to whom several references occur in the manuscript. For the rural chapter in general see J. Scammell, 'The Rural Chapter in England from the Eleventh to the Fourteenth Century', *EHR*, 86 (1971), pp. 1–17.
62 R.E.G. Cole, ed., *Chapter Acts of Lincoln Cathedral 1520–36*, Lincoln Record Society, 12 (1915) pp. 47–8; Par. Thame c.5, fo. 77v.
63 D.D. Bertie c16/17, 19, 37.
64 D.D. Bertie c16/21–24.
65 D.D. Bertie c16/21.
66 PRO, Prerogative Court of Canterbury Wills (hereafter P.C.C.), Bennett 4.
67 PRO, C1/509/11.
68 Par. Thame c.5, fo. 55v.
69 *CPR, 1476–85*, p. 211.
70 D.D. Bertie c16/37.
71 PRO E179/161/171.
72 D.D. Bertie c16/23, 24.
73 PRO E179/161/198.
74 Par. Thame c.5, fos 30v–31v.
75 P.C.C., Porch 35.
76 Par.Thame c.5, fos 72v–73.
77 Ibid.
78 Par. Thame c.5, fos 9–9v, 10v–11, 12.
79 Par. Thame c.5, fo. 34v.
80 PRO E179/161/167; D.D. Bertie c16/20.

81 Par. Thame c.5, fo.46v.
82 Par. Thame c.5, fo.52; C.L. Kingsford, ed., *The Stonor Letters and Papers*, Camden Society, 3rd series, 29, 30 (1919), II, pp. 2, 68, 72, 118, 131, 144–5; D.D. Bertie c16/37.
83 Par. Thame c.5, fos 38, 38v–39.
84 Par. Thame c.5, fo. 51; D.D. Bertie c16/21, 22, 23.
85 Par. Thame c.5, fos 74v, 76, 77v, 78v.
86 Par. Thame c.5, fos 36v, 79v.
87 Par. Thame c.5, fo. 68.
88 Par. Thame c.5, fo. 78v.
89 Par. Thame c.5, fo. 53.
90 P.C.C., Bennett 5, 10; Par.Thame c.5, fo. 66v.
91 Par. Thame c.5, fo. 70.
92 PRO C1/55/71.
93 For example, Par.Thame c.5, fo.20v.
94 Par. Thame c.5, fo. 77; MS D.D. Par. Thame b.2, p. 3.
95 Par. Thame c.5, fo. 44v. This is presumably the story of SS Fabian and Sebastian (*ex info.* Dr C.H.Clough).
96 Throughout the manuscript there are entries of 6s.8d. paid to the churchwardens for burial within the church. Such fees normally went to the clergy, and in the case of Thame must therefore have been conceded by the prebendary and the vicar. The churchwardens evidently did not receive offerings for burial in the churchyard, although such occasions are frequently alluded to in the receipts for 'waste of torches'.
97 Par. Thame c.5, fos 2v–6v.
98 Par. Thame c.5, fos 13v–14.
99 Par. Thame c.5, fos 38–9.
100 This aspect of the churchwardens' responsibilities is not discussed here as it made almost no impact upon the accounts. The regular attendance of the churchwardens at the chapter can be inferred from the manuscript, but there is no indication of their rôle.
101 See Z. Razi, *Life, Marriage and Death in a Medieval Parish: Economy, Society and Demography in Halesowen 1270–1400* (Cambridge, 1980), pp. 122–3.
102 Most recently by C. Burgess, '"A Fond Thing Vainly Invented": an Essay on Purgatory and Pious Motive in Later Medieval England', in S. Wright, ed., *Parish, Church and People*, pp. 77–8.
103 S. Butler, *Characters and Passages from Note Books*, ed. A.R. Waller (Cambridge, 1908), pp. 117–18.

Index